THE OBJECT
ADVANTAGE

BUSINESS PROCESS
REENGINEERING
WITH OBJECT TECHNOLOGY

THE OBJECT ADVANTAGE

BUSINESS PROCESS REENGINEERING WITH OBJECT TECHNOLOGY

IVAR JACOBSON
MARIA ERICSSON
AGNETA JACOBSON

Objective Systems SF AB
PO Box 1128, S-16422 Kista, Sweden

Objectory Corp.
PO Box 2630, Greenwich, CT 06836, USA

ADDISON-WESLEY PUBLISHING COMPANY

Wokingham, England • Reading, Massachusetts • Menlo Park, California • New Yo
Don Mills, Ontario • Amsterdam • Bonn • Sydney • Singapore
Tokyo • Madrid • San Juan • Milan • Paris • Mexico City • Seoul • Taipei

ACM PRESS BOOKS

This book is published as part of ACM Press Books — a collaboration between the Association for Computing Machinery and Addison-Wesley Publishing Company. ACM is the oldest and largest educational and scientific society in the information technology field. Through its high-quality publications and services, ACM is a major force in advancing the skills and knowledge of IT professionals throughout the world. For further information about ACM contact:

ACM Member Services
1515 Broadway, 17th Floor
New York, NY 10036-5701
Phone: 1-212-626-0500
Fax: 1-212-944-1318
E-mail: ACMHELP@ACM.org

ACM European Service Center
Avenue Marcel Thiry 204
1200 Brussels, Belgium
Phone: 32-2-774-9602
Fax: 32-2-774-9690
E-mail: ACM_Europe@ACM.org

OTHER TITLES IN THE SERIES

The programs in this book have been included for their instructional
value. They have been tested with care but are not guaranteed for any
particular purpose. The publisher does not offer any warranties or
representations nor does it accept any liabilities with respect to the
programs.

Many of the designations used by manufacturers and sellers to
distinguish their products are claimed as trademarks. Addison-Wesley
has made every attempt to supply trademark information about
manufacturers and their products mentioned in this book.

Cover designed by Viva Design of Henley-on-Thames
Text design by Sally Grover
Typeset in 11.5/13.5 pt Palatino by CRB Associates, Drayton, Norwich
Printed and bound in the United States of America

First printed 1994

ISBN 0–201–42289–1

British Library Cataloguing-in-Publication Data
A catalogue record for this book is available from the British Library.

Library of Congress Cataloging-in-Publication Data is available

Foreword

By James Martin

The most important aspect of the job of an IT organization today is to play a leadership role in Enterprise Engineering. By doing so, IT professionals can maximize the contribution they make to corporate competitiveness and success.

The management structures and work procedures of most enterprises were designed before modern technology. The procedures need radically reinventing and the management structures need replacing. The jobs of most people need to be fundamentally redesigned so that people add more value in an age of computers and technology.

Terms like 'Business Reengineering' and 'Business Process Redesign' have become popular but are imprecise. Often their proponents advocate one method for change when multiple change-methods are needed. To advocate using one method, like that of Hammer or Deming, for all situations, is like advocating one medicine for all illnesses. The professional Enterprise Engineer should be able to select and integrate multiple change-methods. The intent of Enterprise Engineering is to identify the most valuable change-methods and synthesize them. The integrated family of methods is greater than the sum of its parts.

It is only when different approaches are integrated that it becomes clear that most corporations have the wrong procedures, most computer systems being built today are the wrong systems, most TQM efforts miss their true potential and most corporations have major learning disabilities.

Businesses are highly complex and in most cases have never been 'engineered'; they have grown in an *ad hoc* fashion like a fungus growth. To engineer corporations their procedures need to be charted, or modeled. Only when complex procedures are modeled with clarity can they be rebuilt in an optimal fashion. The models may be built by IT professionals but they should be understood and owned by the business people. To make them easy to understand and change, object-oriented modelling should be used. This book describes an approach to object-oriented modelling for business redesign.

The models of a business should be convertible as directly and easily as possible into the software needed for running the business. Particularly important, when the business changes, or executives adjust business policies, the software should be changeable quickly and easily. Tools are needed which integrate enterprise modelling into code generation for systems. Object-oriented business modelling should be linked to object-oriented design and code generation.

In *The Object Advantage* Ivar Jacobson presents an interesting technique for modelling the business. He looks at a company's usability, identifying customers as users of the business, and suggests that the business model should be designed to offer them the 'usable' company.

What is unique about Jacobson's approach is that he goes beyond simply describing the idea of a reengineered company. Instead he gives the reader a formalized, how-to method that integrates the work of reengineering a business, its processes and its information systems. By linking his techniques for object-oriented business engineering to his object-oriented software engineering method, Jacobson provides actual deliverables and in doing so he has made a valuable contribution for a wide range of businesses and information providers.

James Martin
August, 1994

Foreword

Foreword by Dan L. Jonson

If I had to choose the single most important consequence of the advent of what we call the New Economy, it would be the need for true enterprise architecture. Since the dawn of corporate computing, executives have operated under the assumption that corporate business problems could be solved by hiring enough IS professionals. Most executives believed, and many still do, that the basic reason for prior and present problems was a poor information management structure not up to the task of effectively operating in an environment of rapid and near constant change. What they didn't see or understand was the simple fact that IS resources are just that — *resources*. To be truly effective, these assets must be transformed from a potential to a kinetic state and applied to a conditional business process in a fluid business environment to generate the expected value. Moreover, for a company to remain competitive and improve customer loyalty, it must create the proper alignment of strategy, process, and technology. This cannot be accomplished without the creation of an accurate and multi-layered blueprint, thus the significance of enterprise architecture as the keystone component in a company's successful adaptation to the New Economy.

Corporate restructuring, currently referred to as 'business reengineering' is one of the most widely discussed topics of the early 1990s. Examples abound of dinosaurs who have been able to turn themselves from the brink of extinction, like Chrysler Corporation, while many remain in the throes of redefinition and chaos, like IBM and GM. While hundreds of pages have been dedicated to the discussion of process change and reengineering, a review of contemporary literature reveals that it is broadly prescriptive. Recommendations as to what companies must do to adapt to the New Economy are made in expansive general terms. These authors provide the 'what' and 'why' of business reengineering, but not the 'how'. This void is being filled by the publication of this significant reference work by Ivar Jacobson and his co-authors Maria Ericsson and Agneta Jacobson. I would like to take this opportunity to thank the authors for a magnificent and commendable work in an area completely neglected by the academic world and the entire IS industry.

During my entire professional career within the international insurance and reinsurance community, I have been baffled at the way large companies have managed their IS and technology departments. Little or no effort has been expended to interface these resources with actual business issues that faced corporate executives and line managers to solve real structural problems. Many years of frustration dogged my pursuit to identify a powerful, yet simple enough environment that would allow implementation of a modernized and more efficient enterprise structure for our industry. Until I discussed these issues with Ivar Jacobson and his team, I did not realise that the required tool for the accurate design of business processes was a powerful and well matured object-oriented modelling methodology. Further, I achieved an enlightening as to the magnitude of Ivar's long-time pioneering work at both the L M Ericsson Group and Objectory AB. The OOSE methodology, as described in *Object-Oriented Software Engineering: A Use Case Driven Approach*, provides the initial building blocks for successful realization of any industry specific business model. The *Object Advantage: Business Process Reengineering with Object Technology* elevates this proven and dependable methodology to a higher level by exhibiting 'how' to do it. This technique, together with the Objectory tool, now become the most important elements in successfully building an improved enterprise architecture and providing a seamless transition between the resulting business model and the process to develop the required information resources. Now business leaders with even modest vision can learn to anticipate and even control the future through the development of ideal enterprise models. They can now profit from, rather than be surprised by, global competition and rapid change.

I firmly believe that this work, with its logical framework and practical recommendations, will have a profound impact on governments and corporations worldwide, as they seek excellence, efficiency and profitability. It is an authoritative guide on how to realize the ultimate adaptive enterprise architecture and thus maintain *the* competitive advantage through skillful and forward looking management.

Dan L. Jonson
August 1994
Deep Creek Lake, Maryland

Preface

Background

In a very short time, business process reengineering (BPR) has become one of the most popular subjects at conferences on business management and information-systems design. It may become the number one buzzword of the Nineties. BPR, as defined by Hammer (1993) is 'the fundamental rethinking and radical redesign of business processes to achieve dramatic improvements in critical, contemporary measures of performance, such as cost, quality, service and speed'. BPR implies that you take a comprehensive view of the entire existing operation and think through why you do what you do, why you do what you do the way you do it, and why ... In short, BPR requires that you question the entire existing operation and try to redesign it in a way that uses new technology to serve your customers better.

The number of books on BPR increases all the time. During 1993 and 1994, several important books were published on this subject. Several of these present, in a convincing way, the principles behind BPR. The book that received perhaps the greatest success within this area is *Reengineering the Corporation* (1993) by Michael Hammer and James Champy. This book has a very simple, but clear message: if you are to survive, make your company process managed. This clear, articulate message enables the reader to understand the meaning of reengineering, that one must perform it and, in principle, what it entails to perform it.

What is this book about?

This book, however, is not yet another book on these principles. This is a book that describes how you can, in practice, redesign a business according to BPR ideas. The difference between having assimilated the principles and being able to apply them in practice is very great indeed.

The risks involved with performing a reengineering project are significant. There are estimates that 50 to 70 percent of companies that try it fail. I think the risk of failure is even higher. BPR risks fall roughly into two categories: risks associated with the change process, and risks associated with the technology used. It has been estimated that 80 percent of the failures are caused by 'soft' factors, such as motivation, management commitment, leadership, the need for expert guidance, and so on. Most books and methods on BPR tackle these soft factors, creating best-selling authors and prosperous consultants.

I am convinced that BPR's success rate can be dramatically improved if its methods offer more concrete guidance. I don't underestimate the need to address the change process; that need remains. But I believe you can almost guarantee successful BPR if you have a formal reengineering process in hand. At Objectory AB, in Sweden, we have lengthy experience in reengineering many companies' software-development organization to adopt an object-oriented process. Our experience is unambiguous: a formal reengineering process and less hand-waving is a must for success. A similar message is also brought to us by James Martin (1994) in his recently published book-series *Enterprise Engineering — The Key To Corporate Survival*. James Martin not only articulates the basic principles for reengineering, 'Change or Die', but he also offers a comprehensive set of techniques, an 'integrated engineering approach', to manage the necessary changes in a company.

Ingredients of a formal reengineering process

A formal reengineering process includes:

- A description that specifies every activity and deliverable involved. This process description must be adaptable to the reengineering project. For instance, the size and maturity of the organization and the type of process you are reengineering will influence the process description.

- Deliverables, in the form of business models, that focus on the company's architecture and dynamics. These are different from traditional business models, which fail because they model the company as a computer with a database and a program that manipulates the database. The business models should be presented in an engaging language so that everyone involved – the CEO, executives, process owners, process managers, process operators, resource owners and customers – can understand them, not just the reengineering team.

- A process for the development of an information system that is truly integral to the reengineered company. A truly integral information system is one that is developed in parallel with new business processes and both influences the design of those processes and is influenced by them. This is often the most overlooked element of BPR. IT organizations are generally not as competent as other engineering disciplines in fashioning their product (information systems). The Software Engineering Institute (SEI) at Carnegie Mellon University estimates that 85 percent of all software development done in 1989 was done without any real method. A good word for this type of work is 'hacking'. Here is a rich source of failure. A tight, seamless relationship is required between the process that develops the business model and the process that develops the information system. These processes primarily involve concepts, models, tools and document-ation. Only if this is done do you increase your chances of success. Establishing this relation enables business people to communicate with IT people and IT people with end users. It also eliminates the separation between the business models and the information system's requirements models and tears down language barriers.

Who needs such a process?

In the first place, the reengineering team needs a formal process to be able to redesign their company. They need tools with which they can visualize, explain, test and evaluate their ideas, solutions, decisions and actions. They need their special, expressive models of the redesigned company. These models are also used by people building information systems. These people must have clear models of the business which the information system is to support. And they must be able to build models of their information system that must be understood by the reengineering people; otherwise, there is a significant risk that you do not achieve the effects you desire.

The people in the new company also need to understand how the company will operate and what their new job will be. This requires special models that are more straight-forward work descriptions than the models that are dealt with in this book. The difference between these models and the reengineering team's models is similar to the difference between a user guide for an information system and documentation of the same information system (design documentation, program code, test specifications and so on) produced by its developers. We will not describe these simpler models in this book.

Our technique

We have called our reengineering technique object-oriented business engineering based on use cases. It stands on the following fundamental ideas:

- Use cases are a simple, natural way to identify business processes. A customer is a user of a company, and he or she uses the company through a business process. Each way of using the company is a use case.

- Object orientation is an excellent way to clarify the inner workings of a company — its processes, products, services, resources — and how those things depend on each other.

- The business model of the redesigned company and the requirements model for the information system must be seamless. This is achieved by pairing object-oriented business engineering and object-oriented software engineering — a use case driven approach (OOSE), which work in harmony. For more details on OOSE see *Object-Oriented Software Engineering — a Use Case Driven Approach* (1992) by Ivar Jacobson.

Why we have written this book

We have seen it as our mission to present a framework for a formal process for reengineering a corporation. The framework can be used to test the ideas in a smaller scale. Furthermore, it can be used as a source of inspiration to develop such a process. But it is not, and we wish to emphasize this, a process itself. A lot more work than can be accomplished by a number of individual authors needs to be done. The various procedural tasks must be refined, the different modelling languages must be described in more detail, guidelines must be developed, documentation must be clarified. You will need support from reengineering tools, which will be very expensive to develop if they are to used by professionals. These tools must be developed as an integral part of the process; process and tool stick together through thick and thin.

Our experience

When, 27 years ago, I developed the first generation of what later became object-oriented software engineering, using my technique I made a model of a large company. The basic ideas behind my methodology were inspired by the way that Ericsson Telecom developed electro-mechanical systems. So I used the methodology for designing a small hardware system to make a model of Ericsson as a corporation. Having done that I felt comfortable about introducing the methodology to the development of combined hardware and software systems. This happened in 1967. Since then I have worked primarily in the field of software development.

My methodology has undergone major improvements, the most important of which were presented in my PhD thesis. Every new idea, a new language construct for example, was always first applied to the design of an organization. By using modelling constructs that were applicable for software as well as for organizations, I considered the constructs to be natural — they would be able to survive because they were not overly technical. Thus, the ideas behind this book have been tested for many years, but they have been applied in practice for just seven years. In 1987 we used the first version of object-oriented business engineering within Objectory AB (our Swedish corporation) to develop Objectory, a software development process. This was presented in Jacobson (1987). At that time we used a slightly different terminology. We used the term 'factory' to stand for a business system. Objectory was an invented name that combined the words 'object' and 'factory'.

Objectory AB developed in 1989 a specialized version of Objectory to be used for business engineering within Swedish Telecom. The experience from this work and from the work of Objectory AB's other pioneering customers, such as Citibank in New York and Avemco Corporation in Frederick, Maryland, has extended our understanding of business modelling in general, and specifically of using use cases and objects within business engineering. Thus on one hand our experience of business engineering is far less than our experience of software engineering. This will be clear to you as you read this book. Therefore we recommend that you exercise caution when using the ideas presented. Try them out on a small scale before you use them in practice. And, please, if you learn something new, let us know about your experiences. On the other hand, we probably have more experience than most other people trying to combine business engineering ideas with object technology. This leaves us with the confidence to write this book.

On the organization of this book

The book consists of three parts:
The first part of the book is an introduction. It consists of three chapters. Chapter 1, Business engineering, summarizes the fundamental ideas and motivations for BPR. We will outline what the new business will in principle look like, what the risks are, and how they can be reduced. Furthermore we will give our picture of how, in the future, a modern business should manage business engineering issues. You may skip this chapter if you already are familiar to BPR. However, we think that our framework for business engineering in general is wider than BPR and can be used for the long-term organization of work on business development. Chapter 2, What is business modelling?, presents the basics of business modelling. It answers the question in its title and explains why you need models of your business. Furthermore, it describes who

you should develop business models for. At a first reading you may skip this chapter. However, we believe that the handler concept, models for handlers and the architecture of a model are important contributions to business modelling in general and worth reading the second time round. Chapter 3, What is object-orientation?, introduces the basics of object-orientation in the context of business modelling. This chapter describes the elementary concepts of object-oriented modelling such as objects, instances and classes, associations between objects, and inheritance between classes. This chapter should be skipped if you already are familiar with object modelling in general.

The second part is the core of the book and consists of Chapters 4–10. Here we describe object-oriented business engineering based on use cases. Chapter 4, Object-oriented business engineering – an overview, introduces our approach. Chapter 5, Architecture, describes the architectural style of our approach. A business model should emphasize the architecture of the modelled company. In this chapter we present the architectural design that we believe allows the right kind of decisions to be made about the company. Here we introduce use cases to model business processes, and objects to model internal processes. Chapter 6, Reversing the existing business, describes how to make a model of the existing business and Chapter 7, Forward business engineering, describes how you redesign your business to be process-managed. Chapter 8, An example, examines the results of using object-oriented business engineering to redesign Objectory AB, a real organization. Even though Objectory AB is a small company, the basic ideas behind approach are made clear and demonstrated. Chapter 9, Building the supporting information system, gives an overview of object-oriented software engineering, first using plain English and then by using object-oriented business engineering. In this chapter we describe the transition from business modelling using object-oriented business engineering to requirements modelling of the supporting information system. We describe how an elegant object model of the business is related to a use case model of the supporting information system. Chapter 10, Managing object-oriented business engineering, describes how you organize your reengineering work and the new company. The chapter describes the different roles that you will need in your reengineering team, and the different roles that people will have to play in the new company. Planning for the reengineering project is also discussed. Finally, we present some agreements for moving to a process-managed organization between different parties.

In the third part, Chapter 11, Scaling up to large businesses, we describe how our approach can be scaled up so that it can be used by large companies.

Acknowledgements

Our approach has been used in practice by several people. The feedback we have got from these people have been of utmost importance to us. In particular we would like to thank Bob Becker, Karl Frank, Dan Jonson, Håkan Lidström and Anders Rockström. Our former president, Mark Broms, has given us a lot of insight into how to implement a process-managed organization, what kinds of roles you should look for, and their different responsibilities. We would like to thank Björn-Erik Willoch who has given much concrete advice and insights, and who has supported our writing of this book. Many of our reviewers have given us very valuable critisism for which we are very grateful. We would particularly like to thank Gene Forte and Bengt-Arne Vedin. Furthermore we would like to thank Angela Burgess and David Howe for helping us with the English. The following colleagues of ours have made valuable contributions to the book: Christian Ehrenborg, Johan Aronsson, Per-Arne Gussander, Sten Jacobson, Lasse Johansson, Patrik Jonsson, Kit Molander, Per Sundqvist, Nils Undin and Lars Wiktorin. We are very grateful to Objectory AB for allowing us to publish this work. And, last but not least, we would like to thank our families for their support and encouragement.

Whilst writing this book one of the authors, Agneta Jacobson, gave birth to a little girl Jennifer, which at the same time made another of the authors, Ivar Jacobson, a grandfather. Congratulations to all three!

On behalf of all three authors,

Ivar Jacobson
June, 1994
Nybrogatan 45C, S-114 39 Stockholm

Ivar Jacobson   ivar @ os.se
Maria Ericsson   maria @ os.se
Agneta Jacobson

Contents

chapter 1
Business engineering

1.1 Introduction

More than 200 years ago, the economist Adam Smith formulated a theory to describe industrial practices that were already centuries old, having been used by the Venetians to construct ships in the 15th century. Smith's *The Wealth of Nations*, published in 1776, presented a number of principles for organizing industrial work that were revolutionary at the time. All work should be divided into primitive tasks simple enough so that each could be performed by an individual worker. Each worker would not be required to learn many other tasks and could thus specialize in a few tasks. This idea was very simple to understand and implement. These principles were – and are – very effective when applied to the mass production of similar products by a largely unskilled, uneducated labour force using simple tools.

Today's companies are largely founded on principles that can traced to this early theory. Yet almost everything is different about industry today. Products are customized, not mass produced. The labour force is highly educated, and competent people want responsibility and challenges. The market for products is much broader, and competition for customers much more aggressive.

But the most dramatic change in industrial practices involves the production tools and techniques themselves. Of all the modern tools, information technology (IT) is overwhelmingly the most important. IT is not only the foundation for many other important technologies (personal and portable computers, networks and mobile communication, robotics, shared databases, and so on), it is also the way you will offer your customers information. Information has either already become, or will soon become, an important part of the products and services your company markets.

Why, then, do we continue to base our industrial practices on archaic ideas? To survive in the new world, we must fundamentally rethink they way our industries are organized. It is high time to bury the old way of thinking and replace it with a new approach. A new approach that takes advantage of the new type of human resources and technologies. This new approach is the cornerstone of business engineering. In this chapter, we will discuss the fundamental principles of business engineering and its most important application – namely, to reengineer or redesign an existing company.

This application, which has been called business process reengineering (BPR) by various authors, has the greatest initial effect on any business, and it is therefore the most frequently discussed in business-development literature. In the business world, business (process) reengineering is the buzzword of the nineties. Everyone talks about it, everyone has their own interpretation of what it means, and everyone claims to be doing it. In truth, few have applied it successfully.

1.2 What is business engineering?

We begin with a simple definition of 'business engineering', which we shall further clarify in this and later chapters. Then we define 'process', a key word in business engineering. Finally, we relate a company's business (that is, its products and services), to its processes.

1.2.1 The business engineering concept

Business engineering is a set of techniques a company uses to design its business according to specific goals. The set of techniques includes

- Step-by-step procedures to design the business.

- Notations that describe the design.

- Heuristics or pragmatic solutions to find the right design, measured in terms of the specific goals.

In short, business engineering seeks to organize a commercial undertaking in a competitive way. At first glance, this does not seem to be anything new. Entrepreneurs have always tried to position themselves competitively. However, today's definition incorporates what is perhaps a new way of thinking — viewing the construction of an enterprise as an engineering activity. We see companies or businesses as something that can be formed, designed or redesigned according to engineering principles.

Furthermore, the notion that you can compete more effectively if you use modern engineering principles — principles based on streamlined processes — to design your company is a radical one. It will change the way your company operates. The risks are great, as we describe later, but the improvements you can achieve by applying this new way of thinking are quite dramatic. By 'dramatic' we mean on the order of 10 times: more like a 90-percent reduction in cost or lead time or a 90-percent increase in quality and customer satisfaction, not 10 percent.

1.2.2 What is a business process?

Put simply, a business process is the set of internal activities performed to serve a customer. The purpose of each business process is to offer each customer the right product or service (that is, the right deliverable), with a high degree of performance measured against cost, longevity, service and quality. The term 'customer' should be used in an extended meaning. It can literally be simply a customer, but it can also be another individual process in the environment that is external to the company, such as a partner or sub-contractor.

Processes are nothing new. Every company has always had processes. The problem has been that we haven't been able to describe them as easily as organizations. Organizations have names ('sales' and 'production'), and a responsible person's name is attached to each one ('president', 'division chief'). Processes are usually invisible and neither described nor named. Processes arise more naturally than hierarchies because they come into being when people realize that they must cooperate to achieve the result promised to the customer. Processes cut

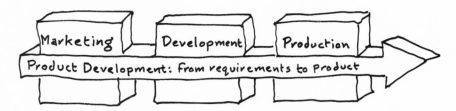

Figure 1.1 *Processes cut straight through the traditional organization structure.*

straight through traditional organizations (Figure 1.1). Davenport has expressed this very well: 'Whereas an organization's hierarchical structure is typically a slice-in-time view of responsibilities and reporting relationships, its process structure is a dynamic view of how organizations deliver value.'

To better grasp the processes that a company offers, you can name them descriptively. Hammer (1993), for example, suggest naming processes according to their start and end status, such as 'product development: requirements to product', and 'sales: lead to order'. Names such as these intend to separate processes from departments. Later, when people are used to thinking in terms of processes, you can substitute simpler names. We suggest you use either the gerund ('selling', 'developing') or progressive form ('performing sales', 'performing development'). However, avoid these forms when referring to departments.

Business engineering, then, requires that we organize our work not according to organizations or tasks, as Smith suggested. Instead, we must consolidate related tasks into business processes. When a process is divided among organizations, the interface must be clearly defined. This situation can be conducive to conflict at both the organizational and personal levels. The effort required to join parts of a process is great, and it can easily obscure what must really be done. A large part of what is called internal company politics is concerned with reaching an agreement on this interface. Managers expend a great deal of energy manipulating situations in order to stake out their own turf. In Swedish, the rather vulgar expression 'pinka in sitt revir' says, in essence, that managers behave like animals that must mark their territory. Managers use this expression to describe not only what their colleagues do, but also what they do themselves. In other words, they realize this behaviour is beneath their dignity, but they don't know how to avoid it.

Company politics involves the struggle for more money, more staff and thus more power. Since time immemorial, men have been raised to compete, not cooperate, in contrast to the way women are raised. Perhaps this is one reason so few women occupy the highest ranking executive positions in today's organizations. Some people, including Carlzon (1987), who pioneered the theories of business engineering and implemented them by totally redesigning Scandinavian Airlines Systems (SAS), have said that process-oriented organizations will better suit women's work style: 'The new leadership role should open up many more possibilities for women in business'.

Processes have another advantage over the traditional organizational approach: You cannot measure or improve a hierarchical structure in any absolute sense, but you can measure the cost, time, output, quality, and customer satisfaction associated with a process. As Davenport (1993) has written, 'A process is a specific ordering of work activities across time and place, with a beginning, an end, and clearly identified inputs and outputs: a structure of action'. To this definition we would add that an output may be either a product or a service. An example of a product is a new car, while the repairs to a car constitute a service. And these inputs and outputs can communicate either with a specific customer or with another individual process in the environment − not with another internal process, which Davenport has stated on occasion.

Another interesting definition of a process related concept is 'value stream', defined by James Martin (1994). A value stream is 'a set of end-to-end activities which collectively creates value for a customer'. Martin has selected a term other than the common word 'process' because this word has so many meanings, and also because it has been extensively misused. We use the word 'process' as an everyday word without any precise meaning. Later, in Chapter 5, we will describe how we model business processes as use cases and internal processes as objects.

A customer-oriented process is expressed in terms of meeting an individual customer's needs, not the needs of all customers. By primarily concentrating on processes that provide value to customers and not merely to other parts of the business, we arrive at what we should actually be doing. When you adopt this focus, you discover that much of the work previously performed was not performed to satisfy a customer, but to provide something to some internal activity. A customer is satisfied by giving him the right product or service, with high quality and with short lead times, at the right price.

Carlzon, former president of SAS, organized his front troops into teams, one team for each flight. The team bore responsibility for the process 'flying: from checking in to returning baggage on arrival'. The team was made up of personnel who worked inside the plane as well as personnel on the ground. The latter were, for instance, technicians and baggage handlers, who of course were no longer on the team as soon as the plane left the runway. This was a completely new way of organizing commercial flights as compared with the procedures in older functional organizations. Carlzon describes very vividly how correcting a minor fault, such as a loose moulding, might be carried out in the old and in the new organizations. Earlier, the purser was obliged to make a formal report of the fault, whereupon a very costly and time-consuming procedure was initiated, involving managers in several line organizations. In the new organization however, the purser could simply ask a technician on the team to screw in the moulding, thus eliminating the problem altogether.

1.2.3 How do processes relate to products?

Products are goods that are designed, manufactured, sold and delivered; processes handle products. In the Western world, we traditionally focused on products, not processes. You might say that we formed our processes to handle products we had already designed. We now realize the folly of that approach: product and process must be formed in a coordinated, integrated fashion.

In the early 1950s, when it was still a small company, the Swedish furniture retailer IKEA developed a unique business concept. In those days, good furniture was sold in fine stores located in the city centre. Volumes were low, so prices were unavoidably high. Ingvar Kamprad, IKEA's founder, wanted to sell his furniture to everyone, regardless of income and residence. To reduce prices, Kamprad had to increase sales volume and reduce distribution costs. He wanted to get rid of the middleman and sell directly to the customer, who would transport and install their furniture. His solution was simple and ingenious. The furniture was constructed and packed so it required less storage space, was cheaper to transport and simple to assemble. Customers could fetch the furniture themselves, either at an IKEA warehouse or at a local railway station, transport it to their home, and assemble it there. Using this method and selling via postal order catalogues instead of from expensive shops, Kamprad managed to cut costs substantially. Kamprad realized he could change the entire sales and distribution process and dramatically improve his company's competitive situation. To succeed, at least two things had to be achieved. First and foremost, the customers had to accept the idea of fetching and assembling furniture. Second, the furniture had to be designed so that the distribution process was feasible: It had to be suitable for assembly and disassembly and compactly packed. Kamprad decided this was feasible, and time has proven him right. He changed the way many people furnish their homes. Today, IKEA is a multinational company (turnover in 1993 was US$4 billion).

It is obvious that a company's products must be designed in harmony with the company's processes. The most important processes, of course, are those that take care of the company's customers.

1.2.4 How do processes relate to services?

Processes allow companies to offer services, just as processes handle products. In this respect, services do not differ from products. Traditionally, we have considered products to be tangible; services, intangible. Products are paid for individually; services, by the work unit (days, hours). However, this way of thinking leaves a large grey zone in which services are packaged and described as a product (air travel, for example). In addition, manufacturing companies are beginning to see the financial wisdom of backing up their products with a set of services.

Thus, the line between product and service is blurring. In the context of business engineering, it is appropriate for the sake of clarity that services and products be handled as two different kinds of deliverables. A deliverable is an output from a business that has a value — material or immaterial — to a particular customer. In this definition, things we have traditionally defined as services become a special kind of deliverable.

1.3 Why do we need business engineering?

The most fundamental driving force behind every company is the need to better its own financial position. Put simply, a company must make money. A company can make more money by doing what it intends to do in the most cost-effective way possible. That is to say, you must reduce the cost of your business processes. Eliminate superfluous internal work. Make more employees more productive through empowerment and training. A company can also make more money by selling more of the products and services it produces. Improve quality. Shorten lead times. Give customers what they want. To accomplish this, you can no longer simply throw more resources at the problem; that approach has become too expensive and ineffective.

The world in which entrepreneurs live is different from what it was just 10 years ago.

First, the customer has taken control. They are much more aware of their position and the choices open to them than they were even in the early 1980s. They no longer accept being perceived as part of a collective, but expect to be seen as individuals. As Hammer (1993) says: 'There is no longer any such notion as the customer; there is only this customer'.

Second, customers have a new attitude towards products and services. Each individual customer wants products that are:

- adapted and configured to satisfy his/her needs,

- delivered in a way that is practical to him/her, and

- delivered when he/she is available to receive it.

Third, the global market means competition comes from all over. Customers want to buy products that are widely accepted in the world, not just locally. It is no longer sufficient to have a decent product and a good price. You must be able to measure yourself against all your competitors, no matter where they are.

To survive, you must adapt to a new way of doing business that involves constantly adjusting to a changing environment. This cannot be done by steering a multilayered corporate hierarchy from the top. It requires business engineering. Companies must organize themselves to cope with constant change. Companies themselves will not be 'stabilized'. They will change constantly, to satisfy customer requirements, address increasingly tough competition, improve internal processes, modify the range of products and services they offer, and give personnel tangible goals and the freedom to reach those goals in a creative manner, within a given framework.

That framework is provided by focusing on customer-oriented business processes.

1.4 What does the new company look like?

Obviously, there is no single answer to this question. There are many different ways to design a new, modern company, of course. And there are many different ways in which the same design can be implemented, that is, included in the company. However, we can give you some hints as to what you might expect.

On the one hand, you will be surrounded by the same people. A few individuals with especially vital skills and experience have been recruited. Some of the previous staff have left because their positions were no longer tenable or they could not accept the change in the nature of their assignments. Generally speaking, however, the same people are with you.

On the other hand, the company is no longer what it was. People have different tasks and new values. They are rewarded in new ways. They have begun to be more involved, to take on more responsibility. They are perceived as being more knowledgeable, more service-minded.

Customers are discovering that they are more important as individuals, and that it is pleasant doing business with the company. Sounds too good to be true? What has happened? Something revolutionary, surely. In fact, it is true. Carlzon has called it 'flattening the pyramid' and challenges us to 'turn the traditional corporation upside down'. At the very least, we can imagine turning the organization on its side, as Figure 1.2 shows.

The traditional, hierarchically functional organization has managers at several levels. At the bottom of the organization, where most of the actual work is performed, the 'grass roots' workers serve the customers. The customers are at the very bottom. In the new organization, customers stand to the side of the organization, as if they were its equals — its partners. The 'grass roots' workers have become process operators, the interface to the customers. Middle managers have become process team leaders.

What is the difference between the old and new organizations? Let's compare how project work is performed in both organizations.

In the old organization, a project leader is put in charge of an assignment that may slice across functional units. When the project leader approaches the line managers of the various units to recruit employees to help carry out the assignment, he usually receives a less-than-friendly

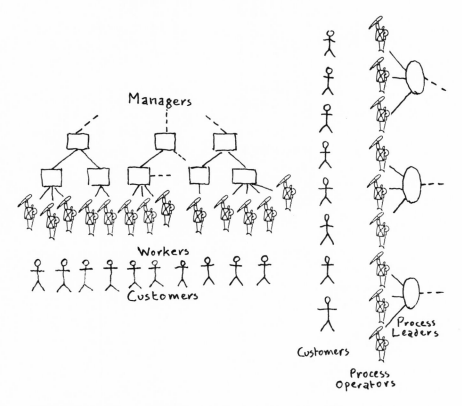

Figure 1.2 *Left, a traditional hierarchical organization. Right, a new organization.*

reception. Line managers have several roles. Among other things, they are expected to ensure that things are done right – and that the right things are done – within their unit. They must also take care of their personnel and developing their skills. Line managers know project leaders are necessary, but must also keep their guard up so they don't lose resources. Negotiations between managers and project leaders are never-ending in scope: Anyone who has ever worked on a project knows it is necessary to report to both the project leader and the line manager, who don't always convey the same message. Conflict is unavoidable.

In the new organization, a process leader also recruits others, who may come from different functional units, who will be required to complete the project. In a similar fashion, a process leader recruits and organizes personnel into teams containing the required competence. The members of the team are process operators, each one offering various skills. The team's work consists of a number of activities that are linked together in a 'natural' way. The job is carried out to the specifications of a particular customer, and results in something of value for the customer in question. In today's terminology, the job is a 'project' (for example, product development: from requirements to product). We call the job a 'process'. A process has both a beginning and an end, and when it is complete the available resources can be used for some other purpose. Thus there may be several instances of the same process going on concurrently. Each process has a process leader; each process may also have process operators. Process leaders report to a process owner, who is an executive. The process owner defines the process, and sets and monitors its goals, whereas a process leader 'runs' an instance of the process.

Thus far, no appreciable difference is apparent between the line organization and the process-oriented. However, there are decisive differences between the two.

In the first place, a process-oriented organization views not only traditional projects as processes, but other jobs as well, even more routine and repetitive jobs. For example, 'sales: from lead to order', might be carried out by only one salesperson. When the salesperson is finished with one customer, he/she takes on the next. Thus, the sales process is cyclical: When one assignment is finished, a similar one is begun. The organization can coordinate assignments among salespeople in several ways. For example, each area may have a single salesperson or one sales coordinator may participates in all instances of the sales process. Another example of a cyclical process is 'flight: from check-in to baggage return'. Here, the same team, augmented by ground personnel, begin work with a new flight as soon as they have completed work with the one before it. In line organizations, these jobs are invisible. They are not projects, yet they cut across several functions and they are performed despite line organization. In the new organization, such jobs are elevated to a visible, identifiable status, where they can be discerned for what they are: processes.

Another major difference between functional and process-oriented organizations is the lack of middle managers. No manager is forced to guard a functional area and assume responsibility for what is done and how it is done. Managers — in the form of supervisors — are no longer necessary. Small organizations can do without managers, and large organizations are flattened in comparison with today's situation. The process leader is directly responsible to top management (who are not shown in the figure above) and reaches agreement with them about what his/her process can cost. The assets (read, 'money') management provides are to be used by the process leader to deploy resources — be they human, hardware, or software — from within or from without the company. The top management has responsibility for the theory of how work shall be carried out and for coordinating various processes so interfaces operate smoothly and the same assignments are not performed at more than one place in the organization.

A process-oriented organization groups its employees according to their areas of competence. For each of these areas, one individual — a resource owner — is responsible. A resource owner:

● Takes care of his/her personnel.

● Coordinates resource requirements from process leaders for the entire area of competence.

● Develops resources to meet the demands of process leaders.

● Manages trainees and assumes responsibility for their personal development.

● Ensures that each staff member has a basic salary commensurate with his/her tasks.

A resource owner has people but no money, and a process owner has money but no people. One of a resource owner's most important tasks is to negotiate and sell employee skills to process owners to get money to cover his/her costs (salaries, and so on). In this organization, resource owners can offer the right people to the right process owners. A resource owner reports, as does a process owner, directly to the company's top management.

In the new organization, employees will tend to view their work in more positively. Together, they help to fill the customer's needs. They are required to do what is asked of them, not what their functional role dictates, so their assignments become more multifaceted. They feel less supervised and more empowered, and they begin to see themselves almost as small-scale entrepreneurs. Furthermore, because it is easier to measure customer satisfaction over the long term, it is easier to reward staff members with bonuses, for example. Advancement opportunities are more plentiful and more distinct, and are based on the individual's ability to perform the new job. Good process leaders and resource owners are important and highly sought after. A line organization, in contrast, might reward a good technician by advancing that person to a managerial position. The result may be that we get a poor manager in exchange for a good technician. In a flattened organization, there is no need for us to make this mistake. There is always an acute need for knowledgeable, competent personnel, and in the process-oriented organization, there are always opportunities to reward them.

Carlzon (1987) tells this story. Two stonecutters were standing hewing square blocks out of granite. When they were asked what they were doing, one of them replied in a bored tone: 'I'm cutting this stone into square blocks'. The other answered proudly: 'I'm helping to build a cathedral'.

In the reengineered company, every staff member has a vision of what the entire team's ultimate goal and the way it shall be achieved. Everyone knows how success will be measured. Everyone understands and appreciates the value his or her co-workers bring to the team and the business, and everyone is aware of his or her own part in the greater context.

1.5 Business engineering, business (process) reengineering, and business improvement

How does the concept of business engineering stand in relation to terms that border on it, such as business (process) reengineering and business (process) improvement?

1.5.1 Business engineering framework

Most people are most interested in business reengineering, because it is the first thing you think of when business engineering is mentioned and because its effects are the most penetrating and dramatic ones (when successful). Business improvement, which deals with long-term maintenance of developed organizations, is not as eye-catching, mostly because it is something companies constantly engage in.

Although this book is devoted to business reengineering, we shall try to establish a framework that encompasses business improvement. We shall discuss this framework in more detail later. Here, our discussion is more general, in that we view business engineering as an umbrella concept for both business process reengineering and business improvement. Put simply:

Business engineering = business reengineering + business improvement.

1.5.2 Business reengineering

Business reengineering implies that you takes a comprehensive view of the entire existing business and think through why you do what you do, why you do what you do how you do it, and so on. Thus, you questions the entire existing business — or at least its most important processes — and try to find completely new ways of reconstructing them, 'new ways that use the new person in a better way' (Carlzon, 1987). New ways, we might add, that seek to use new technical gains (for example, modern information technology) to serve its customers better.

This is what we call business reengineering, as does Hammer (1993). Others, including Johansson (1993) and Willoch (1993) call it business process reengineering. Davenport (1993) calls it process innovation, 'major reductions in process cost or time, or major improvements in quality, flexibility, service levels or other business objectives'. Carlzon (1985, 1987) — whose ideas on this theme predate any other author we cite — called it 'flattening the pyramid'.

But why have we eliminated the word 'process' in our term? Because we see 'process' as a superfluous term. In the future, business reengineering will mean reengineering business processes, and nothing else. As a rule, reengineering can proceed for many years before the better part of a company's processes have been fully redesigned. The work is thus divided into phases, and each phase has a clearly defined objective. The most important objective of the work as a whole is to achieve dramatically improved performance of critical, measurable process parameters. Hammer and Champy (1993) claim that 'reengineering is the fundamental rethinking and radical redesign of business processes to achieve dramatic improvements in critical, contemporary measures of performance, such as cost, quality, service and speed. [emphasis added]'

'Dramatic' and 'major' are words that describe reductions or improvements that are ten-fold, not merely 10%. 'Fundamental' means that instead of asking how the company might carry out its work in a better way, one asks fundamental questions about the company. Hammer and Champy describe business reengineering as 'starting all over, starting from scratch'. It is a conscious decision that underlies the idea of making dramatic improvements and not merely insignificant, marginal changes in the existing organization.

After a business reengineering project is complete, the company's ability to do business should have improved dramatically. According to Johansson *et al.* (1993), the company should have reached a 'breakpoint'. However, radical changes in processes cannot be carried out in a routine fashion; we can only expect to achieve them by using special initiatives, such as task forces. Such a task force is organized like a project, that is to say, made up of members whose background is cross-functional. Since these people are recruited from different organizations, and because they are given freedom of authority regardless of their functional niche, the necessary conditions for developing the most effective processes possible are created.

1.5.3 Business improvement

Once a company has reengineered its processes, they must be maintained and improved. This requires new objectives and new efforts to reach these objectives. Usually, these objectives are more modest in scope, and the work required to attain them does not have as dramatic an influence on the company's performance. Now, the work of change is local and does not span the entire business. Moreover, it involves trimming costs and lead times and monitoring service and quality. Nevertheless, business (process) improvement is continuous and is of great importance to the entire organization in the long run.

Davenport (1993) used a table (see Table 1.1) to describe the difference between business improvement and business reengineering.

Table 1.1 *The differences between business improvement and business reengineering.*

	Business improvement	Business reengineering
Level of change	Incremental	Radical
Starting point	Existing process	Clean slate
Frequency of change	One-time/continuous	One-time
Time required	Short	Long
Participation	Bottom-up	Top-down
Typical scope	Narrow, within functions	Broad, cross-functional
Risk	Moderate	High
Primary enabler	Statistical control	Information technology
Type of change	Cultural	Cultural/structural

Source: Davenport (1993)

This table uses several important parameters and assigns them values in order to characterize the differences.

As the table indicates, reengineering a business process should be performed only once. After it is installed in the company, it is subject to improvement, of course, but normally you should not have to reengineer it within the next few years. The table also says that business improvement today is usually carried out within a single function, whereas business reengineering is a corporate concern. The more every-day improvements are carried out discretely by individuals in each functional area.

Another interesting aspect of the table is that business reengineering's most important enabler is listed as information technology. We want to amplify this: It is impossible to overestimate the importance of IT to enabling reengineering. IT integrates different organizations within the company. A good information system binds together the different activities within a process and can make even complex processes flow more smoothly as the work is successively dealt with by different areas of the company.

There is no razor-sharp division between business improvement and business reengineering; however, for instructional purposes it might be appropriate to make a clear division between them, especially now

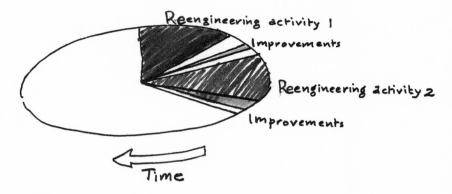

Figure 1.3 *Life cycle of a business process.*

when new ideas about corporate organization are gaining currency. We regard business improvement and business reengineering as similar occurrences, but of different scope. Therefore, they are given different profiles, as our greatly simplified model of the life cycle of a business process illustrates (Figure 1.3).

Starting at the top, the size of each slice indicates the scope process-change activities. The first big slice depicts a radical change in the process that takes some time. Then a series of smaller slices depict several minor improvements made to the process. The next big slice indicates that you might have to reengineer the same process in the future, even if your reengineering activities have been very successful. As a rule, however, subsequent reengineering measures will not be as revolutionary. Thus, your company develops.

Of course such a simple model cannot express how all the company's processes are developed in parallel. As you expect, they are very dependent on one another. And the company may want to introduce new processes now and then. So it is important that you build your company so that it can remain robust in the face of change, which means that changes can be incorporated with minimal effect on the existing company. This would seem to be self-evident, but the fact is that few traditional reengineering methods provide support for it. The information system that supports the business must, in turn, be developed so that it can tolerate radical changes with consequences that are no greater than would be reasonable, given the scope of the change. Unfortunately, this is customary in traditional IT development.

1.6 Risk management

The risks of failure in a reengineering project are extraordinarily great. Hammer estimates that between 50 and 70% of the projects don't succeed — that is, they do not achieve dramatic improvements.

1.6.1 Critical success factors

Kathleen Flynn (1993) presented certain factors for success that she discovered in connection with a large-scale reengineering project:

- *Motivation.* The motive for initiating a reengineering project must be clearly defined and stated. Hammer (1993) calls this the presentation of a 'case for action'. Top management must be convinced absolutely that the reengineering effort will lead to a dramatically improved result, and they must understand that the result will shatter certain structures for good. To ensure the success of the effort, management must commit themselves to it completely, allow it to envelope the company as a whole, and assign their best forces to the reengineering team. Furthermore, they must be prepared, in the words of Johansson *et al.* (1993) to 'break the china'. Ultimately, it is human beings, using various tools, who will enable the processes. Therefore, people must understand why the project has been set in motion (in other words, they must appreciate the problems that beset the business), accept their new tasks, and be trained to carry them out. Therefore, they must be given time and a reasonable pace to succeed.

- *Leadership.* A conductor who is part of the company's executive management, has wide-ranging authority, and enjoys the trust of the organizations involved, must spearhead the project and assume responsibility. Even before the effort is launched, the leader must be aware of the difficulties in building up the new company: He/she must resist pressure from a balky organization and fight to convince people that the project is not only vital but essential to survival. He/she must neither capitulate nor accept simpler, more marginal alterations. Finally, he/she must push the effort forward and demand, within reason, a timely result.

- *Organization-wide ownership.* The organizations involved, including personnel at all levels, must persuaded to assume common ownership of the work that will bring change. In this effort, the most important group is the middle level, the level Willoch (1993) calls 'permafrost'. It is relatively easy to explain the new way of working to grass-roots staff, but people who have advanced to a managerial position find it much more difficult to understand what the new company can offer them. Willoch defines three categories of middle managers. Tigers are the young careerists who, although they participate enthusiastically in reengineering, also have a tendency to focus on their own goals and successes at the expense of the project's overall aims. Donkeys are older staff members who have attained their career objectives and want stability in the company; they can seriously slow down a reengineering project. Sharks have developed the routines and instructions that guide the company's operations and often possess the real power in an organization; they can cause the greatest problems by sabotaging any real change in the fundamental 'truths' that govern the organization's life.

- *Vision.* The company's new goals must be articulated and made comprehensible for everyone involved.

- *Focus.* The work of changing the company shall focus on the highest-priority goals, and resources shall be directed towards these goals. (Never bite off more than you can chew ...)

- *Well-defined roles and responsibilities.* Besides the people who are knowledgeable about the business that will be reengineered, others familiar with how one goes about changing a business must participate.

- *Tangible products.* The results of the reengineering work shall be concrete deliverables such as reformulated goals and missions, new work flows, a process model, an organizational plan, and a data model.

- *Technology support.* Support in the form of methods and tools is indispensable to the work of reengineering. Business engineering usually involves constructing an information system to support the new business. This is an area of risk that is most often overlooked. IT organizations are generally not as competent in fashioning their own products (information systems) as humans are in exploiting other engineering disciplines used to build houses, bridges, automobiles, and electronic devices, for example. The Software Engineering Institute (SEI) at Carnegie Mellon University estimated that 85% of all software developed in 1989 was done without any real method. A good word for this is 'hacking'. Here we have a rich source of failure.

- *Expert guidance.* Mentors can help people who are new to reengineering. However, it is important that consultation is, in fact, supportive, not controlling: the consultants must not render passive the company's own staff. Goldratt (1992) describes in a compelling novel how this support can be proffered by posing the correct questions — questions that induce the reengineering team to think in terms of the correct issues.

- *Risk-taking.* As Carlzon (1987) has said, 'One must dare to take the leap'. Comedian Flip Wilson put it even more bluntly: 'You can't expect to hit the jackpot if you don't put a few nickels in the machine'.

1.6.2 Reducing the risks

Ideas and principles alone are not sufficient to succeed in business engineering. Hammer and Champy (1993) suggest business engineering can be achieved through training and qualified consulting. But this is still not sufficient.

Business reengineering risks fall roughly into two categories: risks associated with the change process, and risks associated with the technology used. It is generally accepted by those in the industry that 80% of the failures are caused by 'soft' factors, (such as motivation, management commitment, leadership, the need for expert guidance,) and we believe that this is a reasonable estimate. Most books and methods on BPR tackle these soft factors, creating best-selling authors and prosperous consultants.

While we don't underestimate the need to address the change process, we are convinced that the success rate can be dramatically improved if reengineering methods offered more concrete guidance. In fact, we believe you can almost guarantee successful reengineering projects and reduce the dominance of these 'soft' factors, if you use a formal process. At Objectory AB, in Sweden, we have lengthy experience in reengineering many a company's software-development organization to adopt object-oriented processes. Our mission is to help customers change their development process from whatever it is to being object-oriented. Our experience is unambiguous: A formal reengineering process and less hand-waving is a must for success. A reengineering team needs a common perspective and a common language to pilot their work to a successful result. As much as possible, you want to achieve similar results regardless of who does the job and independent of any particular individual. This calls for a common, repeatable process. Creativity, business acumen and experience are of course individual attributes, but process should be common knowledge.

A formal reengineering process includes:

- A process description that specifies every activity and deliverable involved. This description must be adaptable to the reengineering project. For example, the size and maturity of the organization and the type of process you are reengineering will influence the process description.

- Deliverables, in the form of business models, that focus on the company's architecture and dynamics. This is the subject of Chapter 2.

- A process for the development of a truly integral information system. A truly integral information system is one that is developed in parallel with new business processes and both influences the design of those processes and is influenced by them.

- A tight, seamless relation between the process to develop the business model and the process to develop the information system. Primarily, these processes describe concepts, models, tools, and documentation. Establishing this relation enables business people to communicate with IT people and IT people with end users. It also eliminates the separation between the business models and the information system's requirements models and tears down language barriers.

Nevertheless, there is a overriding condition that is altogether decisive. Being able to use the same technique for business development and information-system development is not an end in itself. This was also possible with traditional techniques. No, it is paramount that the technique you use is an excellent modelling tool for both the business and the information system. It is not enough that it can be used – it must be ideal for both. No compromises can be accepted. Only if this condition is met can you use the same technique for these separate applications.

1.7 The future of business engineering in the corporate world

How will business engineering be viewed in the future by the corporate world? We believe that most companies are altogether too unsystematic in clarifying and communicating why they do what they do, and why they do it that way. We have become slaves to what we are doing, and we find it difficult to raise our head and ask 'Why?' Usually the only descriptions of the company you have are organizational charts upon which appear the names of various executives. This tells you nothing really, except: 'Regardless of what this company is involved in, these are the organizational units that carry it out, and these are the executives who keep track of what's going on. In some way, they manage to persuade a number of workers to perform what needs to be done.'

A company is a complex system. You must be able to get an overall view of it and understand it if you are going to work in it, if you want to change it to adapt to new circumstances, or if you want to support it with modern technology. Hierarchical organizational charts simply do not reflect the true network of relationships, information flow, material flow, and dynamic interactions that make a company 'work'.

Modern companies must embody a corporate culture in which employees are constantly prepared to implement improvements into the business. A company should be able to institutionalize its incremental development and make special innovative efforts when the time is right. To do this, a modern company needs correct and current business models. We believe you should organize the work of describing the company and its processes as a process – the business-development process (Figure 1.4). In order to serve its purpose, the business-development process uses competence from various areas of the company, and it carries out reengineering projects in line with directives from the company's top management. In contrast, incremental improvements in business processes are at the business-processes level, by individuals who make up the process teams.

Introducing a business-development process is no guarantee that radical, sweeping changes will be put in motion and generate a dramatic increase in profit. Business development is not enough by itself; making dramatic profits demands insight and talent. However, by being organized in the right way, the company prepares itself for a leap forward.

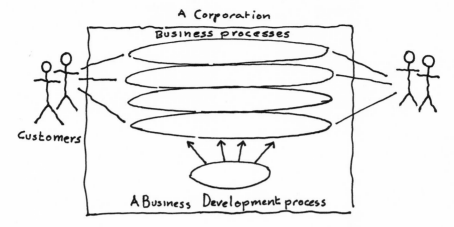

Figure 1.4 *In each company, there should be a business-development process (or possibly several) to support the company's business processes.*

The business-development process, which is carried out by a team with a similar competence level as the reengineering team, is meant to develop the company at the express directive of corporate management. The process shall maintain models of the existing company and measure how well the company is managing its business processes.

You may be very skeptical of a special process being in charge of defining and selling the new processes. Many managers have experienced, that without broad participation within the company there will be widespread attempts to undermine anything such a process team proposes. Special process teams tend to become insular and arrogant over time, negating their very purpose for existence. Yes, this has and can happen if it is not managed correctly. It is important that you distinguish between improving existing processes and either creating new business processes or making major changes to existing ones. From a pragmatic standpoint, the workers and managers closest to the customers and the production line are likely to have excellent ideas as to how the process can be improved and they should themselves take care of their own processes. The business-development process should only care about the new or radically changed processes. Furthermore, this process should be led by someone who has the confidence of the process owners and resource owners of the processes concerned.

The people involved in the business-development process must have data about the business processes' lead times, qualities, resource requirements, productivity, and so on, or should at least know how to get it. Furthermore, they should be able to benchmark the company against other companies, seeking out information about other companies against which the company wants to be measured and from which they might learn something. These might be competitors, of course, but it is difficult to learn anything from them. As a rule, companies benchmark against companies in other market segments but with similar role patterns. Companies in other segments can even see something positive in exchanging information, and will gladly share their experiences in return for future exchanges.

When management wants to implement major changes, the following business-development process is triggered:

- Information about the existing organization is collected. At this stage, getting the right information is very important, or you run the risk of making changes without having full knowledge of the consequences.

- The business-development process team develops a model (or several of them) of how the new company is expected to operate.

- The model is communicated to those who are currently responsible for the corresponding processes and, after it has been modified, it is approved.

- The model is implemented in the company as various types of resources. Besides human resources with varied competence and experience, there are also mechanical resources. Of these, the most important is information technology.

- Information systems are built to support the business processes. These systems must be developed in harmony with the business processes. The development work is not carried out in sequence, but in parallel.

After this initial reengineering effort, the new processes begin to work, and continuous process improvement happens at a more moderate pace. Skeptics of disciplined, methodical approaches to business engineering should be assured that working with the processes continuously is of the utmost importance. There are two main reasons for this:

- Continuous improvement helps you maintain knowledge about what your processes look like and the reason for the primary purpose of each process – to produce something of value for the customer. A large initial cost in a new reengineering project is to describe the existing organization in terms of business processes.

- Continuous improvement helps you maintain your knowledge about what business reengineering and business improvement is and means. Otherwise, the next time you will enhance your organization, you will have to start from the beginning and learn everything anew.

1.8 Summary

Thanks to modern information technology, we can radically change the way a company operates and achieve dramatic improvements. This new way of changing a business is called business reengineering. Customers become more satisfied, the company becomes more competitive, and personnel become more competent and responsible. In this chapter, we have tried to give a brief introduction to business engineering, why you should use it, and the basics of how the new company will look. We have also discussed the risks reengineering poses and how they can be reduced. Finally, we have given a picture of how we think a modern company shall handle business engineering issues in the future.

In reengineering projects, there is a considerable risk factor attached to building the information system that will support the business processes. We are forced to admit that most of the IT world does not have even a decent chance of building a 'good' information system; that is, one that supports the company's business, is accepted by its users, and is tolerant of change. The available techniques for building systems of this type are in their infancy when compared with the engineering techniques used to produce houses, bridges, and automobiles. However, a small segment of the IT world has seen the emergence of a new technique based on object orientation.

Object orientation is the most promising technique to produce a 'good' information system. Object orientation is really nothing new; Ivar Jacobson and others have been working with it for more than 25 years. Unfortunately, however, the technique is not widely known, and today only a small segment of the IT world makes use of it. Object orientation alone is not sufficient. Actually, it is only a basic technique, similar to chip technology for hardware. Chips are not sufficient in themselves to build a good hardware system — you must choose the right chips and put them together in an intelligent way. In the same way, one must find the right objects and then put them together in an intelligent way to use object orientation.

Our approach to business reengineering is to proceed from the business processes. We find them by starting with the customer and other surrounding influences, then we consider what they can use the company for to develop what we call the company's use cases. We model business processes with the help of our use-case concept, then use object-thinking to make clear, comprehensible models of the company. In other words, first the use cases, then objects! We use the same thinking to model the information system. We start with the users, find all the use cases, then build an object model of the system. The advantage of working in this way is that if we, when we model the company, use the same way of thinking that we use when we model the information system (both are systems), we will get a high level of traceability between the two models.

But perhaps we are proceeding too fast. Let's continue this discussion in smaller steps. In Chapter 2, we describe in general (without introducing objects) what we mean by modelling a company, explain what we must be able to express, and what we use these models for. In Chapter 3, we introduce the object-oriented way of thinking, the foundation for the remainder of the book.

1.9 References

Carlzon J. (1987). *Moments of Truth*. MA: Ballinger Publishing Company

Carlzon J. and Lagerström Th. (1985). *Riv Pyramiderna! en bok om den nya människan, chefen och ledaren*

Chamberlain W. (1993). CIO, Reengineer Thyself. *Chief Information Officer Journal*, September/October, pp. 21–5

Davenport T.H. (1993). *Process Innovation, Reengineering Work through Information Technology*. Boston, MA: Harvard Business School Press

Flynn K. (1993). Critical Success Factors for a Successful Business Reengineering Project. *CASE World Conference Proceedings*, October 1993, Boston, MA

Goldratt E. (1992). *The Goal*. NY: North River Press Inc.

Hammer M. and Champy J. (1993). *Reengineering the Corporation: A Manifesto for Business Revolution*. NY: HarperCollins

Johansson H., McHugh P., Pendlebury J. and Wheeler III W. (1993). *Business Process Reengineering. Breakpoint Strategies for Market Dominance*. Chichester: John Wiley & Sons

Martin J. (1994). *Enterprise Engineering – The Key to Corporate Survival*. Vol. I–V. UK: Savant Institute

Willoch B.E. (1994). *Business Process Engineering. Vinnende arbeidsprosesser og organisasjonsstrukturere i forandringens decennium*. Norway: Fagbogförlaget

chapter 2
What is business modelling?

2.1 Introduction

Every company is a complex organism. It is created, begins to live, grows, becomes successful, faces difficulties, pulls itself out of crisis, renews itself, continues to grow, and so on. At any given moment, the picture a company presents is only part of the truth about it — there is so much more hidden within its complexities. It is impossible to capture completely the essence of a company's being. Fortunately, it is not really necessary to do so. However, it is desirable to examine a company's being in depth and detail so that everyone concerned with it will have sufficient information to make decisions that will be the best possible ones in every situation. Even sufficient information, of course, does not guarantee success. Good intuition is of course necessary for any entrepreneur, and as a rule you must resign yourself to using your intuition if you wish to be successful. However, knowledge reduces risks. Very successful companies usually have succeeded in seeing to it that all their employees have individually adapted knowledge about the company: about its strategies, visions, goals, processes, products, services, resources and the relationship between these factors. Companies strive to clarify themselves for their various interested parties.

The problem is to be able to transfer knowledge about all these important things to all those people who should be aware of them. Man has for a long time known that complicated things are easier to understand if they are visualized in some way, not just described in words. A formal way to visualize something is to build a model of it. In this chapter, we introduce the 'model concept ' and discuss the types of models suited to different purposes. We shall also show how these different models can be linked together to give an overall picture of a company. But remember, a model should never be considered to be the 'truth' − it is only a (more or less correct) map of it.

2.2 What is a model?

Almost all creators express themselves with models. We build models when we want to build cars, bridges and buildings. We draw circuit diagrams when we want to shape and define electrical devices, computers, machines and tools. We use formulas to understand physics, chemistry and mathematics. In virtually every discipline, we use different techniques to clarify what we are doing − it is natural to most of us to work this way. Modelling is the unifying term we use to express what we are doing.

A model clarifies − for a person or group of people − some aspect of or some perspective on a thing or an event. To accomplish such a general purpose, there are different kinds of models and different kinds of model descriptions. The two main types of model descriptions are static and dynamic. A static description shows model structures; a dynamic description shows the flow of events. Thus, it is quite natural to use different models to describe different aspect of a company, and it is important to determine what aspect a given model is supposed to express. Obviously, it is neither possible nor desirable to express all aspects at once. For example, in Figure 2.1 we show some of the parties who have an interest in a company. We describe these parties as *handlers* of the company. Customers are handlers. Usually, customers are not all alike, and they should not be perceived as being alike. You must regard them as many different individuals with different needs, and you must allow them to perceive the company in different ways.

The company's Chief Executive Officer must have an overall picture of all the aspects of the entire company: business concept, customers, processes, products, personnel, investments, finances, visions for the future, etc. This overall picture must be tremendously well integrated. In order for management to be able to make the right

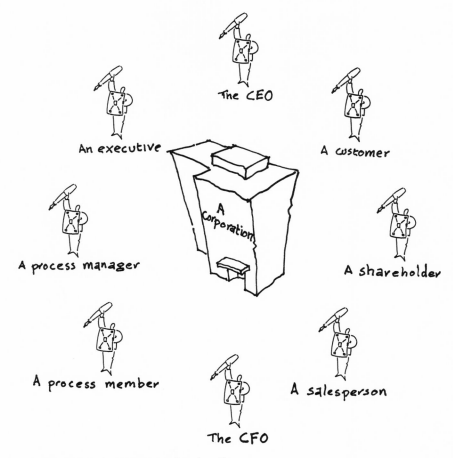

Figure 2.1 *A company and its handlers.*

decisions in any given situation, models must be developed that clearly describe all the facets of the company and how they relate to one another. This is, in fact, possible to do to a limited degree. In models that are to be used by top management, the main characteristic in terms of importance is comprehensibility: essentials must emphasized, details suppressed. In the same way, we can relate models to each of the company's handlers. As with the CEO, each handler requires exactly the information they need to get a comprehensive view of the situation and to know what detailed action they must take. This, at least, is desirable. But in certain situations, even though it may not be possible to predict in detail what must be done, the handler must be aware of the circumstances and be able to choose a course of action that they find suitable. By 'the exact model that is necessary', we mean a model that satisfies the handlers' need for exactly the amount of information they find essential to carrying out the work at hand – no more, no less. This statement, however, should not be taken too literally. Obviously, it is sometimes advantageous for a staff member to know more than only that which narrowly concerns him/herself; in that case, it is clear that he/she needs the information in question. On the other hand, it is also clear that the staff member should not be given more information than is necessary, that is, information which is neither of interest nor use to that employee.

Several handlers might need access to the same model. For example, the CEO must know what has been communicated to the shareholders. It is also important that the process leaders and corporate management have the same overall picture of what the company is engaged in, so the two groups can speak to each other in a common language. Finally, although it might be obvious, it is important to emphasize that different models must be consistent. The picture the CEO has of a company's economy and finances should be consistent with what the CEO has observed in reality, even if it represents something that has taken place in the past. The business processes that corporate management see as being offered by the company must be consistent with the actual processes the process leaders and their staffs are involved in. And the resemblance should not be in name only.

In summary, people have always made models. Models of a company are essential to clarifying what the company is about, and it is important to know exactly for whom a given model is made. The company's handlers are identified, and for each category, a model of the company is made. Each model describes an aspect of the company, that is, the aspect that is of value to the handler in question. A model must convey the information about the company that its handlers need – no more, no less. Finally, the integrated models of a company must be consistent with one another.

2.3 What is a business model?

A company's handlers are usually many in number, and – in theory – you could develop a model to suit each of them. In fact, this is more or less what happens. Shareholders receive one kind of description of the

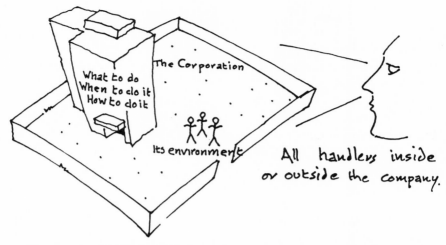

Figure 2.2 *A business model shows the company's function in the world to different handlers in the company.*

company, sales personnel another, and customers yet another. But this is not done systematically and deliberately. These models are probably not entirely consistent with each other, because usually no one actually coordinates their development. In general, companies cannot manage a task of this scope, nor do they see the need for it. But to make the most of a company's potential, you must concentrate on those very aspects that are the most difficult to view comprehensively, aspects that require training, clarification, improvement, change — in other words, aspects that must be kept alive.

One such important model is the business model, in which we clarify the company's function in the world. A business model shows what the company's environment is and how the company acts in relation to this environment. By environment we mean everything the company interacts with to perform its business processes, such as customers, partners, subcontractors and so on. It shows employees at every level what must be done and when and how it should be done. We speak of the business model as a single model, but it doesn't have to be. It can be several models integrated consistently (Figure 2.2).

A key element in the business model is a description of the company's architecture. By 'architecture' we actually mean the architecture of the company model — its most important static structures. These are the structures we want to emphasize. They are relatively long-lived and changing them requires a conscious effort, which is why we call them static. They include the company's functions, that is to say, its divisions, departments, and so on. However, a simple organizational chart is a poor indicator of a company's architecture. Other important static structures are processes, deliverables, and human and mechanical resources. Structures are composed of elements. Each element is linked to other elements. Elements have an owner, someone in the company. Elements are tangible: they have substance, can be assigned a value (sometimes several values), and have limits. We do not consider dynamics – the flow of events within a company – to be part of the architecture. In defining the architecture, we do not take into account how the elements work together, what they do in a given situation, or how they cooperate to carry out assignments. That a flow of events (such as a process) is present is a question of architecture, but the way in which events flow is not. The actions and decisions that make up a flow of events are details that describe individual processes. They are of interest in themselves, and understanding them is necessary if you are to understand the individual process. Therefore, in some cases it is very important to describe the dynamics of the business and to include them in the business model, but they are not an architectural element.

A usable business model must be limited. To describe an entire company's business, it must suppress a body of details. Furthermore, a considerable part of the business' resources are used to carry out processes that everyone thinks should be done, but no one needs a model of. A model is a picture of precisely what you want to show, illustrate, explain, understand, discuss, or modify – nothing more and nothing less. Usually, you develop a business model for only those parts of the company that make up the key business processes. Key business processes are those that customers encounter and those through which the company makes its money. Although the flow of events is not part of the architecture it is certainly in some cases very important to describe the dynamics of the business, that is to say that they should be included in the business model. But a business model shows only what is or is perceived to be interesting and important to its handlers. Everything else should be omitted.

Despite the fact that, for practical reasons, you should not develop a business model for the entire company, we want to offer you a technique that is powerful enough to do just that. This technique is a modelling tool in the broadest sense. It can be used to model the overall view of an entire company and it can be used to define the company in detail. Use this tool pragmatically, to develop models that are sound representations of what you want to do. We must not become slaves to our tools, we must master them.

All in all, a business model shows the company's function in the world, what it does, how and when. The model should emphasize the architecture, that is, the static structures in the company, besides explaining the various flows of events, that is, the dynamic behaviour of the elements in the architecture. The modelling technique shall be forceful in that it should be possible both to show easy-to-understand surveys of the company and to describe parts of the company in detail.

2.4 What does a business model look like?

To give you some idea what a business model could look like, we shall present various views of one. Let us begin with what is perhaps the most well-known model, the one that employees usually show when they present their company (Figure 2.3).

The model of a reengineered company would describe the company's processes, shown here as ovals, and the environment, the customers, suppliers, and partners, in which the processes are used (Figure 2.4).

A third view of a company could describe how the company's various functions (for example, departments) must work together, to

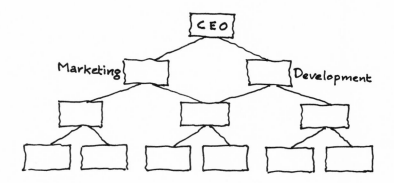

Figure 2.3 *A model of the hierarchical line organization in a company.*

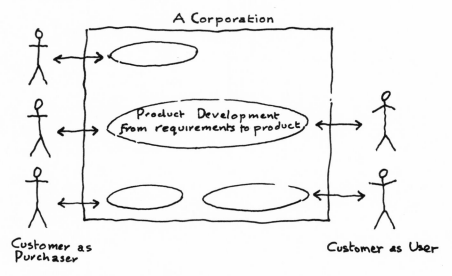

Figure 2.4 *A model of the company's processes.*

carry out a process (Figure 2.5). In this model, customers outside the company are served by four functions inside the company that are linked with arrows. The direction of the arrows shows the event flow from function to function for one process.

There are many other business-modelling techniques; these are just three examples.

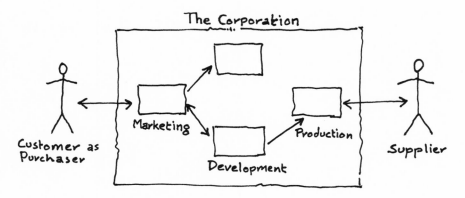

Figure 2.5 *A diagram of how different functions cooperate in a process.*

2.5 A few words about the traditional way of modelling

The business process reengineering literature describes very few business modelling techniques. Johansson (1993) describes a simple technique for describing sequential processes and lists a few other techniques. Tsang (1993) and Sheleg (1993) describe a technique based on business events for reengineering a company, but don't support their ideas with a modelling technique. This is symptomatic, and results either from an unappreciation for the value of modelling or (more likely) the lack of access to a good business-modelling technique. In fact, all the generally available business-modelling techniques belong to the same family of information-systems modelling techniques. Although we shall not go into them at any length here, we can name a few of the best known.

- Structured Analysis and Structured Design (SA/SD) (Yourdon and Constantine, 1979, and Yourdon 1989), is one of the most famous methods of developing information systems. SA/SD stresses that a system provides its users with one or more functions – the so-called functional-decomposition approach. SA/SD offers a number of techniques, such as data-flow diagrams, state-transition diagrams, entity-relationship diagrams (in the analysis phase), and structure charts (in the design phase).

- Integrated Computer Aided Manufacturing Definition (IDEF) was developed by the United States Air Force from ideas that surfaced in the mid 1970s. This technique inspired the US Department of Defense to create IDEF1 (1981), which was in turn developed into the Federal Information Processing Standard IDEF1X. IDEF offers support at several levels by means of the 'model of the business', the 'model of the information system', and the 'technology model'. Business modelling is supported by entity-relationship diagrams for data, and a special type of data-flow diagram that hierarchically describes the functions of the system.

- Structured Analysis and Design Technique (SADT) (Ross 1985) uses notation that resembles the data-flow diagrams in IDEF to describe an information system's functions as well as its data structures, again by decomposition.

All these techniques come from the computer world. It is as though we learned to think in a way that works for computer systems, and we realized we could apply the same way of thinking to describe an organization. We are thankful we have not yet seen a model meant to be applied to human beings that is expressed in COBOL. We do think some people would appreciate a model like that, however, because then they could simulate the company directly. And in fact such a model is not such a great leap from models expressed with any of the popular techniques based on information-systems modelling. When you program in Fortran, COBOL, Pascal, C, or similar languages, you assume there are two types of occurrences to work with: data memory and program memory. A data model refers to what is placed in the data memory. A program refers to what is placed in the program memory. When a computer runs, it follows instructions in the program memory to manipulate data in the data memory.

Most of the techniques based on information-systems modelling are all based on this paradigm. When you describe an information system, you assume it contains two types of things: things that resemble programs (things that can be activated to function and instruct) and things that contain data (passive things that hold information that can be retrieved, read, and replaced). In other words, you describe an information system as an abstraction of a computer.

We believe information systems should be described so they are easy for people to understand, with abstractions that people can comprehend. We think it is bizarre to apply the way of thinking that governs computer systems to business processes. It forces human brains to think like computers. We find this unacceptable. In the next chapter we shall introduce object-thinking, the basis for a modelling technique for people, not machines.

2.6 Why do we need business modelling?

As we have stated, a company is a complex system. It is difficult to view even a small company in the context of its entire 'universe', understand its parts, the interfaces among its parts and all the important details. And there are a great many 'universes' here, made up of parts and with interfaces between them. There are functions, processes, resources, finances, customers, suppliers, and so on. Larger companies are virtually incomprehensible. No one really has a clear picture of all the separate entities.

It is a wonder any large company can function and survive, but there are several reasons they do. The most important reason is that companies, in spite of everything, change rather slowly and organically. People grow into their roles, and changes are made only to the degree people feel that they can comprehend the consequences. As long as a company does not need to change its strategy fundamentally, there is an inertia inherent in the company that will enable it to function. But if the company faces difficulties and major changes have to be implemented, there is an acute risk that people will not really understand what they are doing, or why they are doing it, or whether there is something else they might do instead. As a rule, boards of directors are slow in discovering that things are going badly; but if nothing is done, the very existence of the company may be at stake. The usual solution is to show the company's CEO the door, and hope that his successor will be able to change the course the company is on. We simply take a chance, wagering the entire bankroll on the turn of a card. This is analogous to what many companies are actually doing when they develop software according to the 'hacker' mentality. Sometimes it works like a charm and they succeed, but most often it doesn't work at all. A change of leadership will, in many cases, be sufficient to reverse a negative course, but if the company's problems are of a more profound nature, a change at the management level will not be enough.

Take IBM in 1993, for example. One of the world's largest company is shaking at its foundations, and no one knows how its future will turn out or what the new IBM will look like when the dust has settled. For more than a decade now, it has been obvious to most future-watchers where the software industry was heading. Obviously, IBM did not heed these signals, but clung fast to its old strategies. In all likelihood, if IBM had changed course 10 years ago it would never have found itself in its present crisis. And when a company finds itself in a crisis situation, usually the only available recourse is to take chances, to keep on 'hacking'. Time is short, and the company is bleeding to death. There is nothing more that can be done in a systematic fashion, and you are obliged to reengineer in the dark.

But it does not have to be this way. By working more systematic-ally with good business models, you can guarantee that your company is comprehensible from top to bottom throughout the organization. You can describe your company, explain it, clarify new thoughts and ideas, evaluate them against the existing company, draw up scenarios on the environment – customers, competitors, products, and so on. IBM should have been able to simulate different industry scenarios and see the effects they would have had on IBM. Scenarios that showed the PC becoming very powerful, the demand for mainframe computers being drastically reduced, the rise of client-server computing (which was actually a well-known technique already in the beginning of the 1980s), the demand for open solutions and universally compatible software, etc. By evaluating what scenarios like this would mean in the long run – what effect they would have – IBM might have chosen another course and kept itself vigilant in the face of these eventualities. At least to outsiders, it looks like IBM did not have full control of its business processes.

Thus, we need business models to manage a company's development in a systematic way instead of by taking chances. It is important that these models capture the right factors in the company, revealing what is essential and suppressing what is nonessential. Even with perfect business models there is always a risk factor and many uncertainties. Business models can help to reduce risks, avoid avoidable errors and increase the probability of success. In the next section, we shall comprehensively examine the requirements we have on a business model to ensure that it serves the company in a worthwhile way.

2.7 Who should have a business model, and why?

A company influences many different categories of people, and each of these categories (as we mentioned in Section 2.3, What is a Business Model?) should have its own model of the company. Here, we limit our discussion to the most important categories and describe their requirements only briefly. We also want to show the people in each category have only one view of the complete model – a view of the information they need and nothing more. Finally, we discuss how all views should be consistent.

2.7.1 Customers and partners

Fundamental changes in a company's business cannot be done unless everyone in the environment is engaged. Customers, as well as other important collaborators (or partners), have expectations with regard to the company, just as the company has expectations with regard to customers and partners. Often the most radical ideas for reengineering come from customers or partners. A model that engages the environment must focus on a view of the company as seen from the environment, a view that shows what the company has to offer the environment and vice versa. In this context, it should be apparent that how the company has internally organized its work, functionally and hierarchically, is of no interest whatsoever to the environment. On the other hand, the environment is vitally interested in the company's business processes and its interfaces with customers and partners. Also of interest is the company's geographical distribution: where it is located, and which processes are in force in which locations.

2.7.2 Executive management

Executive management formulates a company's visions and goals. To do so, it must have a clear picture of how these factors are implemented within the organization, so the models it uses must stress the company's architecture. These models should give executive managers not only an overview of the company's business processes and how they relate to one another, but also a comprehensive view of every single process. For each business process, managers must be able to identify visions, goals, costs, lead times, quality of output to the customer, and so on. Furthermore, they must be able to allocate resources (process owners, process leaders, and resource owners) to the models, and they must be able to budget and evaluate their budget against the later outcome.

2.7.3 The reengineering team

The staff assigned to redesign the company must have access to the most thoroughly detailed models. These people need the same overview models that management needs – in fact, they will communicate with management using these models. However, the reengineering team also needs detailed descriptions of each stage of every active process. They must be able to judge what type of resource, and how much of each type, is needed. They must be able to identify potential bottlenecks and how to eliminate them. More than these complete descriptions, though, the reengineering team needs methods and tools by which to develop their models. The team must be able to visualize the company, comprehend and redesign it at different levels of abstraction, prototype it, establish all the resources necessary to implement it, and document it. Finally, they must be able to 'sell' the new company, redesigned to accommodate a new organization. Among other things, these methods and tools must allow the team to:

- Visualize the company and the world around it. They must be able to try out various scenarios to see how business processes can be extended, either by taking over tasks currently performed by customers or putting customers in charge of tasks currently per-formed by the company. The team will have to work with alternative process architectures and simulate their effects.

- Work with different design alternatives once they have chosen a process architecture. In this case, design means designing the business processes so that they are deploying the troops (human resources) in the most effective way possible. The reengineering team must be able to make decisions about design at different levels, from the comprehensive architectural level (such as the functional structure and the types of resources that should be on hand) down to the detailed, dynamic level of events. Studying business processes in action will reveal conflicts – bottlenecks, gridlocks, inconsistencies – in the flow of events among processes.

- Describe the company's deliverables in the context of how, when, and during which processes they are handled. Every product and every product type has a life cycle that should be clear to everyone who works with it.

- Adapt the chosen architecture design to the existing organization. For a company that is widely distributed geographically, with affiliates and subsidiaries in many countries, it might be preferable to reengineer the company in stages, one or a few processes at a time, and leave the rest of the company more or less intact.

- Describe how the final design will be implemented using both human and mechanical resources.

- Present the reengineered company so that everyone understands the consequences of the new organization, their new task and how they are to carry them out. This is another model, but in this case the requirements of formality (completeness, consistency, clarity, etc.) are not dominant. Instead, simplicity is most important – this model must be quickly understood by staff without much training and much interference in their work.

2.7.4 The process owner

As a rule, a process owner is chosen from executive management. If this is the case, he/she will have the information as described in Section 2.7.2, Executive Management. Of course, each process owner must understand their own process in detail and, even if they do not personally document the process, they should contribute actively to its design. In addition, every process owner must understand the neighbouring process or processes in a general way.

2.7.5 The resource owner

The company's various resources are each handled by a resource owner. A resource owner must have all-around familiarity with the business processes and know how they are implemented in terms of human resources. Each resource owner must be able to offer the right kind of resources – with the right kind of training, competence, experience, etc. – to the processes they support.

2.7.6 The IT organization

Here, we refer to a company's IT organization as a single entity. We do not break down the many different types of resource needs within the IT organization. A business model serves as an important input to building the supporting information system. But it is actually more complicated than that. As we mentioned in Chapter 1, it is simply impossible to develop a business model for a company without simultaneously developing – albeit with some displacement in time – the information system as well. The development of the business models and the information systems must be done interactively. To build an information system, you need access to much information about the business. For example, you must know:

- The users (or resources), both within and without the company, who will use the information system.

- All the business processes and how each of them shall be supported by the information system.

- The types of document that are produced while a business process runs and what is done with each of them. In brief, the IT organization usually needs the same level of formal description as does the reengineering team. IT people are now generally used to using formal techniques in their work, so they gladly accept this type of technique.

2.7.7 Human resources

Again, the reengineering team must present and explain the new organization so that everyone concerned understands the consequences, knows their new assignments, and how they shall carry them out.

2.8 Working to develop a business model

Trying to capture how an existing company operates is to perform a reverseengineering activity. Usually, you do this to get a firmer footing so that you can significantly improve some aspect of a company in the future. A model of an existing company is also important when you try to understand and explain how the company, or some process in it, operates. For example, if you want to dramatically improve lead times through reengineering, a model can identify bottlenecks, resources needs and costs associated with different stages in the process. But producing a model of an existing company is time-consuming and expensive. Also, it can be arduous because everyone tends to interpret what they actually do in such different ways. It can be difficult to get a consensus on this model. Therefore, it is very important to delimit what you shall model and how detailed you shall model it. Proper scoping, in other words, is the key. Concentrate on describing the parts of the business that can be radically improved by reengineering. Thus, even if your modelling technique allows you to describe the whole company in every conceivable detail, it is important to be pragmatic and model only that which can be valuable to the reengineering task.

Describing a new company is a forward-engineering activity that begins with the formulation of goals and visions. After that, different scenarios are sketched. For each scenario, a process overview is produced that encompasses customers, suppliers, and so on, as well as processes. The various processes are simulated — either by playing them out as a kind of corporate game or by simulating them in a computer system. Finally, the chosen alternative is implemented as various kinds of resources within (and sometimes outside of) the company.

2.9 Summary

The most common business model is the hierarchical organization chart, complete with the various managers' names. This model is vastly insufficient if we want to develop and/or change a company. Instead, we need models that show the company in the context of its customers, suppliers, partners, etc., models that show the company's business processes and how they work to generate products and services to the outside world. We must be able to identify conflicts among processes so they can be eliminated. And we must be able to develop these models systematically, so we don't have to take chances when deciding on major changes. We have discussed those who require a business model of their company and what they will need to 'read' from their model. We have talked about customers, partners, executive management, the reengineering team, process owners, resource owners, the IT organization, and other participants. Each of them requires a different model. The reengineering team needs the most developed and detailed model, while the others need segments or simplified descriptions of it.

2.10 References

Ross D. (1985). Applications and extensions of SADT. *IEEE Computer*, April

Sheldon R. (1993). Object-oriented business engineering. *First Class The Object Management Group Newsletter*, **3**(3), August/September

Sheleg W. (1993). Business process reengineering driven by business events. *Database Newsletter*, **21**(5), September/October

Tsang E. (1993). Business process reengineering and why it requires business event analysis. *Case Trends*, March, pp 8–15

Yourdon E. (1989). *Modern Structured Analysis*. Yourdon Press/Prentice-Hall

Yourdon E. and Constantine L.L. (1979). *Structured Design: Fundamentals of a Discipline of Computer Program and System Design*. Englewood Cliffs, NJ: Prentice-Hall

chapter 3
What is object orientation?

3.1 Introduction

Object orientation is a special approach to the construction of models of complex systems, in which a complex system, consisting of a large number of occurrences, is regarded as a set of objects. The relations between these occurrences are seen as associations between objects; their properties are attributes of the objects. In addition, the occurrences can have static as well as dynamic characteristics. An occurrence that affects another when a certain event takes place is described as communication between the objects.

Object orientation is often presented as a revolutionary new technique, but this is not the case. Object orientation is a proven technique that has been in existence – and in use – for some time now, particularly in software technology. The forerunner of all object-oriented programming languages is Simula, which was developed in Norway during the 1960s. As early as 1967, Simula incorporated all the essential properties that today's object-oriented programming languages contain. For various reasons, however, object orientation did not attract attention until the early 1990s. Only a tiny percentage of all system development is carried out using object-oriented techniques, but there is a discernible trend towards increased investment in this area among larger companies throughout the world.

Over 25 years ago, we used the object-oriented technique to model many different kinds of systems. It was used to describe both organizations and systems constructed entirely of hardware. In fact, our experiences with these areas of application convinced us that the technique could be developed further: it could be generalized and applied to other systems. We found that we could base our arguments on models of organizations and hardware systems, and transform them into arguments relating to software, even though, in those days, support was not provided by any programming language. Although Simula had been developed at about the same time, it had not received widespread recognition. We (Jacobson, 1992) independently developed a technique for building an object-oriented design model of software, which we later implemented in assembler language. In achieving this, we demonstrated that the programming language itself is not crucial in modelling software. The most important consideration is how the resulting model looks: it should be constructed in such a way that it can be understood easily and modified to suit specific needs.

In this chapter, we first describe in general what is meant by object-oriented models, then discuss the various properties of an object-oriented model in more depth. This leads to a discussion of why object-oriented modelling provides such good system properties and why this type of modelling is so well suited to modelling not only software but also businesses. Finally, we describe how object technology has developed to its present state and our vision of its future development.

3.2 Object-oriented models

To summarize what we said in Chapter 2, a business model of a company shows the company's function in the world, what the company does, and when and how it does it. It emphasizes the architecture, but it also describes the separate courses of events that take place within the company.

Companies deal with real events and occurrences. They produce various deliverables — whether products or services — which are built up of other occurrences. These occurrences, which can be either material or immaterial, are tangible enough to have a price. They can be sold, produced and delivered, and the customer's satisfaction with them can be measured.

All of these occurrences are modelled as objects. Because there is a close relation between the real-life occurrence and the objects in the model (often a one-to-one relationship), the semantic gap between reality and the model is a small one (Figure 3.1).

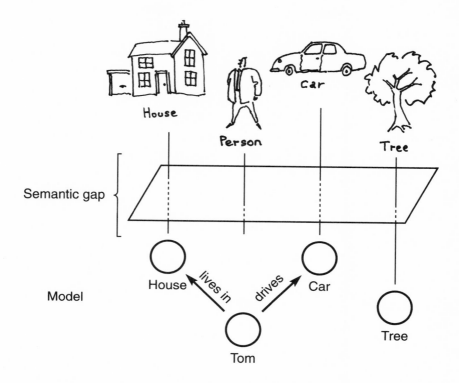

Figure 3.1 *Because occurrences in the real world are directly mapped to objects in the model, the semantic gap is small.*

It is not only the occurrences that are represented by objects. The relations between the occurrences are also shown as associations between objects.

This reasoning supports the idea that it is natural to represent the static structures of occurrences and their relations in an object model. This is widely known, and is used in data and conceptual modelling. Object orientation takes this reasoning a step further by also allowing occurrences that change dynamically to be modelled as objects. Objects, therefore, can demonstrate certain behaviour in relation to their environment: they can be activated, they can change, they can activate other objects, and so on.

A good argument for using object orientation to model companies is that it models the company in a way that is very close to the real thing. There is a very minor *semantic gap* between reality and the model. Object-oriented models are therefore natural and easy to understand. They also have – as we will discuss later – a number of other important properties that become evident in the modelling process; thus, object-oriented models are widely accepted as a means of describing complex systems in general.

There are a great many books that deal with object orientation in the software context, so in this chapter we will focus on describing how this technology can be applied to modelling companies. We begin by listing some of the most important properties of object-oriented technology. Later, we discuss in more detail what these and other properties mean in the context of object orientation.

- Objects and occurrences in the company are modelled as *objects*. An object encapsulates information, and can offer behaviour towards other objects.

- An object belongs to a *class* of similar objects. In describing the class, each object that belongs to that class is also described.

- One class can reuse another class by means of *inheritance*.

3.3 What is an object?

An object is an occurrence that is meaningful to our company and that we wish to describe in its environment. The word 'object' is used in many situations, and its meaning shifts accordingly. However, we define an 'object' as an occurrence that can contain information and offer behaviour. Other objects can make use of the object's behaviour to obtain or alter information that is attached to the object.

Here are a few examples:

- A bank account is an object in a bank; an office is another object in the bank, as is a customer.

- An insurance policy is an object in an insurance company. As in the bank, objects such as offices and customers also exist.

- A car is an object in a central automobile register. A car is also an object in the billing system of a vehicle manufacturer.

Thus we can see that objects are found in the domains that we want to describe. All occurrences in the enterprise under consideration are potential objects. These objects are of one type, but there are also other types: types that describe the work tasks in a company; for example, depositing and withdrawing money are two objects in the bank. Whereas the objects 'customer' and 'account' in one bank may be similar to corresponding objects in another bank, it is less likely that objects such as 'depositing' and 'withdrawing' would be the same in different banks. The latter type of object describes how the task is carried out.

It is not unusual to find, in completely different domains, objects that have the same name: customer objects are found in both banks and insurance companies; cars occur in both car registers and car manufacturers. Are these objects identical? As a rule, they are not. Obviously there may be many similarities; for example, a customer object, whether in a bank or an insurance company, will contain information such as the customer's name, address and social security number. Normally, however, objects differ in two principle aspects:

- Different kinds of information are attached to them. In a car register, a car object contains information about the owner, the model, the year of manufacture, taxation, and so on, whereas the manufacturer's car object has information about the purchaser, the date of manufacture, the car's colour and its optional extras. These differences are due to the different purposes of the objects.

- They are used in different ways. In the central car register, the car object is used to record changes of ownership, for example, or to find out who is the present owner, or to send out car tax bills. On the other hand, in the manufacturer's system, the car object is used to invoice the purchaser, to answer questions about delivery dates, or to provide a description of the car's appearance and features.

Thus, an object is characterized by what it is used for and by the information that is attached to it. Naturally, these properties are closely related.

The information is captured by what we call the object's *attributes*.

Figure 3.2 shows a Customer object whose Name attribute has been given the value – that is, holds the information – 'Jim Smith'. A Customer object has many other types of attribute, such as social security number, address and telephone number.

The use of an object is captured by its behaviour or by the *operations* that it can offer to other objects in its environment. Operations are the 'tools' that other objects use when they want to do something

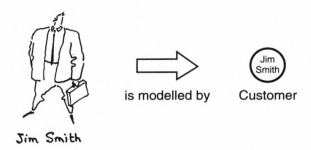

Jim Smith

Figure 3.2 *A customer in a bank is modelled as an object.*

with an object. In fact, an object can only be reached by other objects via its operations.

How does one object use another? This is usually modelled by one object sending a message to another. However, because the word 'message' has so many meanings in the programming context, we prefer the word *stimulus*. When one object sends a stimulus to another, the receiving object is invoked and, depending on the stimulus, the receiver selects a suitable operation to perform. Normally, a receiver can perform several different types of operations. Each stimulus has a name that clearly determines the operation to be performed. While performing the operation, the receiving object can read and change its attribute values, and decide to do one thing or another. It may, in turn, need to use other objects and may therefore send stimuli itself.

We can see that an object's attributes are contained within the object itself. This property, which is essential to object orientation, is called *encapsulation*. The only way of reaching the information in an object is by using its operations. The values of its attributes are always completely hidden from the object's environment.

It is not only its attributes that are hidden from the object's environment. The detailed structure of the operations is also hidden. The only thing that is available to the environment is the type of operations that can be invoked in the object; that is, the names of the operations that stimuli sent to the object can convey and the various types of information that each operation requires in order to be performed. The names and types of information are called the operation's *signature*. The combination of signatures that an object can offer is called its *protocol*.

We can develop these ideas further by describing the collaboration between objects in terms of *contracts*. A contract specifies the stimuli that can be communicated between two objects. Once a contract has been

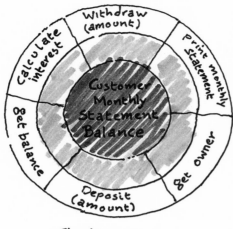

Checking account

Figure 3.3 *The Current Account object.*

established between two objects, the sending object (client object) can only send stimuli that are defined in the contract, and the receiving object (server object) must respond correctly to the stimuli defined in the contract. This topic is discussed by Meyer (1988) and, in more detail, by Wirfs-Brock (1990). According to Wirfs-Brock, a contract between two objects implies that a number of requirements are placed on the objects in the contractual relation. The requirements placed on the server object are called that object's *responsibility*. Usually, an object has several responsibilities, one for each contract it shares.

Therefore, it should be possible to describe an object in two different, but related, ways. First, there is an external description, which shows how others can use the object and the responsibilities the object has towards other objects. This description contains only the object's protocol (how it can be used), and we call it the object's *specification*. The second description specifies the object's various attributes and how each operation is realized. This description is called the object's *implementation* (Figure 3.3). The core of the Current Account object in Figure 3.3 consists of the object's implementation, shown in grey. The object's shell, shown in white, is its protocol.

What do we gain by this approach? The internal design of an object can change without the object's environment being affected. If we add an attribute, or change the importance of an attribute in an object, it will not affect the use of the object. Only if the object's protocol is changed will those who use the object be affected. We might need to make a number of changes that are local to the object, and will therefore only affect the object's core. In other words, these changes will only affect the attributes and the realization of the operations; they will not affect how other objects use these operations. If we did not collect attributes and operations in objects, but left them separate from each other (as in most non-object-oriented methods), changes of this type would not be merely local, they would spread to many different places in the model.

Another common type of change is to introduce into the model a new type of object that resembles an existing object, but differs from it in one or several respects. Of course, we want to be able to reuse as much as possible of the existing object's properties, and only describe what distinguishes the new type of object from the existing one. In many cases, such an addition to an object-oriented model can be introduced with the other objects being unaffected, or affected only slightly. This means that a system can be adapted easily to a new application, for example, a company can expand to another country or region. In Section 3.7, we describe how this can be achieved using the object-oriented technique.

To summarize:

- Objects have attributes and operations.

- The environment — that is, other objects in the system — can use the object's operations, but cannot directly reach the object's attributes to get their values.

- The object encapsulates both the attributes and the operations' inner structure.

- The object's set of signatures represents its protocol.

- An object's environment is not affected by changes made in the object's internal design, as long as its protocol is not affected.

3.4 Objects are linked

An individual object does not make a system. A system is made up of a number of objects. A model of a commercial organization usually consists of many objects that are related in some way. In a model of this kind, we

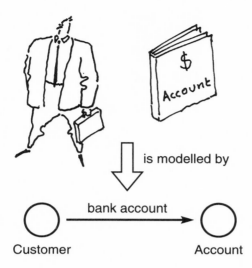

is modelled by

bank account

Customer   Account

Figure 3.4 *Jim is the holder of account number 132 463522. This is modelled by the object Customer, which has an association to the object Account.*

show the relations between the objects by drawing associations between them. For example, we might want to show that an object uses another object, or that it knows another object. There are different types of associations, which clearly express the particular way in which given objects are related.

Let us return to the bank example, and look at some examples of the relations between objects. We can model a customer having an account with the bank (Figure 3.4).

To describe this situation in the object model, we define the Customer object as having an association to the Account object. This association states that a certain customer has a certain account. The Customer object has attributes such as name and address, but to describe which account a certain customer has, we must express it as an association to the Account object. Furthermore, we give the association a name that describes the role played by the indicated object.

This type of association between two objects is static and is used to locate one object in relation to another. We call this kind of relation an *acquaintance association*. An acquaintance association can be changed, for example, by the customer closing an account and opening another. This would mean that the acquaintance association pointing to the old Account object is deleted, the old Account object itself is deleted, a

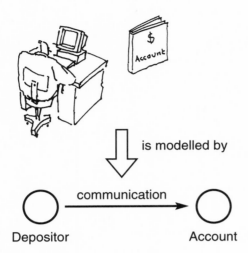

is modelled by

communication

Depositor   Account

Figure 3.5 *Depositing money into an account can be modelled with a communication association.*

new account is created and a new acquaintance association is set to point to the new Account object.

There is another type of relation that is used to describe how one object uses one or more operations in another object; that is, the first object communicates with the second. Let us examine more closely how we can model the act of a customer making a deposit into his account. We describe the task itself – the act of making the deposit – by using the Depositor object. Depositor uses an operation in the Account object to increase the sum of money in the account. In the model, this is expressed as a relation between Depositor and Account. The relation is called a *communication association*. The communication association is dynamic, because it is only used when an object is active and sends a stimulus to another object.

When a customer wants to deposit money, Depositor helps to carry out the task by sending a stimulus to the customer's account, with information about the sum of money that is to be deposited. Account then increases the total sum by that amount.

We model this by establishing a communication association between Depositor and Account (Figure 3.5).

In summary, we can give a more formal definition of *association*. An association is a directed binary relation, which means that it will always link two objects. It is always the associating object that knows and acts upon the associated object, never the other way round.

A process in an organization can be illustrated by showing which objects are involved in the process, and how these objects are related to one another. More examples of this are given in Chapters 4 and 8, but let us study the example from our banking system here. We can begin by looking more closely at how the bank handles the act of someone borrowing money. As this description is only an example of how the process works, it has been simplified.

Example 1

The loan process starts when a person completes a loan application form and gives (or sends) it to a bank clerk. The clerk checks the customer database, to find out if this person is already a customer at the bank. If the person is not an existing customer of the bank, the clerk registers the person in the database.

The clerk continues the process by working through several different types of checks upon the customer. The clerk runs a credit worthiness report and checks whether the customer is insolvent. If the customer seems to be free of any registered complaints, the clerk determines whether the customer will be able to afford to pay the interest on the loan, using the information given in the application form about salary, savings, existing loans and monthly expenses. The clerk calculates how the loan would affect the customer's budget and compares the result with the minimal limit for which the bank allows loans to be carried through.

If everything seems to be in order, the clerk gets in touch with the customer and arranges a meeting.

> At the meeting, the customer is informed of the terms of the loan: the interest, amortization and possible mortgage (if the amount is above a certain limit). The clerk prepares a contract, which the customer has to sign in order to get the money. When all of this is taken care of, the clerk updates the customer database. A loan account with information about amount, interest, amortization and mortgage rules is created and connected to the customer in the database. The clerk gives a copy of the contract to the customer and puts the original in the central archive at the bank.

This description is by no means complete. We have not described, for example, what happens in those circumstances when the process deviates from the normal course of events. What happens, for example, if the customer's credit is not so sound? Nevertheless, this description — together with a view of the objects that will realize the process — should help you to have a better perception of the type of objects found in an organization.

Proceeding from our description of the loan process, we have outlined how the process might be modelled in terms of objects. Figure 3.6 shows these objects and how they interact.

When we consider this view of the objects that participate in the process, certain questions come to mind. For example, it might seem somewhat confusing that we have shown not only the customer, but also an object called Customer Data. The customer is the person who initiates the entire loan process by submitting an application for a loan to the bank. On the other hand, the Customer Data object models the information about the customer that is available at the bank. It is often the case that a business system needs to keep information about its users; that is, its actors. Therefore, it is common to get 'pairs' of actors and objects as in our example.

Another question that arises when looking at this view is how the objects will be implemented. The objects Customer Data, Account and Loan Regulations are realized at our bank with the help of one or two different databases to which the bank officials have access. The Bank Information Bureau object models the use of a global computer system to which all banks have access.

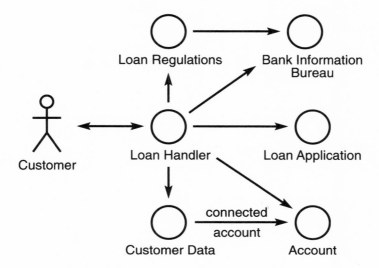

Figure 3.6 *An object model for the loan process.*

The Loan Handler object is responsible for the tasks that need to be performed by the clerk in the loan process. These tasks may be divided into a number of smaller areas of responsibility: for example, Loan Application Receiver (which receives the loan application and registers the customer in the customer database), Credit Checker (which validates the customer's credit status), and Contract Negotiator (which handles the terms of the contract and negotiations with the customer). However, at our bank it has been decided that all of these tasks should be handled by the same resource. In this way, the customer will only need one contact at the bank, instead of having to go from one clerk to another. To make sure that only one person will be responsible for these tasks, only one object is modelled for them: Loan Handler.

To make it easier to understand how the objects communicate with one another to carry out the process, we describe the course of events in terms of the objects that perform the process. By reading the following description in conjunction with the object view shown in Figure 3.6, you will see how the flow of the process proceeds through the participating objects.

In the example given here, we have only used one type of object. In Chapter 5, we will describe three different types of objects: interface objects, control objects and entity objects. In a model built using these three types of objects, instead of only one type, it is easier to understand the responsibilities and roles of the individual object types, by simply looking at a view corresponding to the one shown above.

Example 2

When the Loan Handler receives a Loan Application, the Loan Handler checks the customer database to find out if the applicant is already a customer at the bank. If the person is not registered in the customer database, the Loan Handler will enter Customer Data for this person.

The Loan Handler continues by working through several different types of checks upon the customer. The Loan Handler requests a credit worthiness report from the Bank Information Bureau. If the customer seems to be free of any registered complaints, the Loan Handler moves on to determine whether or not the customer will be able to afford to pay the interest on the loan, using the information given in the Loan Application. This includes information about the customer's salary, savings, existing loans and monthly expenses. The Loan Handler calculates how the loan would affect the customer's budget and compares the result with the minimal limit for which the bank allows loans to be granted. This information is found in the Loan Regulations object.

If everything seems to be in order, the Loan Handler gets in touch with the customer and arranges a meeting.

At the meeting, the customer is informed of the terms for the loan: the interest, amortization and possible mortgage (if the amount is above a certain limit). The Loan Handler prepares a contract, which the customer has to sign in order to get the money. When all of this is taken care of, the Loan Handler updates the customer database. A loan Account, with information about amount, interest, amortization and mortgage rules, is created and connected to the Customer Data in the database. The Loan Handler gives a copy of the contract to the customer and puts the original in the central archive at the bank.

3.5 Objects can form aggregates

We often want to express the fact that an object consists of one or more separate objects. For example, in the model of the banking system, we might want to model an object called Inventory. Inventory consists of all the different occurrences in the bank that can be counted as belonging to the bank's inventory. In this sense, Inventory is an aggregate, made up of a number of designated smaller parts. In Figure 3.7 we have shown, for the sake of simplicity, only two types of occurrence that are part of the bank's inventory, namely furniture and computers. If we examine a computer more closely, we see that it can be broken down into three constituent parts – a display screen, a processing unit (CPU) and a hard disk – which we might want to keep an eye on and thus model as separate objects.

Once an aggregate is defined, a number of rules can be applied to it automatically. In our example, we might say that since Computer is part of Inventory, Inventory cannot be considered to be part of Computer.

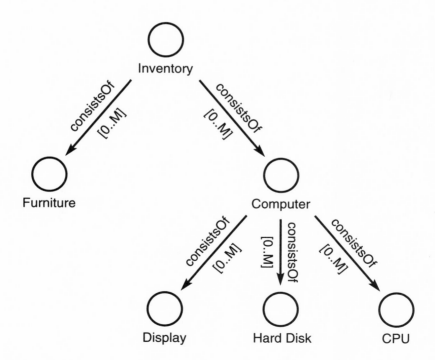

Figure 3.7 *An aggregate.*

We can also say that since Display is part of Computer and Computer is part of Inventory, Display is therefore automatically part of Inventory.

Aggregates can be especially useful to show, for example, how products in a company are built up of smaller parts, which in turn can be made up of still smaller parts.

3.6 Objects belong to a class

In a company, there are normally several objects of the same type. For example, in a bank, there are a great many customers. Each of these customers is an object, and if we study them carefully, we can see that their responsibility with regard to their environment is identical. In other words, the Customer objects have identical operations and their attributes are the same. What distinguishes one customer from the next is the values that its attributes assume.

To avoid having to describe every single occurrence of a customer, it is sufficient to describe, just once, the properties of a typical customer: his or her attributes and behaviour (Figure 3.8). Each separate object belongs to a *class*, and in this case, Jim, Mary and Chris all belong to the class 'Customer'. Each class has a name and a description. The description contains a template that all objects in the class follow. Usually, there are several objects that conform to the description of a particular class. These objects are distinguished from each other by their attributes, which have different values. We can say that a class has a template for the attributes that should be present, and that the objects use the template to structure their attribute values. The template gives names to the attributes, and these names are used by the objects themselves to manipulate their own attribute values. Each object knows to which class it belongs, so each can conform to the class description. In our bank example, each Customer object knows that it belongs to the class 'Customer'.

Since all objects of the same type have the same operations, it is also sufficient to describe their operations only once. They are described, together with their class, in the class description. When an operation is to be performed on an object — when an object receives a stimulus — the object turns to its class to identify the operation to be used. The operation specifies what the object is to do, which attribute values are to be used, and which operations (its own or belonging to other objects) are to be carried out.

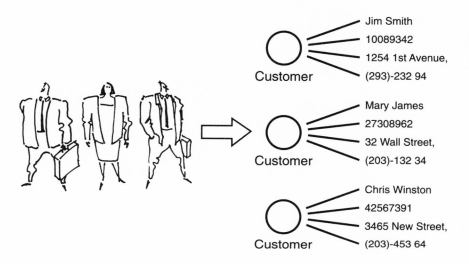

Figure 3.8 *Jim, Mary and Chris are all customers at the bank. They each have identical sets of attributes, but their attributes all have different values.*

When an object is created, the class to which it will belong is also specified. This means that the class template is copied and inserted into the object. The object is given a unique identity, and initial values are set for all of its attributes. During the object's lifetime, the values of its attributes can change as operations are carried out on it. All objects that are created to conform to the description of a particular class are said to be *instances* of that class. When instances are created, the class is said to be *instantiated*. Thus, all accounts in the bank are instances of the class 'Account'.

We also differentiate between class associations and instance associations. A class association links two classes, whereas an instance association links two instances. An example of one type of association that is usually an instance association is the acquaintance association. In our previous example of an acquaintance association, we mentioned that a certain customer knew which accounts he or she had access to. This knowledge is modelled as an association between the two instances Customer and Account, which means that it is an instance association. An example of a class association is an inheritance association, which we will examine in Section 3.7. All instances of the inheriting class contain all of the properties described in both the inheriting and the inherited class. Class associations are indicated by dashed arrows and instance associations by solid ones. It should therefore always be possible to determine

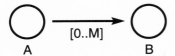

Figure 3.9 *An instance of class A associates with an instance of class B. The association has the cardinality [0..M].*

whether the objects that we are referring to are classes or instances. If the association between two objects is a class association, then the two objects must be classes; if it is an instance association, then the two objects must be instances.

It is often desirable for an object to associate with several instances of a certain class. This can be described in terms of *cardinality* in the association. In Figure 3.9, the cardinality implies that an instance of class A can associate 0 (zero) to many – although here it is not specified how many – instances of class B.

One usually says that objects have a life cycle: they are born, they live and they die (Figure 3.10). The life cycle can be described at various levels of detail, but a convenient way of showing the states that an object passes through during its lifetime is by drawing a state transition diagram. Its purpose is to simplify the picture of what happens to an object. State transition diagrams describe the states an object goes through, the stimuli it can receive in each state, and the stimuli that lead to a state transition.

Many objects have very simple state transition diagrams, similar to that in Figure 3.10, but there are, of course, objects that have extremely

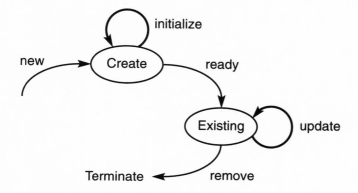

Figure 3.10 *The life cycle of an object.*

complicated states and state transitions. In such cases, we need a state transition diagram with more illustrative notations. See, for example, the section on state transition diagrams in Jacobson *et al.* (1992).

An object should not be removed until all references to it have been taken away. This is quite obvious, otherwise these references would all be invalid. When there are no existing references to an object and the object is to be deleted, all of its attribute values will disappear, as will its relations to other objects and the actual object itself.

We can summarize as follows:

- An object belongs to a class.

- The class specifies what the object can be used for; that is, the operations that can be performed on the object and the attributes of the object.

- Each object has information about the name of its class and assumes different values for its attributes during its lifetime.

- Changes in an object's attribute values occur as operations manipulate the object's attributes.

- The same operations are common to all objects belonging to the same class.

3.7 One class can inherit other classes

Earlier, we mentioned that objects can be related to each other. We have already mentioned acquaintance associations and communication associations. These are relations between individual objects; therefore, they are called instance relations. Classes can also be related to each other through so-called class relations. The most interesting class relation is called the *inheritance association*. A class can inherit another class. This means that an instance of the inheriting class will obtain all of the operations and attributes that are described for both the inheriting class and the inherited class.

The use of inheritance relations is another example of how we can reuse existing descriptions. If two or more classes have similar properties and differ only slightly, the properties they have in common can be factored out and described in what is called an *abstract class*. (An abstract class is a class that will never be instantiated.) The classes from which the common properties were factored out may now inherit the abstract class. Because the commonly-held properties are extracted, they can all be described in one place. This means that when modification work is performed, it is only necessary to make changes in the description of the abstract class to modify some of the commonly-held properties, instead of having to change the descriptions of every class that shares these properties. If a property that is not held in common, but belongs to a class that inherits the properties of the abstract class, is modified the other classes will not be affected; the effect will only be felt by the class that has these specific properties. The act of factoring out commonly-held properties from existing classes and placing them in abstract classes is called *generalization*.

Let us look at an example of generalization. At the bank, there are two types of accounts; current accounts and savings accounts. The holder of a current account may withdraw more money than there actually is in the account. The amount of money by which the account can be overdrawn is regulated by a credit line. The holder of a current account receives a monthly statement. The holder of a savings account usually gets a better rate of interest on the amount in the account. However, the amount of allowed withdrawals is regulated, and the holder usually receives a quarterly statement. If we want to model this, we would have a class Current Account and another class Savings Account. These classes have some different and some common properties. Instead of describing the common properties in each of the two classes, we can describe these properties once in a class called Account, and let Current Account and Savings Account inherit Account (Figure 3.11).

In Figure 3.11, we can see that the common properties of Current Account and Savings Account have been factored out into the class Account. The classes Current Account and Savings Account describe their unique properties. In Current Account there are additional attributes (the credit line and the monthly statement) and three operations describing withdrawal, how to calculate the interest and how to print the monthly statement. In Savings Account the additional attributes hold information about the number of withdrawals that have been made on the account and the quarterly statement, and three operations describe withdrawal, how to calculate the interest and how to print the quarterly statement. Both Current Account and Savings Account have operations named withdraw and calculate interest. However, how these operations are carried out differs in the two classes, which is why they cannot be

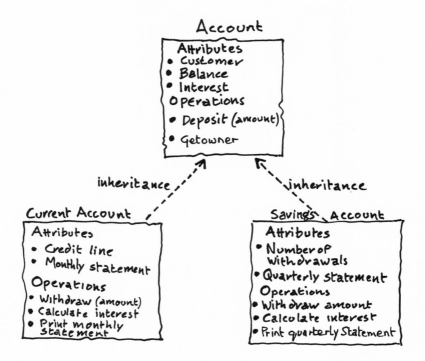

Figure 3.11 *Factoring out commonly-held properties into an abstract class: generalization.*

factored out into the class Account, but are described in each of the separate classes.

Another common type of inheritance involves a class reusing properties of the more general class and adding or changing one or more of these properties. If, for example, we need to create a new class and there is already a class in existence that has several of the required properties, we can allow the new class to inherit the existing class and describe only the unique properties of the new class. This type of inheritance is usually called *specialization* (Figure 3.12).

In some banks, computer support has been introduced to automate the tasks required for checking credit in the loan process, which were previously performed manually. Computer support also implies that it is possible to carry out automatically various estimates of the financial consequences that the loan will have for the customer. By specializing the class Credit Checker, we will be able to reuse all of the properties that we want to use at the banks that introduce computer support: we do not

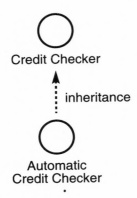

Figure 3.12 *Specialization of the class Credit Checker.*

have to describe these properties in Automatic Credit Checker as well. Instead we can concentrate on describing the new properties relating to the computer support in the class Automatic Credit Checker (Figure 3.12).

When we create a new class in a system, we might want to reuse properties from more than one class. One way of dealing with this is allowing the new class to inherit properties from several other classes. This is called *multiple inheritance*.

Let us look at an example of this (Figure 3.13). At the bank, there are separate registers that include all of the information needed about customers and employees. These are modelled by the classes Customer and Employee. However, the bank management has decided to have a set of favourable conditions for employees who wish to use the bank's services. These conditions should obviously not be modelled in Customer (since all customers are not employees of the bank) or in Employee (since not all employees are using the bank's services). Thus, the new class Employed Customer is created. However, we do not want to describe all of the properties of Customer and Employee in this new class as well. If we apply multiple inheritance, we can allow the class Employed Customer to inherit the properties of both Customer and Employee.

A disadvantage of multiple inheritance is that it tends to make the model more difficult to understand. Conflicts may arise – for example, a class might inherit the properties of two classes that have operations with the same name, but different descriptions. Which of these descriptions will apply to the inheriting class? There are various ways of handling

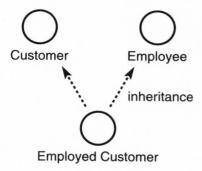

Figure 3.13 *Multiple inheritance.*

conflicts of this type. One is to define a new operation with the same name in the inheriting class, and describe the behaviour of the inheriting class there. Another is to explicitly select the inherited operation to be used in the inheriting object. However, it is important to understand that even if these conflicts can be solved, the solutions may well diminish the intuitive significance of the model. Therefore, multiple inheritance should be used with caution.

The inheritance mechanism helps us to make a model of our organization that can tolerate change. Because commonly-held properties are only described in one place, any changes to these properties will only have to be made in one place.

Furthermore, inheritance mechanisms are very useful for specializing businesses that are located in geographically separate places. Even if these businesses actually perform the same type of work, it is almost certain – for various reasons – that they will be dissimilar in several respects. Instead of trying to force a business to work in exactly the same way as another, or beginning the modelling process from scratch, inheritance can be used to reuse as much of the existing model as possible. In this way, modelling is made considerably easier.

3.8 A summary

Against the background you now have, we can proceed to a more detailed picture of what an object-oriented model implies. We present below a brief description of the concepts central to object orientation.

- An *object*, or rather an instance of a class, has an inner state that is aware of its own class. The state of the object is called the object's information. An object can be used by other objects. When one object uses another, we say that it sends a stimulus to the other object. The receiving object accepts the stimulus and performs an operation. Performing an operation means that the object inspects its values, alters its own inner state, or uses other objects.

- A *class* is a template for all objects — that is, all instances that are created by the class — and defines what these objects can be used for. The class describes the operations that the object can offer, the various activities that belong to each operation, and the different attributes that each object has. An object's inner state — its information — is determined by the value of its attributes and associations. An object performs an operation by obeying the definition of the operation of its class.

- An *object model* of a system consists of a set of classes — the classes of the system — and a set of associations. We have mentioned two types of associations. An acquaintance association implies that the object knows another object. A communication association implies that the object can use another object — it can send a stimulus to this object.

- A class can *inherit* another class. It can also inherit several other classes, which is called multiple inheritance. Inheriting another class means reusing the definition of that class, in terms of operations, associations and attributes.

Finally, a short note about terminology. In object-oriented contexts, it is usual to use the term 'object' in a broad sense, without specifying whether one is talking about instances or classes. This is done to avoid cluttering the descriptions unnecessarily. We therefore adopt this practice, but only where it is clear from the context what is meant.

3.9 Why is object orientation necessary?

Thus far, we have introduced the basics of object orientation. We have described the central concepts and explained their individual char-acteristics. Together, these concepts provide the most important properties found in various systems models, which allow the models to be comprehensive, understandable, changeable, adaptable and reusable:

- *Comprehensive*: because it is possible to break down the classes hierarchically, we can obtain an understandable overall picture of the business being modelled.

- *Understandable*: the business is described in terms of objects, which often have a direct link to occurrences in the real world.

- *Changeable*: changes are usually local to a given class. They can, therefore, be introduced without affecting other classes in the model. With major modifications, several classes may need to be changed; a good structure, however, allows even changes of some magnitude to be kept relatively local. As the protocols between objects are well defined in the respective objects' classes, one object can be exchanged for another as long as their protocols are the same.

- *Adaptable*: it is possible to specialize, with the help of the inheritance mechanism, existing classes. A model can be adapted to different situations, for example different countries, by inserting the adaptation in classes that are specializations of more abstract classes.

- *Reusable*: classes can be built and handled as components. When new classes are created, properties in already defined classes can be reused.

3.10 Object orientation as a platform for the future

Object orientation is a universal technique that can be applied to many types of system: artificial, man-made systems as well as natural systems. Of late, this technique has found wide acceptance in the software industry. It is already being used for just about all types of software: systems for banks and insurance companies, defence systems, process control systems, robot systems, telecommunications systems, geographical information systems, presentation systems, and so on. It is used for technical systems as well as purely administrative ones, and is equally applicable in systems with stringent real-time requirements and those that handle huge amounts of data, or have maximum requirements for reliability, and so on.

The widespread development of object orientation throughout the field of computer technology has paved the way for its global acceptance in a vast range of applications. Today, practically all research and development look towards object orientation as a means to more effective ends. Contemporary methods of system development are object oriented, and we can safely say that the only programming languages that will survive are the object-oriented ones; old languages such as COBOL, Ada and C are being 'dolled up' to accommodate the requirements of object orientation. The trend for new databases is that they are object oriented, as are all of the user interfaces being built today. Future operating systems, as well as the computer architectures of tomorrow, require support for object orientation all the way down to their very cores.

In other words, more and more areas of computer technology are converging on object orientation, as Figure 3.14 tries to show. This has made it possible to apply the technique in nearly all types of application area. First, when products are being made using what is basically the same technology, developers in different areas can begin to communicate with each another in a meaningful way, learning from one another and exchanging experiences. The difference between building an administrative system and a purely technical one is less than people have assumed. Differences have arisen primarily because people were using different kinds of artefacts, such as methods, languages, operating systems, and so on that had their own nomenclature and their own approaches to program development. As more and more developers use object orientation, these boundaries are being eroded, and we can now help each other to further this technique, independent of the application areas in which we are active. It is no exaggeration to say that there is now a consensus that acknowledges object orientation as the platform most development organizations will choose by the end of the century. From this platform, we can make a joint effort towards the techniques that will be needed to build the computer-based systems of the future.

To understand where object orientation is going, it is important to keep our goal in mind, and to see our efforts now and in the future in a wider context. With management concepts that emphasize quality, productivity and lead time, we are striving to become as knowledgeable as the engineers who construct buildings, roads and machinery. All our efforts, therefore, are directed towards a far-reaching goal: to build the best possible software systems in an industrial way, using computing techniques in the same way that other engineers use their various techniques.

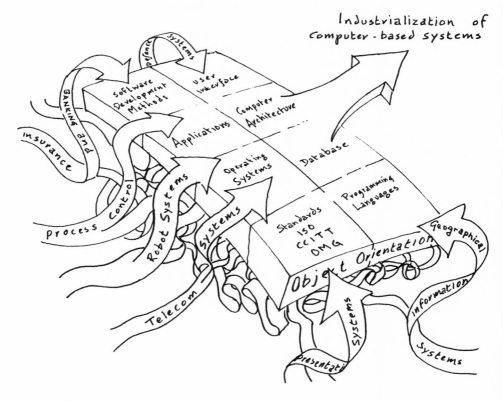

Figure 3.14 *The evolution of computer-based systems.*

Today, software experts seem to share the opinion that future software will be built on object-oriented ideas. Object technology has shown itself to be a winner, and those who adopted this technique early now have a huge lead that will take others many years to close.

Hoping that object orientation will be replaced by something else in a few years is not realistic. It is more likely that within almost every area of development, we will be converging our efforts in the direction of object techniques.

3.11 Object-oriented business modelling

The application of object-oriented techniques has consequently come a long way in developing all kinds of computer-based systems. There are a great many methods available for building object-oriented systems. We do not intend to list all of them here, but refer instead to what are perhaps the most well known; among them: Shlaer and Mellor (1988), Coad and Yourdon (1990), Booch (1991), Rumbaugh *et al.* (1991), Wirfs-Brock *et al.* (1990), Martin and Odell (1992) and Jacobson (1992). The Object Management Group (1994) published a survey on object-oriented methods. A method for the development of object-oriented software is characterized by describing how one or more models – analysis and design models – of the software system can be developed to function as a kind of abstraction of the code in the system. Methods are not usually bound to a particular programming language, but instead can be applied to the whole class of object-oriented languages. Because these models of the software – as well as the software itself – are object oriented, there is an advantage to be gained from the seamless transition between the models and the code. Thus, it is easy to trace an object in one model to the corresponding object in another model. This also means that the good properties that characterize object orientation are present throughout the development of the software system.

Modelling of businesses and information systems makes similar demands on results. A business is at least as complex as a software system and, in both cases, one wants to achieve models that are comprehensive, understandable, changeable, adaptable and reusable. Modelling in a simple way that is easily understandable to everyone concerned, both inside and outside the organization, is a central requirement in business engineering. If the results cannot be understood by all parties, then you have definitely missed the objective of developing the business.

The object-oriented approach is very close to the way in which human beings themselves view the world, which is why object-oriented modelling provides – for the moment – the best support for building good models. For this reason, many attempts are being made today to model businesses using object-oriented technology (Shelton, 1993).

By first modelling businesses in an object-oriented way, then building the IT support system according to object orientation, we can achieve further advantages. Besides producing sound models, we can link the business model and the system model together, simply and effectively. Objects in one model correspond to objects in the other. This is especially true of objects that are handled in businesses, such as products or their constituent parts. Thus, traceability between the models (business and system) is achieved, which reduces the risk of introducing errors into the transition between the two models. Having the developers of businesses, systems and software speaking the same language is of great benefit, in that it allows them to discuss their respective models with one another and thus verify that they are doing the right things.

We believe, however, that it is not sufficient merely to use object orientation. Although object-oriented thinking is essential to being able to describe the innermost core of a business or a system, we must also be able to describe what the business or information system does or what we want it to do. Thus, thinking in terms of *use cases* is an important complement to object-oriented thinking. A use case is a sequence of transactions in a system, initiated by a user of the system. A use case has a complete flow of events, that is, it has a well-defined beginning and an equally well-defined termination. Basically, use cases have the following purposes:

- To describe the business or the information system in terms of what people, whether customers or users, can do with it, and how they can use it. This description will give a very clear picture of the requirements that the business or the information system must meet.

- Use cases link together different models of a business or an information system, for example, the analysis model can be linked to the design model.

- They have an important role in the link between a business model and its information system.

3.12 Summary

A complex system is modelled using a set of connected objects. These models are said to be object oriented if they are characterized by the following:

- the existence of objects

- the existence of classes, to which the objects belong

- that one class can inherit another class.

Today, object-oriented technology is being used very successfully in software and in every type of system built by man. These systems are comprehensive, understandable, changeable, adaptable and reusable. Because the same approach is used both for realization of software systems (in the code) and for abstract models of the system (analysis and design models), it is easy to trace properties between the two models. The risk of introducing errors into later models, as a result of not fully understanding the intentions behind earlier models, is reduced.

Object-oriented technology is also highly applicable to modelling organizations and their business processes. If the same technique is used to model a business as is used to build the supporting information system, the transition between the two activities will be both easy and distinct.

As a universal technique, object orientation is spreading into more and more areas of technology, and being used in more and more application areas. Object orientation is expected to be the technique that will be used by the end of this century for virtually every type of software system. It is likely to become the dominant technique for the development of businesses as well.

3.13 References

Booch G. (1994). *Object-Oriented Analysis and Design with Applications* 2nd edn. Redwood City, CA: Benjamin/Cummings

Coad P. and Yourdon E. (1991). *Object-Oriented Analysis* 2nd edn. Englewood Cliffs, NJ: Prentice Hall

Cox B.J. (1986). *Object Oriented Programming — An Evolutionary Approach.* Reading, MA: Addison-Wesley

Jacobson I. (1992). Object orientation as a competitive advantage. *American Programmer*, **5**(8)

Jacobson I., Christerson M., Jonsson P. and Övergaard G. (1992). *Object-Oriented Software Engineering — A Use Case Driven Approach.* Reading, MA: Addison-Wesley; New York: ACM Press

Martin J. and Odell J.J. (1992). *Object-Oriented Analysis and Design.* Englewood Cliffs, NJ: Prentice Hall

Meyer B. (1988). *Object-Oriented Software Construction.* Englewood Cliffs, NJ: Prentice Hall

Object Management Group. (1994). *Object Analysis and Design: Description of methods* (Hutt A.T.F., ed.). New York: John Wiley & Sons

Rumbaugh J., Blaha M., Premerlani W., Eddy F. and Lorensen W. (1991). *Object-Oriented Modeling and Design*. Englewood Cliffs, NJ: Prentice Hall

Shelton R.E. (1993). Object-oriented business engineering. *First Class — The Object Management Group Newsletter* **3**(3)

Shlaer S. and Mellor S.J. (1988). *Object-Oriented Systems Analysis*. Englewood Cliffs, NJ: Prentice Hall

Wirfs-Brock R., Wilkerson B. and Wienter L. (1990). *Designing Object-Oriented Software*. Englewood Cliffs, NJ: Prentice Hall

chapter 4
Object-oriented business engineering – an overview

4.1 Introduction

Our technique for business (process) engineering, first published in Jacobson (1994), is called object-oriented business engineering – the use case approach. In this chapter, we will concentrate on how object-oriented business engineering can be applied to reengineer a business enterprise. Towards the end of the chapter, we will discuss how object-oriented business engineering can be used to handle business improvement, the long-term continuous maintenance of a business.

4.2 Object-oriented business engineering in context

Within every business enterprise, we envision a resource, assigned by top management, to develop and maintain the company's business processes. It is this resource that applies object-oriented business engineering. In smaller companies, this resource may not be clearly articulated; instead, it is performed by management. To make our reasoning plainer, we have given a name to this resource, business (process) development (Figure 4.1). Business development develops the

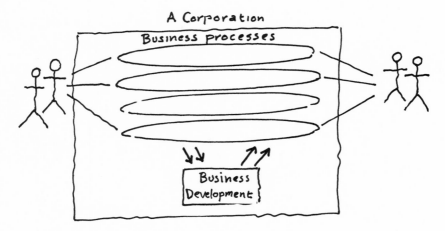

Figure 4.1 *In a company, there is a resource that performs business development.*

business enterprise. Its input includes new and changed objectives; its output is a changed company.

Business development is no ordinary business process. For one thing, it has no external customer. It could be described as an internal process, but we want to avoid using the term 'process' for internal organizational elements. Instead we view business development as an object, or rather, as an aggregate of objects. (In Figure 4.1 we have portrayed business development as having the same form as a business and, for the moment, we are satisfied with this.) Business development can be a part of many different tasks in a single company. Among these tasks are business (process) reengineering – the one of most interest – and business (process) improvement. Other tasks are engineering a new business and the merging of two companies. In this chapter, we concentrate on describing how business development, with the help of object-oriented business engineering, performs business reengineering. At the end of this chapter, we also touch on how business development can use object-oriented business engineering to facilitate business improvement.

4.3 Business reengineering overview

A reengineering project is usually described as consisting of four primary activities:

- Developing Business Vision. In this activity, the company creates a vision of how its business processes shall be developed so that it can attain its strategic objectives.

- Understanding the Existing Business. Here, the company is surveyed and charted to show how it functions at present.

- Designing the New Business. This activity is carried out to develop the new and changed processes, as well as the information system that will support them. Prototyping and testing of the new processes is part of this activity.

- Installing the New Business. Here, the new design is installed in the business.

Although it is important to have a simple model of how reengineering will be carried out, we think that this model is too simple (Figure 4.2). The order of these activities is not sequential, but at least partly parallel, and some of them are iterated. Furthermore, to be able to visualize the new company, you must first understand the existing one. And to know what you must understand about the existing company, you need a vision of what is to be done. Therefore, our model is slightly different. It shows reengineering work being performed within the framework of business development, and it emphasizes that reengineering consists mainly of two steps: reverse-engineering the existing

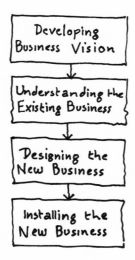

Figure 4.2 *A simplified reengineering project.*

company and forward-engineering the new company. Intuitively and a little naively, we say that:

> business reengineering = reverse business engineering + forward business engineering.

Understanding the existing company is a reverse-engineering activity; it implies that we make an abstract model of the business and the processes we wish to improve. Designing the new company is a forward-engineering activity. We call these activities reversing the existing business and engineering the new business, as shown in Figure 4.3. This figure is also a simplified model of how reengineering work is carried out. The arrows primarily show how the different activities convey information to one another and to the environment.

A reengineering project can be initiated in many different ways and in many different situations. In our overview, we assume that the project was started in response to a reengineering directive, which explains why something must be done and specifies what the project should achieve. The reengineering directive triggers an activity called envisioning, which visualizes the new business enterprise or the new processes in the

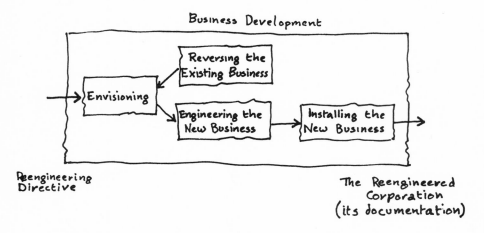

Figure 4.3 *An overview of the main activities in a reengineering project.*

business. In order to achieve this, of course, we must know the company's strategy and understand the existing business. We must at least understand the parts that could be subject to reengineering, so that we can concentrate the work on the things to be changed. This is essential in order to make radical changes in the business without taking unnecessary risks. The results of envisioning are what we call an objective specification, a vision of the future business.

Thus, envisioning triggers the reversing the existing business activity, which produces a model of the existing business. In a mature business, where people understand the importance of having a known and documented processes, a business model already exists that can form the basis for reengineering work. This model was produced when the company was last reengineered, so there is no need to carry out this activity again. However, let's assume here that we have not progressed this far and thus must begin by modeling the existing company.

The work of engineering the new business implies creating one or more new processes, designing them, developing a supporting information system, perhaps simulating or prototyping them, and so on, to produce a model of the redesigned company. The objective specification is one input to this activity. The weight of the entire reengineering project rests on this activity. Also, this activity must be prioritized in terms of lead time, so you can begin to realize the new possibilities quickly.

As a rule, a reengineering project will normally include yet another main activity, installing the redesigned company. In this activity, the redesigned company is incisively implemented in the real organization. This demands special techniques, which we discuss only briefly in Section 4.9. We describe the techniques to carry out the other tasks in our model – envisioning, developing and testing the new business – in much more detail. We will concentrate on describing how we build various formal models of existing and new companies. This is primarily carried out in the activities reversing the existing business and forwarding the new business, described in detail in Chapters 6 and 7. As for envisioning, it can be performed many ways, so there is no point in trying to formalize it. Therefore, we offer a high-level look at envisioning in this chapter only. Nevertheless, the principles that govern envisioning will be made clear.

We emphasize that our plan for carrying out reengineering work is a proposal only, to help you understand the basic idea. You can perform this work in many different ways, and you should select the techniques that best suit your company, taking into consideration the values and attitudes of its management, its size, the nature of its business, its staff's familiarity with modelling, etc.

4.4 The reengineering directive

A directive starts the entire reengineering effort. The company's management should formulate this directive or allow it to be formulated. It should be expressed in high-level terms. The tone of the directive indicates the expectations that surround the project. To force a dramatic change in the business, the directive must concentrate on serious, fundamental problems and point out radical changes that can be expected in the future. The directive should explain the situation the company is in and why it cannot remain there. Concretely speaking, the directive should be able to consist of a 'case-for-action paper', according to Hammer (1993). The case-for-action paper explains why the business must be reengineered. Management must make it plain that it has a case for action. The directive should clarify the following points unequivocally and powerfully:

- The company's environment. Who are the company's customers and competitors? How is the environment changing at this moment?

- The customers' expectations. Why must the company satisfy its customers' needs in a way that differs from the existing one.

- Competition increase. How are competitors meeting the customers' needs?

- The company's business difficulties. What are we doing wrong? Why aren't we doing it right?

- A diagnosis of the company. Why do we have to fundamentally rethink the company's way of working and radically change its operations?

- The risks of not changing. What are the consequences of not reengineering? The directive should be forthright; however, to be believable, it must not exaggerate the situation. Actually, the problems are often already widely known and recognized, although they may not have been catalogued in a clear and concise fashion. It is absolutely necessary that the company's executive management are wholeheartedly behind the directive and support it completely. The staff must be convinced that the company cannot continue on the same course if it is to survive and remain competitive. Furthermore, they must be made to understand that the situation can be dealt with, but that action will have to be taken now.

4.5 Envisioning

Once a reengineering directive has been issued, the envisioning activity should produce a vision of the new company and formulate it in terms of an objective specification. Here, we assume a directive has been formulated. If it has not, then management requires help to formulate it. The work of visualizing the new company is not formalized in the same way as is the work of producing a model of the existing company or the redesigned company. However, there are several steps (Figure 4.4) that should be taken to ensure that the vision of the new company is on the right track. Davenport (1993, pp. 117–35) gives a more thorough description of this activity, which must:

- Ensure that the company's strategic goals fit with its goals for the reengineered company.

- Seek to understand how the existing company functions, in order to specify the new company.

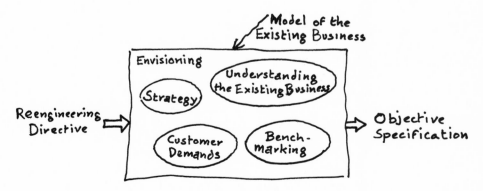

Figure 4.4 *The Envisioning activity in its context.*

- Interview current customers to find out how to improve customer satisfaction with the company's products, services and processes.

- Compare the company with other businesses in the environment by means of benchmarking.

4.5.1 Who takes part in the envisioning work?

The reengineering team arrives at a vision of the new company. This small team includes various handlers. The most important participants are the representatives of the company's key customers. Other participants are people from within the company and, perhaps, a reengineering consultant. A suitable way of working is by means of a series of workshops, with the follow-up work being done by individuals or small teams.

4.5.2 Strategy

The company's business strategy must, of course, suit the way the company works, that is, there must be a strong link between the strategy and the processes the company uses. The strategy must embody the company's long-term goals and align the processes with which it works to those goal. As Davenport (1993) has written, 'Strategy and process objectives must reinforce one another and echo similar themes'. It is especially important to base the reengineering work on a strategy that is fully communicated throughout the company. On this basis, the reengineering team can arrive at a good design and explain its motivation. Davenport (1993, p. 121) develops a number of criteria for a good strategy that is applicable in reengineering:

- A strategy should not be based solely on financial goals. In general, employees tend not to perceive financial goals as being sufficiently concrete, since it is not apparent to them how they can attain the goals.

- A strategy should be formulated so that its effects can be measured. A change in lead time is measurable, as is customer satisfaction, etc.

- A strategy should focus on a limited and realistic business idea.

- A strategy should inspire, not force, employees at every level to create a company that realizes the desired goals.

4.5.3 Customer demands

It is self-evident that the best impetus to improving a business comes from the people the business is meant to serve – its customers. Therefore, you should analyze and quantify each customer's present and future expectations with regard to the company. Oddly enough, it is common that the people in a company do not feel that they have to perform analyzes of this type in a conscious way. They usually feel that they know all the answers, and are quite surprised when it turns out that they do not. Analysis is best performed via interviewing the company's customers in face-to-face, spontaneous interviews or systematically arranged inquiries. The aim is to get some idea of how to expand and improve the line of products and services in order to better satisfy the customer. Interviews reveal the processes that most urgently need to be improved. Johansson (1993, p. 121) recommends market-research techniques to capture the customers' needs and desires.

4.5.4 Understanding the existing business

To be able to envision a new company, you must have a good picture of how the existing company looks. In a company in which business engineering has already been instituted, a model of the current company will exist. If not, a model must be created, in the reversing-the-existing-business activity. In this activity, you reverse-engineer only those parts of the business that are subject to the reengineering directive. It is, therefore, plain that the work of visualizing the new company begins before and ends after the work of reversing the existing business. Therefore, envisioning and reversing the existing business are parallel activities.

4.5.5 Benchmarking

Benchmarking is a technique that is increasingly being used in connection with reengineering, especially as a tool to visualize how the new company should function. In benchmarking, you analyze and exchange knowledge with the best of other businesses, with the objective of validating that your own process goals surpass those of your competitors. Examine companies that do an outstanding job of what you want to do and learn from them. Focus on companies within your own field (your competitors) or on companies in other fields that use similar processes. Select companies that:

- have a good reputation

- give thorough customer satisfaction

- yield high-quality results

- are recognized leaders in their field

- are interested in benchmarking.

4.5.6 How is the work of visualization performed?

The directive initiates the work. The strategy – the platform on which the reengineering team defines a vision – should be traceable to the goals of the prioritized process and the goals derived from the strategy. The strategy must be clearly formulated in incisive, stringent terms, without platitudes. Knowledge of how the existing company and its processes function is essential to creating new processes.

The reengineering team begins the visualization work by deciding what process or processes are most important. Of course, it is important that they focus on areas that will yield the quickest positive results. They should be careful not to spread themselves too thin, but instead gather their forces and concentrate on increasing the effectiveness of the most vital processes. Hammer (1993, p. 122) gives a more detailed description of how to select the processes most suitable for reengineering. He defines three criteria:

- Seek out the processes that are in the most trouble. Hammer presents here an interesting list of symptoms such processes exhibit.

- Choose processes that are vital to the customers and central to the entire company's existence.

- Choose processes that have a good chance of being reengineered successfully.

By benchmarking, get to know how other companies perform, learn to identify your 'best competitors' and 'colleagues'. With this knowledge, you can establish tough objectives and understanding how to achieve them. Visualizing the new business is an iterative task. Take all the time you need to test alternative process scenarios, inspect each process inside and out, think carefully about what has been done thus far, and so on. Build prototypes to simulate and evaluate ideas before proceeding to implement them. This is where the combined creativity in the team blossoms and bears fruit. No suggestion should be deemed too eccentric for presentation; after all, some of the wackiest ideas have given birth to fundamentally innovative solutions.

Concentrate on the most important processes. Taking the most important in order, sketch them and delve deeply into the interfaces among them and their environments. Is a particular interface fixed or modifiable? Can its scope be increased so that work originally done by the customer – or by no one – is now done by the company? Or can the scope by diminished, so that work done by the company is now done by the customer? A process is improved if it serves the customer better, which implies that it becomes simpler, produces better products, offers shorter lead times, etc. For each process, set up measurable goals against which the reengineered company can be measured. Later, when the new company is established, you can use these goals to continuously measure how the processes are functioning and being improved.

The team must also make a rough estimate of the kinds of support the new processes will require, especially information technology. It is important to indicate, at an early stage, which techniques are available for implementing the business. Are you free to support the process with new custom software? Must you use existing software? Or can you purchase off-the-shelf software? Can you find the necessary resources, internally or externally, for the software that must be developed? Is the existing configuration of computer systems, terminals, workstations, networks and so forth important? Is compatibility with the existing information system a requirement?

The result of envisioning activities is an objective specification that provides a vision of the new company.

4.6 The objective specification

The objective specification shall describe a vision of the future company. Thus, another name for it could be vision description. It should:

- Identify and name the reengineered company's new or radically changed business processes.

- Include overview, high-level descriptions of the future processes, emphasizing how they differ from current processes. For each process, the specification should name the customer, supplier, or other type of partner. It should describe the input, activities, and product of each process. These descriptions should not be comprehensive or detailed – they are intended to stimulate discussion about the vision among senior executives as well as customers. Furthermore, these descriptions should present, in straightforward terms, the company's philosophy, as well as its intentions with regard to the new or changed processes and how they are expected to operate. To make plain the company's complexities, the descriptions must be well-written, and may also include simple, self-explanatory notes that explain the processes' relations to the environment. But they should avoid saying the obvious, which means they are usually incomplete. Details and in-depth evaluations can wait until the company redesign begins, in the activity we call forwarding the new business.

- Define measurable properties and goals for each process, such as cost, quality, life cycle, lead time and customer satisfaction. Each goals should be traceable to the strategy. Furthermore, the goals should be somewhat lofty, stretching the company's targets so that they motivate the reengineering team to work more rigorously than they would to make incremental improvements.

- Specify the technologies that will support the processes, with special emphasis on IT support. In this context, the specification should also state if the existing information system – hardware and software – will be used and, if so, the compatibility requirements.

- Describe imaginable future scenarios. To the degree that it is possible, the specification should predict how the processes will need to change in the next few years due to new technologies, new interfaces to the environment, and other types of resources. It should also explore if the processes will need to be adapted to other organizations, such as affiliates or partners of one kind or another. The same (or similar) process may perhaps be installed in different geographical locations. However, it should not speculate to the point of absurdity. On the one hand, you don't want to construct a rigid process structure if you can already predict it will need to change. On the other hand, you don't want to introduce unnecessary flexibility in a process, that is, flexibility that will never be used.

- A list of critical success factors (see Section 1.5.2, Critical Success Factors).

- A list of risks that must be eliminated. Identify potential pitfalls that threaten the reengineering work and determine how to avoid them. Chapter 1 lists some examples.

4.7 Reversing the existing business

Here we mention this activity only to place it in context; we will not explore it in detail until Chapter 6. The work of reverse-engineering the existing company is initiated once you have identified, through envisioning, the priority processes. In this activity, you want to obtain a clear picture of how the processes currently work before you reengineer them. In this way, you ensure that you know what you have and what needs to be changed. Reverse-engineering also helps evaluate future changes in the processes, so you are interested not only in how processes work, but how well they work, in terms of measurable data (costs, lead time, and so on). The task of describing how the existing company works demands a great deal of finesse and common sense, and the results will be critical to the success of subsequent reengineering. We warn, however, against digging too deeply in search of some obscure truth that you cannot, need not, or should not unearth.

Two views of the company should be described, an outside and an inside view. The outside view is from the perspective of the environment;

the inside view describes the internal structure. Both views should be consistent, of course. Every 'what' in the outside view should have a corresponding 'how' in the inside view. The outside view describes the company and its environment in terms of use cases, which model processes that effect the company's users: customers and other external partners. The interface between each use case and its users is important and must therefore be described with special care. A use-case model views a company as a system, its customers as users of the system, and its processes as different ways (use cases) customers can use the system. In the next chapter we explore use cases and related concepts as we describe how to develop a use-case model. The inside view describes the company's functional, hierarchical structure (if there is one), the processes performed, and the various resources used. The functional structure to reveal the interfaces among various organizational units. The reverse-engineering activity produces a model of the current company and its existing processes, or at least the ones that are ripe for modification.

4.8 Engineering the new business

Again, here we intend only to place this activity in context; we will examine it in detail in Chapter 7. Engineering the new business is activated when management has made the decision to initiate a reengineering process based on the objective specification. At this point, the organization that will perform business-development work is already in place, and the rest of the organization has committed itself to supporting its efforts. The actual business-development work can now begin. Engineering the new business has four main activities:

- Producing an outside view of the new company. Now, new or changed processes are described in detail, focusing on their interfaces to the environment. Compared with the objective specification, this description must be more complete and formal. It should leave no doubt about what it means. Again, our means to develop this view is the use-case model.

- Producing inside views of the new company. These 'how' models are all object-oriented, and each of them has its own purpose. You can model each process according to the work tasks it includes and how they are related, or the products or subproducts it affects. These models, which can represent more or less concrete descriptions of the future company, can take into account the company's given organization and geographic distribution. They can also be more abstract and describe a more ideal model of the company. The number of models you choose to produce and what they represent, is a design decision that should be made early in the reengineering work.

- Building an information system to support the new business. We pay special attention to this activity, which can be very demanding and extensive, in Chapter 9. Here we note only that because our software-development approach — Object-Oriented Software Engineering (OOSE) Jacobson *et al.* (1992) — extensively incorporates use cases, it is very well-suited for this task.

- Testing the redesigned company on a small scale before installing it. The result of engineering the new business is a model of the redesigned company.

4.9 Installing the new processes

Once you have developed and tested the new processes, it is time to introduce them into the company. This is a great challenge, because it is necessary to continue running the existing processes while installing the new ones without disturbing the environment in which they both operate. The environment should not notice that things are not running the way they expect. However, a process may need to be changed in order for the customer to experience the company in a new way, in which case the customer must have understood the new process clearly and accepted it fully. In the case of process changes that are completely internal, the customer should not notice any change — the new processes should be compatible with the old ones. There are various ways to install new processes intelligently. As a rule, you set up a pilot project and make sure that it succeeds by selecting an organizational unit with people that have the best chance of becoming a success story.

4.10 Iteration

There is a great deal of iteration between the reengineering activities. During the various activities, you may find ways of doing it that afford far greater improvement potential than you envisioned. When this happens, you must iterate back and change the vision in the objective specification. Discoveries like this can turn up late, even when you are already testing a proposed redesign. The worst-case scenario is that you do not discover until you are installing the redesigned company that it is impossible to carry out the plan. The costs of iteration in this case, of course, are much greater than those of failure of the redesign during the early work. Iteration among different activities, as well as within activities, is not uncommon. However, if you think first and work afterwards, you can diminish the risk of delay and expensive redesign. Good techniques for modelling, such as those presented here, reduce these risks. But if you have to iterate, it is important to follow up and update your models to reflect the changes iteration brings about.

4.11 Business improvement

When the company is reengineered and the new business model is installed, the company enters a new phase of its life. Letis assume the reengineering has been successful and that you have well-documented processes, or at least well-documented new processes. What now? Take it easy? Relax? Not exactly. Carlzon (1985) compares running a business with climbing mountains: 'When a mountain climber reaches the top, he doesn't say, "That's great, now I'm through. I can quit mountain climbing!" He looks around for a new peak to conquer'. When SAS reached its first goal, he wrote, 'It was just because we succeeded so well that, perhaps more than ever, we needed to find a new and more long-term objective to work towards.' Now the long-term work of changing the company really begins. Constantly establishing new goals becomes a challenge for the staff, holding at bay the destructive forces latent in every company. At SAS, they were not prepared for the second stage; only when they had succeeded with the first great effort did they discover new problems: 'The lack of new goals quickly had negative repercussions within SAS. The fine-tuned harmony started to go sour...

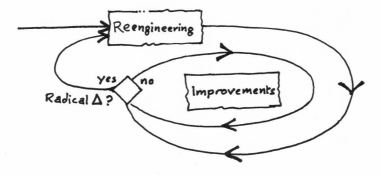

Figure 4.5 *Business development is a continuous ongoing process.*

All the latent forces emerged, all the powers that wanted to get somewhere. Instead of a shared goal, separate goals were being established, for groups as well as for individuals.' Changing a company is an ongoing, neverending process. After the first reengineering efforts — which may have covered only part of the company's business — comes the next phase, and the next, *ad infinitum* as Figure 4.5 illustrates. It is likely that the first reengineering project demands greater attention from management than the following phases; essentially, however, a mature company will always have reengineering activities in operation.

Actually, there is basically little difference between the first phase and those that follow. The differences that exist are primarily in the scope of the improvement work. Major, radical changes are called reengineering, whereas lesser, continuous change is called business improvement. Reengineering is not a one-time effort; it is done many times during a company's life. It will be performed for the processes that the first effort did not encompass and for the already reengineered processes in response to new customer demands, new competition, or innovations in process or technique. Business development is the organization that performs business improvements as well as business reengineering (Figure 4.6). The activities we have described in this chapter — envisioning, reversing the existing business and engineering the new business — are all part of business development.

In Figure 4.6 we have put a dashed line around the activity called 'reversing the existing business' in order to indicate that this activity is discontinued and not resumed when all the processes in the company have been reengineered. By the time this has taken place, a complete model of the company will be in existence. Envisioning is an individual activity. In fact, it is more like a set of activities that are performed in

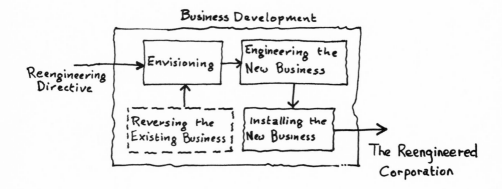

Figure 4.6 *The activities of business development.*

parallel. An activity gathers up proposals for improvements, describes them, evaluates them (Urgent, Important, Less Important), and assesses the cost – in time and money – that their introduction will demand. In another activity that is linked to the project, the proposals that have already been identified are taken and compiled into an objective specification for the new release of the company. Releases must be handled according to a comprehensive overview plan for developing the entire business. As a rule, a company will not be able to make releases with any great frequency. Employees cannot cope with a constant flood of changes. Also, you need time to really try out improvements before applying them on a large scale. It is better to collect the proposals over a period of time and present them, say, once a year if they are not too sweeping in scope. The effects of introducing something that is not ready for introduction can be very harmful. Besides causing serious distur-bances in the business, an immature innovation can substantially damage the confidence that staff and handlers in general have in the people implementing change. This makes it difficult for them to be effective in the future. Furthermore, it takes time to introduce improvements that require changes to the company computer-based support. The constantly ongoing work of improvement we describe here should be managed as a whole. Gather up improvement proposals, without first thinking about how they will be implemented because you should be able to combine worthwhile proposals into releases that are functionally linked and fully integrated, no matter if they are implemented with mechanical or human resources. An important tool when steering the improvement work is metrics. Improvement work should be based on how well goals are achieved. Therefore, you should set measurable goals for each process. If the measured values show that a process or subprocess does not achieve its goals, something is probably wrong with the process.

4.12 Summary

Object-Oriented Business Engineering is built on six key ideas.

- A business has several customers, and it wishes to treat each one according to the customer's individual needs. It offers these customers services and products by means of business processes. Internally, a company should be organized according to these processes, which cut across functional divisions.

- Use cases are a simple, natural way to identify business processes. A customer is a user of a company, and he or she uses the company through a business process. Each way of using the company is a use case.

- A company is a very complex system around which many handlers orbit. In order to clarify its workings for these handlers, the company must be described in the form of models. Usually, different handlers will need different models.

- Object orientation is an excellent way to clarify the inner workings of a company – its processes, products, services, resources – and how those things depend on each other.

- Reengineering a business and developing an integral information system are separate, parallel, tightly linked activities. The design of a business process is greatly influenced by creative IT solutions – it is essential that the two be developed in harmony.

- The business model of the redesigned company and the requirements model for the information system must be seamless. This is achieved by pairing Object-Oriented Business Engineering and Object-Oriented Software Engineering, which work in harmony.

4.13 References

Carlzon J. and Lagerström T. (1985). *Riv Pyramiderna! En bok om den nya människan, chefen och ledaren*

Hammer M. and Champy J. (1993). *Reengineering the Corporation: A Manifesto for Business Revolution*. New York: HarperCollins

Davenport T.H. (1993). *Process Innovation, Reengineering Work through Information Technology*. Boston, MA: Harvard Business School Press

Jacobson I. (1994). Business process reengineering with object technology. *Object Magazine*, May

Johansson H., McHugh P., Pendlebury J. and Wheeler III W. (1993). *Business Process Reengineering. Breakpoint Strategies for Market Dominance*. Chichester: John Wiley & Sons

Shelton R.E. (1993). Object-oriented business engineering. *First Class – The Object Management Group Newsletter*, **3**(3), August/September

chapter 5
Architecture

5.1 Introduction

Making an object-oriented model of a business implies visualizing structures and associations within the business. We can call this the architecture of the business.

For us, the word *architecture* has two meanings: firstly, it refers to the architecture of a specific business and, secondly, to the different types of architecture that our modelling language allows us to show. It is the second meaning that this chapter primarily intends to examine.

By the *architecture of a company*, we mean the most important static, or long-lived, structures within the company. Typical elements in these structures are the company's functions — that is, divisions, departments and so on. Other elements are processes and deliverables at various levels, as well as various kinds of resources, both human and mechanical. One element is linked to other elements to form, collectively, a structure. Each element has an owner — someone in the company. Elements have substance, they are tangible, they can be assigned a value (sometimes many values), and they have limits.

Even though the architecture is the most important thing to capture in a business model, it is also important to be able to express the dynamics in the architecture, that is, what the organization does in different situations. The measures to be taken and the decisions to be made in the course of the different events are interesting and necessary in order to understand the organization's tasks. Therefore, in this chapter, we also examine how to describe a dynamic flow of events that is linked to the architecture of a company.

5.2 What must you be able to express in a business model?

The term *process* is used in many ways. In business modelling, it is used to indicate how a customer can use the business and it encompasses a complete flow of events in the system, which describes how a customer starts, carries out and completes the business process. Davenport (1993) defines a process as 'a structured, measured set of activities designed to produce a specified output for a particular customer or market'. This definition of the term is the one that is most interesting to those who observe the business from the outside, for example the company's shareholders and customers.

The term process is also used in another way. Hammer and Champy (1993) and Davenport (1993) use the same term to describe activities that are entirely internal to the business. These processes do not have any external customer; instead, the value that they produce is meant to benefit other internal processes. Examples of such processes are various kinds of management processes and other processes of infrastructural nature.

We believe it is crucial that a clear differentiation is made between these two different uses of the term process. The first definition corresponds to the business processes of the organization; the second refers to how these processes are divided into internal processes. Essentially, you would want to handle these processes in different ways and, therefore, you should be able to differentiate between them.

Our modelling language must allow us to describe the various types of tasks or internal processes, which every business process consists of, as well as the way in which these internal processes interact to offer a given customer a service or product.

Our concept for the business process is the use case, which is therefore, perhaps, our most important term. Our construct for internal processes is the object, which must therefore be supported by object-oriented business engineering. The relationship between use cases and objects is discussed further later in this chapter. Intuitively expressed, a use case is realized by a set of communicating objects, where one object can participate in several use cases. The use case is the key to finding objects.

Another important concept to discuss is the term *function* or *sub-business*. Very large businesses must be divided into several sub-businesses, each of which covers a particular area of competence. Note that in a process-oriented organization, a sub-business of this type is not a traditional area of responsibility, such as finance or marketing, but an area of competence, such as knowledge about a specific type of product a company produces. A sub-business does not have a manager, but instead has a resource owner, who develops and 'sells' personnel to the process leaders. The process leaders have budgeted resources with which to 'buy' the required personnel. Simply put, by using process owners and resource owners, you will divide traditional responsibility into two components: one leads the organization towards its financial goals, the other develops personnel resources so that the financial goals can be achieved. The concepts of resource owner and process leader are described in more detail in Chapter 10. The modelling language must offer the possibility of expressing how an internal process is realized with human or mechanical resources and from which sub-business these resources will be taken. It is especially important to be able to show how a process can be supported by an information system. There should be easy traceability between an internal process in the business organization and the requirements that must be met by the supporting information system. At this point, we can see that an object corresponding to an internal process in the business corresponds directly to one or more use cases in the information system. This topic is discussed in more detail in Chapter 9.

The terms *product* and *service*, or, taken together, the *deliverables*, must also be capable of being modelled. A deliverable can be built up of other deliverables. A deliverable has characteristics that describe what you can do with it and what it contains. Our construct for describing a deliverable — or rather its type — is an object, with its operations and attributes.

Furthermore, you need to be able to describe the flow of events when a business process is performed. You must be able to describe the inputs from the outside world, and the actions of the process when it receives an input — that is, the operations that will be performed, the decisions that will be made, and the output that the process will send to the outside world in return. Because input and output are the means by which the process communicates with a customer, input and output must be customer oriented. You can, for example, describe input and output in terms of usability, error-free function, standards, and the like.

Finally, there is a requirement that has to do with business modelling in general. However well you develop a company, you can be sure of one thing: it will be subject to change. Therefore, it is important that our language permits flexibility. It must be possible to change the processes but still produce value for the customers of the business. It must also be possible to adapt the processes to new situations. If the company establishes affiliates, it should be possible to specialize the sales process so that it also works in a subsidiary.

5.3 Internal and external models of a business

When you develop a model of a business, regardless of whether you perform forward or reverse engineering, you should produce two types of model: external and internal. We touched briefly upon this in Chapter 4, and we will develop the reasoning further in Chapters 6 and 7. An external model describes the company and the world external to it. It describes the processes in the company that satisfy the customers' interests, and the interests of others outside the company. The interface between each process and its external environment is vital, and must be described with particular care. Since our construct for processes is the use case, our external model will describe the business' use cases. We call our external model a *use-case model*.

An internal model of the company describes each business process: how they are built up of different work tasks (internal processes) and the various types of resources that they exploit or produce. The company can be structured into sub-businesses (functions). The internal model should then be able to show the sub-business to which a given task is assigned; that is, where a resource for carrying out a particular task can be obtained.

Our internal model is object-oriented. We have, however, introduced a few types of object category in order to make our models clearer. We differentiate thus between objects that correspond to work tasks and objects that correspond to things in the business, for example products. We also differentiate between work tasks, dividing them into tasks that imply direct contact with the customer, such as sales, and internal work tasks, for example product planning.

Our internal model can be of two types: ideal or real. The ideal model is a model of the company that does not take into consideration how the model must be realized in practice. It does not consider the fact that the company may already have a fairly well-functioning organization, or that it may be geographically dispersed among, say, several affiliates. The real model takes these factors into account. It also considers the fact that, at present, the organization does not have personnel who have achieved the level of competence suggested in the ideal model. In many cases, it is sufficient to produce an ideal model and then let the organization itself determine how it will have to function in order to realize the model. More details on how to work with these different models are given in Chapter 7.

In Chapter 2, we discussed why a business model of the company is needed, and indicated the groups for which it is intended. We mentioned the requirements placed on the business model by various groups: customers, partners, executive management, the reengineering team, process owners, resource owners, the IT organization and other participants in the process. Taken together, the external and internal models of a business satisfy the requirements placed on such a business model. The external model is a use-case model, whereas the internal model may consist of one or two object models — an ideal model and perhaps also a real model.

5.4 The use-case model

The use-case model will capture the part of the business in which you are interested. It will describe the business and its environment. The business is made up of all the relevant business processes, for example the processes that are appropriate for reengineering. The external environment is made up of, for example, customers, partners and suppliers that take part in the processes. In object-oriented business engineering, these processes are modelled with use cases, while the environment is modelled using what we call actors.

The use-case model also shows how the external environment interacts with the business, that is, how individual actors communicate with use cases within the business.

The model should describe the business as it is seen externally, that is, how it is perceived by those who wish to use it. Therefore, structures inside the business that cannot be seen by the actors should not be described in the use-case model. An intuitive explanation of a use case is that it constitutes a way of using the business.

We now introduce, in a way that is easy to understand, our various modelling concepts – business system, use cases and actors. After that, we can deepen and widen our definitions by describing the difference between classes and instances of use cases and actors, and by describing some powerful types of relations between use cases.

5.4.1 The business system

The modelling concept we use to symbolize a business is the *business system*. The system to be modelled must be identified and delimited with respect to the external environment; in other words, you define what the business system is responsible for and what the environment is responsible for. Therefore, the boundary between the system and its environment is extremely important. When the work of modelling begins, this boundary is indistinct, but when the model is complete, the boundary will be very clear indeed. A system boundary is by no means obvious and can change in different revisions of the business.

To symbolize a business system in the use-case model, we use a rectangle with rounded corners. Each business has a name, which is placed above the rectangle (Figure 5.1). Everything inside the rectangle belongs to the business system, while everything outside belongs to the business system's external environment.

The Restaurant

Figure 5.1 *The business of a restaurant regarded as a business system.*

To illustrate the concept, we show the simple example of a new restaurant business.

Example

Our good friend Knut, a restaurateur, has just opened a new restaurant, The Checkered Tablecloth. He has asked us to help him to get more insight into his business by constructing a business model of the restaurant (Figure 5.1).

Semantically, the model in Figure 5.1 does not yet mean anything. We will fill it with contents by describing what belongs to the external environment and the inner workings of the restaurant itself.

5.4.2 The actors

To construct a correct model of the business, it is important to understand the environment. In the environment, there are, for example, customers, and it is they who place the most significant requirements on the business. We must avoid drowning in the problems that are internal to the business.

An actor represents a role that someone or something in the environment can play in relation to the business. In our models, the environment is represented by actors, and nothing else. Actors are used to represent everything in the environment that interacts with the business and which we wish to model. Actors can be, for example, customers, suppliers or partners. They can be divided into two groups, human and mechanical. Another company's computer system, for example, might be represented by a mechanical actor. On the other hand, the restaurant's employees or its machinery cannot be looked upon as actors because they are part of the business system itself; that is, they constitute resources that are used to carry out tasks within the system. We will return to how resources are modelled in object-oriented business engineering when we discuss layered systems in Chapter 11.

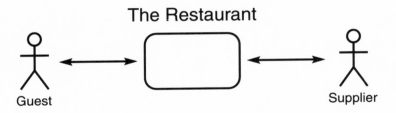

The Restaurant

Guest   Supplier

Figure 5.2 *The business system (the restaurant) with its environment.*

Example

We resume the modelling of the restaurant by adding two actors: Guest and Supplier (Figure 5.2).

The symbol we use to represent an actor is a stick figure (Figure 5.2). The arrows of association that we have drawn between the actors and the business system imply that they can communicate or cooperate with each other.

It is important to understand that an actor represents an abstraction of someone or something that uses the business. An actor can represent many different types of occurrence in the environment. In our example, we have individual Guests at the restaurant, as well as individuals representing Suppliers to the restaurant.

It is also important to differentiate between real people and actors. A real person can play several roles in a business system. Jim Clark, for example, might be both a guest and the supplier's representative.

5.4.3 The use case

A use case is our construct for a business process. The term *use case* is, however, more precise; we want to give it a definition that corresponds to the way users of (customers of) the business view its processes, not primarily as participants in the business would like to structure them.

A use case is a sequence of transactions in a system whose task is to yield a result of measurable value to an individual actor of the system.

Let us look more closely at some of the key words in the definition above:

- *Use case*: the definition above is really a specific flow of events through the system, that is, an instance. There are a great many possible courses of events, many of which are very similar. To make a use case model meaningful, you usually group the courses of events and call each of the groups a use-case class. For example, how you choose to proceed when selling a product might depend on whether the customer is new, where the customer is located, whether tomorrow is a holiday, and so on. All of these alternatives are often best grouped into one use case, called Selling. If you did not group these possible variants, you would end up with an enormous number of use cases, and your model would become difficult to understand. When we say that we identify and describe a use case, we mean that we identify and describe the class.

- *Individual actor*: this expression is perhaps the key to finding the correct use cases, in that it helps you to avoid designing use cases that are too complex. It is important to proceed from individual actors, that is, instances of actors. A good way of finding suitable actors is to name at least two — preferably three — people who could serve as the actor in question. For example, if you were modelling a company that specialized in selling a product, you would realize that an actor called 'the customer' is, in fact, three different customers: firstly, the normal user of the product (and there are many of these); secondly, the buyer of the product — that is, someone who is competent in purchasing, but may not necessarily know what the product will be used for — and thirdly someone who is competent to judge the product in comparison with competing products. It is clear that each of these individuals requires his or her own use case, since they represent different roles that can be played towards the system.

- *In a system*: when we say 'transactions in a system', we mean that the system supplies the use cases. The actors communicate with the system's use cases.

- *A measurable value*: this expression is a very important key to finding the correct level of a use case, that is, one that is not too detailed. A use case must help the actor to perform a task that has identifiable value. It may be possible to assess the performance of a use case in terms of price or cost. For example, applying for a loan in a bank is something that is of value for a customer of a bank.

- *Transaction*: a transaction is an atomic set of activities that are performed either fully or not at all. It is invoked by a stimulus from an actor to the system or by a point in time being reached in the system. A transaction consists of a set of actions, decisions and transmission of stimuli to the invoking actor or to some other actor(s).

We use an ellipse to symbolize a use case. This symbol is chosen to indicate that a use case is extended within a system, where it can cut across several of the business system's inner parts.

Example

We have identified the following use cases for the restaurant (Figure 5.3):

Eating Dinner – a guest comes to the restaurant and is served dinner. The guest can choose from a widely varied menu or may even order a dish of his/her own composition.

Eating Lunch – a guest comes to the restaurant and is served lunch. The guest can choose from a lunch menu that consists of two 'lunches of the day' and several standard meals (*à la carte*).

When the business environment has been identified, you can begin to identify the business system internally. As a rule, this work is done iteratively. In our example system, we would perhaps have identified first the Guest actor, then the use cases Eating Lunch and Eating Dinner. After that, we would have realized that we needed another use case to describe how ingredients were purchased and thus identified the use case Purchasing Supplies and the actor Supplier.

A use-case model, such as that in Figure 5.3, is interpreted in the following way: the business system Restaurant has an environment in the

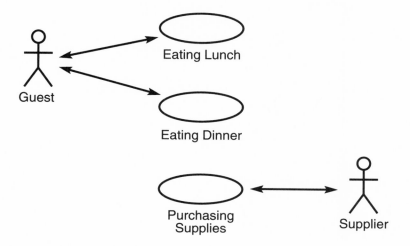

Figure 5.3 *Use cases in the restaurant.*

form of two types of actor – Guest and Supplier. Internally, Restaurant offers three use cases – Eating Lunch, Eating Dinner and Purchasing Supplies. Individual Guests and Suppliers can use these three use cases.

> **On naming use cases**
> The name given to a use case should express what happens when an instance of the use case is performed. The name should therefore be active, often expressed by the gerund form of the verb (Dining) or a verb and a noun together (Having Dinner).

5.4.4 The difference between class and instance

Let us begin by examining the actor. We need to be able to talk about the characteristics that all actors of a certain type share, as well as the unique characteristics that any specific actor of this type may have. In other words, we must be able to differentiate between the class of an actor and the actual actor.

What is it in our model, then, that corresponds to real people, such as Jim Clark and Mary Smith? They are not instances of the actor Guest, since Guest only represents a model of guests in general. However, we can say that Jim and Mary are realizations of instances of the class Guest. An actor represents a role that real people can play. One person can play several roles — that is, realize several instances of the actor.

In the same way, we must be able to differentiate between a class and an instance of a use case. The class is defined by the description we have made of it. An instance of a use case, on the other hand, is defined by the activities performed when a flow of events that follows the description of the use case is executed in the system.

A use-case class can contain several alternative paths through the system, but the instance follows one — and only one — of these paths.

It is important to be able to differentiate between instances and classes for several reasons:

- You must be able to model the idea that the business can serve several parallel flows of events. Several instances of the same use-case class may be performed in parallel.

- You need to be able to identify characteristics that are shared between similar classes, something that is not necessary for instances. An instance obeys its class and can communicate with instances of actors.

- An important part of the use-case concept is making sure that individual customers (instances of actors) are linked to one — and only one — instance of a particular use case. In this way, you can avoid fragmenting the business's responsibility to a customer.

5.4.5 Describing a use case

To provide more depth for the use-case model, detailed descriptions of each use case are written. You do not merely describe in detail the use cases' flows of events, but also how they interact with the environment, that is, the actors.

Example

Let us look more closely at the use case Eating Dinner in the business system Restaurant. When a guest enters the restaurant, he/she is greeted at the door and invited to hang up his/her coat. After that, the guest is seated at a table and given a menu. When the actor Guest has thought over his/her choice for a while, he/she is asked to place an order, or the actor can attract the waiter's attention. The guest gives an order to the waiter, and the order is passed on to the kitchen, where it is prepared. When the order is ready, it is served to the guest. After it has been eaten, the guest is expected to signal the waiter for payment. Having paid, the guest can then fetch his/her coat from the cloakroom and leave the restaurant. The use case is then complete.

The description above is simplified compared with how the use case should be described in reality. We have not mentioned any alternative courses of events, such as the procedure required if a particular dish is not available or if the guest cannot pay. If we try to describe a use case that contains a great many alternative courses of events, our text can easily become difficult to understand. Therefore, it is wise to use some form of structured writing approach. In this case, our example – the use case Eating Dinner – could be as follows:

Basic flow of events:

A. The use case begins when the actor Guest enters the restaurant.

B. The actor Guest has the possibility of leaving his/her coat in the cloakroom, after which he/she is shown to a table and given a menu.

C. When the actor Guest has had sufficient time to make up his/her mind, he/she is asked to state his/her order. Alternatively, Guest can attract the waiter's attention so that the order can be placed.

D. When Guest has ordered, the kitchen is informed what food and beverages the order contains.

E. In the kitchen, certain basic ingredients, such as sauces, rice and potatoes, have already been prepared. Cooking therefore involves collecting together these basic ingredients, adding spices and so on and sorting out what needs to be done just before the dish is served. Also, the required beverages are fetched from the refrigerator.

F.   When the dish is ready, it is served to the actor Guest. When it has been eaten, the actor is expected to attract the waiter's attention in order to pay.

G.   Once payment has been made, Guest can fetch his/her coat from the cloakroom and leave the restaurant. The use case is then complete.

Alternative courses of events:

- *Alternative A*: if the restaurant is full, the actor Guest will find this out at stage A of the basic flow of events. The actor can then choose between waiting in the bar until a table is free or leaving the restaurant altogether. In the first case, the use case will continue at stage B after the waiting time. If the actor leaves, the use case is finished.

- *Alternative C*: if it turns out, at stage C, that a dish Guest wants is not being served that day, he/she will be told, and the waiter should be able to suggest an alternative. When the actor Guest has decided on something else, the flow of events continues at stage D.

By thinking about use cases as state-of-events machines, it is easier to understand how to find use cases and how they should be described. In other words, a use case can be looked on as a state-of-events machine in which the state of an instance of a use case represents which stimuli may be received next as well as the stimuli that can cause the use case to leave its present state, after having completed a transaction, to adopt a new one. An instance of a use case can, when it is initiated, go through a number of states before it is completed.

Various instances of one and the same use-case class can appear to be very different from one another. The steps outlined in the description of the class do not need to have any sequential order forced on them; they can even be carried out in parallel when the use case is instantiated. In troublesome cases, decisions to carry out certain orders can mean that many different activities will be set in motion, to a great degree independently of each other. It might also be necessary to gather a huge volume of data before the work can be carried out. It must be possible to express this without mentioning a particular sequence.

We can also say that a use case can follow different paths through its description, depending either on the choices that are made during its flow of events or on given prerequisites that require the system to act in a special way. For example, an instance of the use case Eating Dinner will react in a particular way if the guest has no money with which to pay; perhaps by requesting identification or even by calling the police. If the guest has money when carrying out another instance of the same use-case class, identification will not need to be shown. However, both of these instances of the use case follow the same description, that is, they will obey the same class.

5.4.6 Interaction between the actor and the use case

Earlier, we mentioned that actors communicate with the system by sending stimuli. In order to comprehend the actor fully, we have to know which use case the actor uses. In the use-case model, we indicate this by means of communication associations between actors and use cases. For example, to show that the actor Guest communicates with the use case Eating Lunch, and vice versa, you would identify one communication association from Guest to Eating Lunch, and another from Eating Lunch to Guest. However, it is not always necessary to denote this with one arrow in each direction. You may use bi-directional arrows if it makes the figure easier to read (see Figure 5.3).

As a rule, associations exist between instances of the actor and the use case. We can show the number of instances that can be associated by giving the association a cardinality.

A communication association between the representations of an instance of a use case and an instance of an actor shows that they interact with each other. The direction of the association is the same as the direction in which the stimuli are sent.

If it is known how an actor behaves towards the system, we can show this in detail by using different types of modelling techniques. We can use interaction diagrams to show how actors and use cases interact during the use case's flow of events. Using state-transition diagrams, we can describe use cases, actors and the interaction between them. A state shows the possible stimuli that are expected at a certain position, and which stimuli will lead to a response. A response could be an output of some sort, such as a value. It might lead to a change of state.

5.5 The object model

The use-case model is an excellent means of both expressing our requirements with regard to the business and providing a good, comprehensive picture of what the business is meant to perform. The use-case model illustrates, in a straightforward way, the function of the business, its environment and the business processes it offers the outside world. Nevertheless, it does not give a clear picture of how the business is structured internally in order to realize its requirements. Neither does it explain how the business processes are realized as various forms of activity, how these activities are linked together into worthwhile process chains, what things are produced or used in the business, or what types of resource are to be used to implement various activities, and so on. If the business is to be understood fully, not least by the reengineering team, a far more detailed picture of it must be available than that provided by the use-case model.

There are also aspects of a business that the use-case model is not intended to express. It is obvious that the business should not engage in anything that cannot be related to the business processes; but it borders on the extreme to think that you will be able to express everything you consider essential in terms of business processes. We see many attempts at business engineering in which people have tried to distort the process concept so that everything could be interpreted as 'a process'. Obviously, there are requirements other than those governing the business processes that must be taken into account, for example product quality rather than process quality alone, the structure of company management, and imparting information to employees. You might call these activities processes, but it would not be especially meaningful.

Object modelling is a means of capturing all of these other requirements that need to be expressed and, in some cases, linking them to objects. Object models at different levels of abstraction and with different perspectives of the company are established to ensure that you understand what is to be achieved with business engineering and to enable well-founded decisions to be made regarding the company's business development.

Object orientation gives the company a solid architecture, an architecture that is comprehensible, alterable, adaptable and reusable. Here, reusability means that you can identify business objects that can be reused to, for example, build up affiliates whose operations are similar to that of the parent company, or to develop companies with new but related business processes.

5.5.1 Objects

What occurrences in the business can be objects? We need objects that represent the things and products that are used during a flow of events in the system. We also need objects that represent the tasks that must be performed during a flow of events. In addition, we have to make sure that there are objects to represent the way in which the system communicates with the outside world.

Example

Examples of tasks that you can identify in the business system The Restaurant are Cloakroom Attendant, Order Handler and Food Preparer. Examples of products and things that need to be handled are menus and orders. Thus, we have identified the following classes: Cloakroom Attendant, Order Handler, Food Preparer, Menu and Order (Figure 5.4).

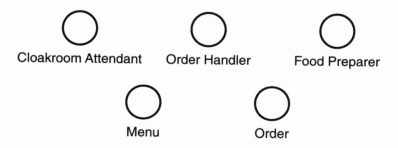

Figure 5.4 *Objects in the Restaurant.*

On naming classes of objects

The name you give to an object class should express, as clearly as possible, the responsibility that instances of the class will have. Classes often have names that consist of several words in order to make the name clearer. It is more important for the name to be clear than short.

It is also important that the name is unique, at least within the object model. Avoid giving classes – or anything else – names that are similar, or that can be interpreted as meaning the same thing.

Class names are usually nouns. If the class represents a task, you can choose a name that has the substantive form of a verb.

5.5.2 Different types of object

Earlier, we mentioned that an object can correspond to tasks, products or things in the business. Tasks can be divided into two types: those that handle the interaction of actors with the business, and those that only perform tasks within the business. It is convenient to identify different types of object in order to clarify their various tasks in the model. We can therefore identify entity objects, interface objects and control objects (Figure 5.5).

Note that the interface objects and the control objects represent tasks in the business, not types of resource. On the other hand, the tasks are realized by people who belong to a certain category of resource. The task of being a food preparer in a restaurant is realized by a person who has been trained to cook. Often, however, several tasks are packed together into one object that will be realized by one particular resource instance. The Order Handler is an example of this – the Order Handler is responsible for both receiving guests and serving them. In most cases, you have knowledge about which components will be used when implementing the model. There is a benefit in making it easy to see these components in the model; if you fail to do this, the object model will be difficult to understand and maintain.

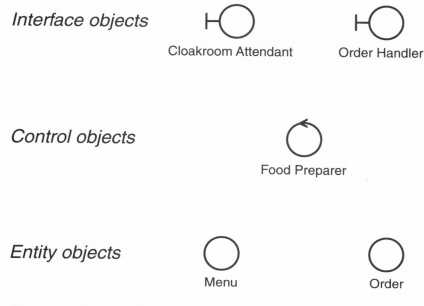

Figure 5.5 *Classes in the Restaurant. Here, we have used different object types.*

 *Interface objects*

Interface objects represent a set of operations in the business, each of which should be performed by one and the same resource. This task involves communicating with the environment of the business. Consequently, you may have certain requirements regarding the communicative abilities of the person who implements the task. An example of such a resource is a salesperson, who should be good at communicating with customers and at negotiating agreements.

An interface object can participate in several use cases. Often, the object has a coordinating responsibility in the process – at least regarding those parts of it that come into direct contact with customers. Any given customer should have as few contacts as possible within an organization. This does not, however, contradict the business theories that recommend everyone in the company to be close to the customer. What it means is that each individual customer's contacts within the company should be as few and as simple as possible.

You can say that the part of the business that has direct contact with the outside world is visible in interface objects, whereas entity and control objects are more independent of their environment.

Control objects

Control objects represent a set of operations in a business, just like interface objects. The difference is that the tasks do not imply taking direct responsibility for contacts with the business environment. Control objects, for example, can represent specialist tasks that are performed without any direct contact with a customer. The name control object arises because the objects are active, controlling or taking part in the control flow that handles the products with which the process works. An instance of a control object therefore often has the same lifetime as the use-case instance in which it participates.

Common examples of control objects in a company are Product Developer and Project Manager.

Entity objects

Entity objects represent occurrences such as products and things that are handled in the business. An entity object does not participate in only one use case; an instance can take part in many courses of events in the business, perhaps throughout the life cycle of the business. Unlike interface and control objects, entity objects are realized in the form of things, not human (or mechanical) resources.

Common examples of entity objects in a company are Product, Invoice and Order.

5.5.3 Associations

The relations that objects and their classes need to maintain in order to perform the courses of events described for the use case are shown by associations between them. An association always links two objects (instances or classes). An acquaintance association usually proceeds from one instance to another and is thus said to be an instance association. The inheritance association always links two classes and is consequently said to be a class association. It may also be required to relate a class to an instance, or vice versa, in which case we call it a meta-association.

As stated in Chapter 3, we consider associations to be binary directed relations. This means that an association always expresses a relation from one object (or class) to another object (or class). Consequently, if you want to show that two objects may communicate in both directions, you will need communication associations in both directions. Notationally, you may use a bi-directional arrow to show this.

References between objects

In our restaurant, it is a natural requirement to be able to find out, from a certain order, the checks that will be issued for it. Thus, in the object Order, there should be a reference to one or more instances of the object Check. A reference of this kind between objects is indicated by an acquaintance association between the objects.

More formally, we might say that an acquaintance association from object A to object B implies that A has a reference to B. Normally, acquaintance associations exist between instances of objects.

An acquaintance association also has a name that reflects the role the associated object has to the associating one. In our example, we have chosen the name 'means of payment' (Figure 5.6).

We can express the number of instances that can be associated by giving the acquaintance association a cardinality. In our example, the cardinality should be allowed to lie between 0 and m. An order can result in either 0 checks if the restaurant decides that the food (the order) is 'on the house' or several if the guests in a party want to pay separately.

On naming associations
The usual method of naming associations is to make sure that the sequence object–association–object together forms a meaning. As class names in general are usually nouns, the names of associations will be verbs. For example, from the sequence Order–handled by–Order Handler, we can construct the sentence 'An order is handled by an order handler'.

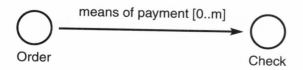

means of payment [0..m]

Order   Check

Figure 5.6 *An instance of Order needs references to instances of Check.*

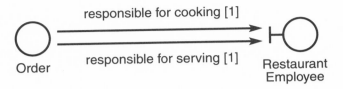

Figure 5.7 *The object Restaurant Employee plays two roles in relation to the object Order: serving and cooking.*

However, we have chosen another strategy, in which we allow the name of the association to express the role the associated object plays towards the associating object. Thus, the name of the association becomes a substantive, often an adjective used as a noun; for example, Order–responsible–Order Handler (see Figure 5.7). It is not quite so easy to form a complete sentence, so we shall instead express ourselves as follows: 'An order handler is responsible for taking an order'.

The first naming strategy, which we can call 'verb name', is similar to that used in data modelling. There, the model is seen as a flat structure, viewed from above. Thus, it is natural to perceive relations as a link between two objects, a binding attraction that goes in both directions. Why then, have we chosen the second strategy? We can give the following reasons.

Firstly, in the object-oriented world, you regard the world as if you were an object. You ask yourself, 'How am I dependent on other objects?' The answer to this question will give you an idea of the roles other objects play in relation to you. Giving relations names that reflect their roles therefore seems the natural thing to do. You can also say that you, as an object, place requirements on the roles other objects will be able to play in relation to you; however, it is not certain that these objects need to know who or what has demanded that they play these roles. Thus, relations normally only exert influence in one direction.

Secondly, giving associations names that reflect the roles other objects play can help us in finding a structure in

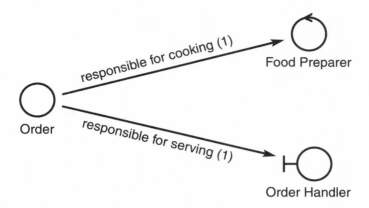

Figure 5.8 *Instead of Restaurant Employee, we choose to identify the objects Food Preparer and Order Handler.*

the object models. If, in our example, we had begun by only identifying the object Restaurant Employee, we would have discovered that the object Order would need two acquaintance associations to this object, 'serving' and 'cooking' (Figure 5.7). These two associations show that Restaurant Employee can act in two roles in relation to Order, which implies that the behaviour exhibited by Restaurant Employee can be divided into two parts. It might also be that the same instance of Restaurant Employee has the task of being both waiter and food preparer, but this is not what we want to show in this model.

A good choice of association name can help us to find a more expressive set of objects, in this case the objects Food Preparer and Order Handler (Figure 5.8).

To avoid confusing the names of classes with the names of associations, the class name is given an initial capital letter, while the association name is all lower case.

Aggregates of objects

The associations called consistsOf and partOf are variants of the acquaintance association. They are used to express that an object is a compound of other objects. A construction of this type is called an aggregate.

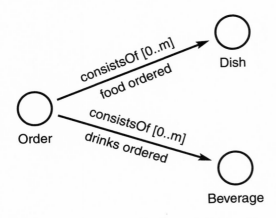

Figure 5.9 *An order consists of a number of dishes and a number of drinks.*

A consistsOf association from an object A to an object B means that A consists of objects of type B (Figure 5.9). The partOf association expresses the opposite situation; that is, that objects of type A make up part of the objects of type B. Normally, consistsOf associations and partOf associations occur between instances.

Communication between objects
Objects need to be able to exchange data with each other when a flow of events takes place. In our example, the object Food Preparer has to find out from the object Order what kind of food he or she should prepare. This type of relation is shown with a communication association between the two objects.

Just as with the acquaintance association, with the communication association we can show the number of instances that can be associated by giving the association a cardinality. The object Food Preparer can communicate with 0 to many instances of Order; therefore, we set the cardinality of their association to [0..m] (Figure 5.10).

A communication association between two objects means that they can 'talk to' each other. The direction of the association shows the direction in which a stimulus will be sent. The communication association is almost always an instance association.

The communication association does not show what kind of stimuli is sent between the objects; this is a level of detail that is saved until we make the interaction diagrams (see Section 5.6.2). The association only shows that communication takes place between the objects. This is why we do not give the communication association a name. In a diagram, you

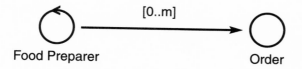

Figure 5.10 *An instance of Food Preparer can communicate with 0 to many instances of Order.*

might put in the type of the association (communication) just to separate it from other types.

Inheritance between classes of objects

In a restaurant, the head waiter is responsible for receiving guests, assigning tables and performing other general activities. An order handler, on the other hand, only monitors one or two tables and performs most of the serving in this area. However, both the head waiter and the order handler can wait on tables, which means that they have common characteristics (Figure 5.11). To avoid having to describe these in more than one place, we can break away the parts they have in common to form a new class, called 'Server', from which the classes Order Handler and Head Waiter can inherit characteristics. We show this relation with an inheritance association between the classes. Another way

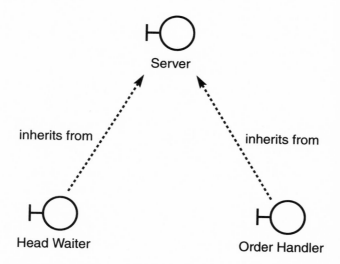

Figure 5.11 *The classes Head Waiter and Order Handler inherit characteristics from the class Server.*

of describing this is to say that the classes Head Waiter and Order Handler are specializations of the more general class Server.

The inheritance association is a relation between classes that shows that when the inheriting class (the descendant) is instantiated, all the characteristics (attributes, operations and associations) that are described for the class (the ancestor) from which it inherits will be present in the instance in question.

5.5.4 Behaviour

By studying the use cases in which an object participates, we can get an idea of the responsibilities the object has towards its environment. The behaviour we describe for the object's class will ensure that these responsibilities are met.

The behaviour of an object can be divided into a number of sequences, which we call 'operations'. For each of these operations, a stimulus initiates the execution of the operation. To be able to carry out an operation, you often need to know certain input and output data, which we call parameters to the operation. The stimulus together with the parameters form what we call the 'signature' of the operation.

The set of operations we have described for a class of objects is called the protocol of the class. This protocol shows how instances of other classes can send stimuli to instances of this class. The structure of the class, as well as the description of how its behaviour will be carried out, is encapsulated in the class itself. This means that you can change the description of how a behaviour sequence or an operation is performed without other object classes being influenced, as long as the protocol is not changed.

It is not always necessary to express an object's behaviour in terms of operations and parameters. If the purpose of the object model is primarily to identify tasks, products and things, and not to describe them in detail, it will probably be sufficient to give a short informal description of the behaviour. The important thing is that the object's responsibilities with regard to the environment is made clear.

Example
The object Order must (at least) be able to show the Dish to be prepared and the Order Handler who is responsible. We

can identify two operations of Order: Which Dish and Which Order Handler. The stimulus that invokes the operation Which Dish has a response parameter that is the name of the dish. For the operation Which Order Handler, the stimulus is accompanied by a response parameter that is a reference to the appropriate instance of the object Server.

5.5.5 Attributes

The characteristics that an object handles and is responsible for are modelled as attributes of the object. An attribute represents a unit of information stored in the object and consists of an attribute association and an attribute type. The attribute association represents the unit that holds the value of the attribute, while the attribute type shows the attribute's structure and type.

The attribute association has a name that, like the names of acquaintance associations, describes the role that the attribute plays in relation to the object. The association can also have a cardinality, so that you can show how many instances of an attribute type can be associated with this particular association. The attribute association is usually found between an instance of an object class and an instance of an attribute type.

It is not necessary to describe, in the object model, every imaginable attribute of the object, but only those that you need in order to understand the object's role and its responsibility in the business.

Why have we chosen this apparently complicated construction to describe an attribute? A common discussion point when modelling is whether to represent a certain occurrence as an attribute type or as an object. By treating the attribute type as something similar to an object, we make it easier to be specific in these discussions.

Example
The object Order has an attribute that specifies which dish(es) and beverage(s) are ordered. In Figure 5.9, we solved this by identifying the objects Dish and Beverage,

and letting Order have consistsOf associations to them. Another solution is to show this relation by means of two attribute associations, one to the attribute type Dish and the other to the attribute type Beverage (Figure 5.12). If the terms Dish and Beverage are only to be handled in connection with an order, this solution is preferable. Both associations can associate 0 to many instances, because an order can contain any number of different dishes and beverages.

5.5.6 Objects have different states

An object can receive various stimuli depending on the values of certain attributes, the operations that have been performed previously, and so on. Depending on where in its life cycle the object is, it will react differently to incoming stimuli. To describe this, we say that the object can have different states. In our simple example, we can study the object Food Preparer. If Food Preparer has references to many − say, ten − objects called 'Order', he/she cannot handle any more orders for the moment. Therefore, we have identified the states 'fully occupied' and 'not fully occupied' for the object Food Preparer.

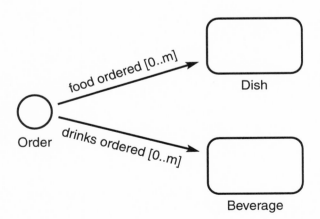

Figure 5.12 *The object Order has two attributes: food ordered and drinks ordered.*

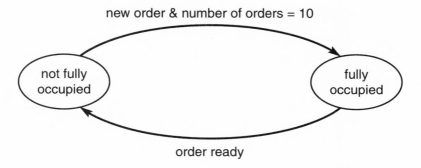

Figure 5.13 *A state transition diagram for the object Food Preparer.*

A state represents what we here call the potential of the object instance. Which of the continuations the object instance will follow from its current state depends on which stimulus it receives. A stimulus will cause the object instance to leave its current state and perform a transaction, but which one depends on the state–stimulus combination.

It is easy to imagine that an object can have considerably more complicated states than those we spoke of in the example above. Thus, it may be wise to visualize the object's potential states and state transitions by drawing a state transition diagram. There are a number of recommended techniques for this; the one to select generally depends on how complex the state pattern can be.

A state transition diagram relates events to states. When an event takes place, the next object state depends partly on its present state and partly on the event performed. A straightforward way of drawing state transition diagrams is illustrated in Figure 5.13; this type of diagram is usually called a Mealy diagram (Sudkamp, 1988).

Example

The object Food Preparer can have the states 'fully occupied' and 'not fully occupied' (Figure 5.13). The stimulus 'new order' in combination with the condition 'number of orders $>= 10$', induces a transition from the state 'not fully occupied' to the state 'fully occupied'. On the other hand, the stimulus 'order ready' in combination with the condition 'number of orders < 10' causes a transition in the opposite direction.

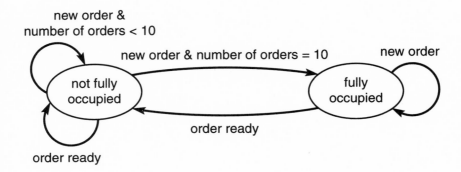

new order &
number of orders < 10

new order & number of orders = 10   new order

not fully
occupied

fully
occupied

order ready

order ready

Figure 5.14 *Supplemented state transition diagram for the object Food Preparer.*

However, not all events cause state transitions. For the sake of clarity you should, in the state transition diagram, show how all vital events affect the object. Our sample diagram could therefore be modified to look like Figure 5.14.

Example
In the state transition diagram for the object Food Preparer, we should depict the effect of receiving stimuli when the conditions have not been satisfied (Figure 5.14).

5.6 Use cases versus objects

The use-case model and the object model are different types of descriptions of the business. The use cases show the courses of events that can be performed, while the objects are more or less an abstraction of the business' implementation. For a particular use case to be executed, a certain set of objects is required in the system. We say that these objects offer the use case. Since different courses of events in the business can handle similar products and things, and contain similar behaviour, it is reasonable for an object to take part in many use cases.

An object model that consists of hundreds of objects, sometimes even more, cannot be easy to understand or deal with: it is too complex. It contains details of how the objects are related to one another internally, how they communicate, which interfaces they use, how they are made aware of one another, and so on. This kind of information makes any description very technical, and there is a great risk that more energy will be devoted to explaining internal collaboration within the business than is spent on trying to understand the business processes. Information of this kind is of course important to have when we make detailed models of business systems; however, it is not necessary to our comprehensive understanding of the use cases.

Finding objects is easy, according to many sources (Meyer, 1988; Shlaer and Mellor, 1988), but finding the right objects is difficult. We suggest that you identify — for each use case — the objects that are needed to execute that particular use case. The object model can then be presented in views showing the objects that participate in the different use cases. If you work in this way, you will have a better chance of finding the objects that really are needed, not just those you think are needed. If you go over every use case in which a certain object plays a role, you will be able to identify the responsibilities the object has in the system by integrating all of these roles (Wirfs-Brock et al., 1990).

Example

The use cases Eating Lunch, Eating Dinner and Purchasing Supplies are each executed by a set of objects. Some of these objects take part in more than one of these use cases; Food Preparer, for example, takes part in all three of them. The total responsibility that the object Food Preparer has in the business is a compilation of the responsibilities the object has with regard to each and every one of the three use cases in which it participates (Figure 5.15).

We mentioned that you can use one or more views of participating objects to show the various objects that offer the use cases. If you want to show in more detail how the objects interact to execute the use cases, you can do this with the help of an interaction diagram (see Section 5.6.2).

Furthermore, it is through objects that use cases influence one another. Two instances of use cases — belonging to the same or different classes — can be realized through the participation of one and the same

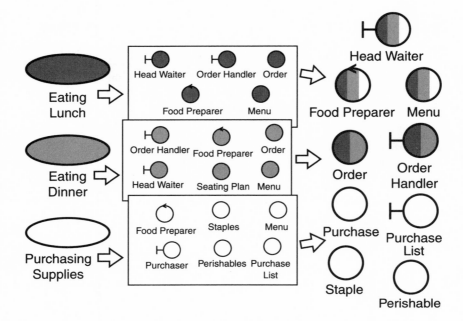

Figure 5.15 *A use case is executed by a set of collaborating objects. By integrating the various responsibilities an object has in different use cases, we can obtain an understanding of the overall responsibility the object has in the business. Some of the participating objects have been left out in this figure for the sake of clarity.*

object instance. In the example given in Figure 5.15, the control object Food Preparer participates in all three use cases. Instances of Eating Lunch and Purchasing Supplies will be running at the same time, and the same instance of Food Preparer might participate in both of these instances. Consequently, conflicts may arise. For example, if Food Preparer is used in two consecutive activities during a transaction in Eating Lunch, it should not be used in Purchasing Orders in between if there is any risk of inconsistency effects. Therefore, a transaction within a use case is something that should be regarded as atomic; it should not be interrupted or divided.

If an instance of an entity object is in use within two different use-case instances, another kind of conflict might arise. If you represent, for example, a document with an entity object, and this document participates in several instances of use cases in a business system, it must be clarified who has the responsibility for the instance. By responsibility, we mean having the right to change the state of the instance. The simple restaurant example we are using, however, does not show this problem clearly. It arises when entity objects are information carriers, like, for example, an Account object in a model of a bank.

5.6.1 Views of participating objects

To illustrate how a particular use case is executed by objects, you can draw views of the objects that participate in the use case (Figure 5.16). These views will express how the objects collaborate to carry out the courses of events that are described for the use case.

A view of participating objects for a use case is intended to illustrate the dynamics in the object model. Therefore, this type of view

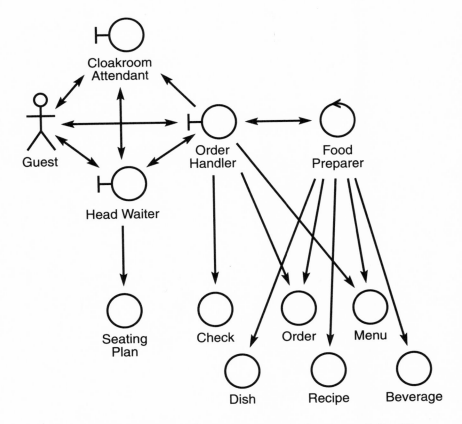

Figure 5.16 *A view of the objects participating in the use case Eating Dinner.*

contains, apart from objects, the communication associations needed to perform the use case. To clarify how flows of events are initiated and by whom, you should include actors and relevant communication associations from actors to interface objects in the view of participating objects.

When developing the object model, you will produce views of this kind (one or several) for every use case. Since an object may participate in several use cases, it will be present in several views of participating objects. All of these views together illustrate the different roles the object has in the model. Another way of putting it is to say that each use case in which an object participates puts responsibilities onto the object.

What about the static relations between the objects? The acquaintance, consistsOf, partOf and inheritance associations, as presented in Section 5.5.3, must, of course, also be illustrated, but this is best done in global views of the object model, not in views that illustrate the flow of a use case.

Because it is human nature to forget why a certain solution to a given problem was chosen, it is important that you document how you intend the use case to 'move' between the objects placed in the view. Therefore, you should make yet another description of the flow of events for the use case, this time in terms of the participating objects. What we are suggesting is not a new use case, only that a use case may have more than one description. Such a description for the use case Eating Dinner might read as follows:

A.   On entering the restaurant, the actor Guest sends a stimulus saying that he/she wants to be served. This stimulus is received by the object Head Waiter.

B.   The actor Guest is asked by the object Cloakroom Attendant if he/she wishes to check in his/her coat. Alternatively, Guest can inform the Cloakroom Attendant of this wish. After that, Guest is greeted by the object Head Waiter, who places Guest at a suitable table according to the Seating Plan. Then, the Head Waiter calls an object Order Handler to take care of Guest. The Order Handler hands over a menu, or verbally describes what is being served. The choices offered correspond to the present instance of the object Menu.

C.   After an appropriate interval, the object Order Handler asks the actor Guest for an order. Alternatively, Guest attracts the Order Handler's attention. Guest gives his/her order and Order Handler checks that the selection is available from the object Menu.

D.   The object Order Handler records Guest's order in a new instance of the object Order. Then Order Handler creates a new instance of the object Check. The Order Handler informs a suitable instance of the object Food Preparer that a new order has been placed.

E.   The object Food Preparer prepares the various Dishes according to Recipes. Food Preparer also takes out the Beverages that were ordered.

F.   When Food Preparer has the food ready, the current instance of the object Order Handler is informed of this and can serve Guest. When Guest has finished eating, he/she is expected to make contact with some instance of the object Order Handler.

G.   Order Handler updates the object Check and presents it to the actor Guest. Guest is then expected to pay. Guest then asks the object Cloakroom Attendant to return any items he/she may have left in the cloakroom, then leaves the restaurant. The use case is thereby completed.

Alternative courses of events:

- *Alternative A*: if, at A, the restaurant is fully occupied, the object Cloakroom Attendant will inform the actor Guest of this fact. Guest will also be told that he/she may wait in the bar until a table is free. When the object Cloakroom Attendant is told by the object Head Waiter that a table is available, Guest is notified. The use case then continues at B. If the actor Guest does not wish to wait, the use case is completed when the actor leaves the restaurant.

- *Alternative C*: if, at C, it turns out that the actor Guest has ordered something that is not included in the object Menu, the object Order Handler informs Guest that the dish is not available. Regardless of whether it is not available because the printed menu does not correspond to what the object Menu actually includes, or because Guest has some special requirements, Order Handler should be able to suggest an alternative order. When the actor Guest and the object Order Handler have come to an agreement, the flow of events can continue at D.

Note that we have chosen to follow the same structure here as we did in the first description of the use case (Section 5.4.5). By doing so, we can maintain traceability between objects and sub-courses of events in the use case.

5.6.2 Interaction diagrams

If you wish to express in more detail how the various objects in the model collaborate to execute a certain flow of events, you can draw an interaction diagram. This diagram shows how a use case is realized by communicating objects. Part of this technique involves identifying the stimuli that are transmitted between objects, as well as the parameters that follow the stimuli. This is known as identifying the protocols between objects.

An interaction diagram shows in detail the interactions that take place between the objects during a use case's flow of events. You show the stimuli that are sent from one object to another.

In an interaction diagram, an object is represented by a vertical column (Figure 5.17). The order in which the columns are placed is not significant, but they should be positioned for maximum clarity. If several instances of the same class participate in the use case, each of those instances can be represented by an individual column if this lends clarity to the diagram. A column most often represents an instance, but might also represent a class. There may also be one or more columns to represent the environment. We call these columns system boundaries.

The chronological axis in an interaction diagram points downwards. It should not be perceived as linear, but as stimuli driven. In other words, the distance between two stimuli in the diagram has nothing to do with the time interval between the events.

At the left edge of the interaction diagram, you usually describe the behaviour sequences that the objects will carry out; these are called 'operation paths'. On the columns, operation paths are represented by rectangles. The descriptions of the operation paths provide the basis for the identification and description of the objects' operations later on. It is not always practical to make descriptions of all operation paths. The structure of the marginal text can easily become too complex, making it difficult to understand to which operation path a certain paragraph belongs. In our example we have chosen to describe operation paths only for the interface objects and control objects since it is in these objects that the control of the stimuli is held.

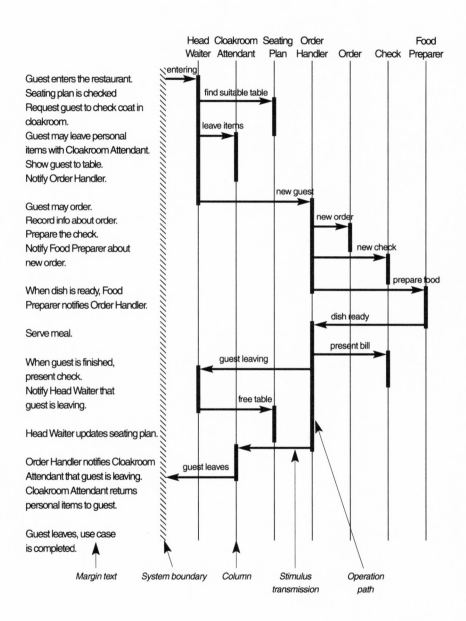

Figure 5.17 *Interaction diagram for the use case Eating Dinner. To make the diagram easier to understand, we have left out some of the objects.*

A use case usually contains several different variants of the courses of events. There is no point in trying to show all of these variants in a single interaction diagram, since it would become too messy. It is better to make several interaction diagrams for a use case, where each diagram shows clearly what happens when an alternative course of events, or a sub-course of events, is performed.

The technique of drawing interaction diagrams has been used for a long time in the world of telecommunications, mainly to describe interactions between different units of hardware. Ivar Jacobson introduced the diagram for the object-based design of software in 1968 and for the object-oriented world in 1987 (Jacobson, 1987).

5.7 Associations between use cases

When a system becomes large, it is important to create comprehensive models of it. A good way to achieve this is first to show the basic use cases in the model, and then to add more advanced courses of events. These can be expressed either as new use cases or as supplements to the basic ones. In order to express that a use case can supplement another, we have introduced the *extends association*. This association is discussed more thoroughly in Jacobson *et al.* (1992).

When you construct a use-case model of a business, it is not unusual to find use cases that have similar descriptions. To avoid overlaps of this kind, we need a tool to help us to show that these overlapping descriptions can be divided into separate, non-redundant use cases. To express this, we have introduced the *uses association* between use cases.

In other words, we have defined two relations between use cases, both of which are of static character. Having the possibility of describing how two instances of business processes interact is also important. However, we have chosen to show that interaction with the help of the object models (see Section 5.8).

5.7.1 The extends association

A use-case description can be rather difficult to overview if it contains too many alternative, optional or exceptional flows of events that are performed only if certain conditions are met as the use-case instance is

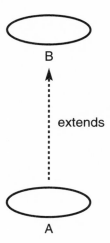

Figure 5.18 *Use case B is extended by use case A.*

carried out. A way of making the description 'cleaner' is to extract some of these sub-flows and let them form a use case of their own. This new use case is then said to extend the old one, if the required conditions are met. Such a construction can be achieved by using the extends association between the use cases.

An extends association from one use case, A, to another, B, means that an instance that conforms to the description of B can, if given conditions are satisfied, conform to the description of A (Figure 5.18). When the flow of events detailed in the description of A has been completed, the instance will once again conform to the description of B.

In the description of the extending use case A, it should be stated – in addition to the flow of events that will be performed – where A is to be inserted in the extended use case B.

When you extract a flow of events using the extends association, you must see to it that the original and fundamental use case, in this case B, still has a course of events that is meaningful in itself. The reason for extracting a flow of events is to reduce the complexity in the description of the basic flow of events. Structuring of the use case model should not be an end in itself.

Example
At The Checkered Tablecloth restaurant, the guests can eat a good dinner including, if they wish, a starter and/or

dessert. If required, they can also order a special arrangement, the Candlelight Dinner, which means that they sit in their own booth, with musical accompaniment during their meal. We have already identified the use case Eating Dinner, which we can now extend by adding the use cases Eating a Starter, Eating Dessert and Candlelight Dinner.

The extends relation will therefore be used to show extensions of complete use cases. Here are some examples of when to use extends:

● To show conditional parts of a use case.

● To model complex and/or alternative courses of events more explicitly.

● To model sub-courses of events that are only performed in certain cases.

● To model the insertion of several different sub-flows in any combination into a flow of events. These sub-flows are treated as use cases in their own right.

In the example in Figure 5.19, the extensions Eating a Starter and Eating Dessert are of the first type, while Candlelight Dinner is of the

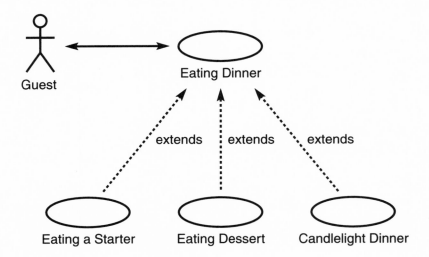

Figure 5.19 *Use cases in the restaurant.*

third type. Other examples of sub-flows that could be modelled as extending use cases are what happens if the guest has no money to pay or if the guest asks for the recipe of a certain dish.

The extends association could be considered as a way of structuring a number of sub-flows. Whether or not we choose to represent Eating a Starter and Eating Dessert as extending use cases depends on whether we clearly want to show the conditional character of these sub-flows in our model. The things that need to be done to give the guest a recipe might be too simple to make it worth administering a whole use case just to describe that extra feature.

5.7.2 The uses association

As you describe your use cases, you will probably find that some of them have sub-flows in common. To avoid having to describe the same sub-flow more than once, you may extract a sub-flow that two or more use cases have in common to a use case of its own. This new use case may then be used by the old ones. This is shown in your model by a uses association from the old use cases to the new one. The uses association helps you to avoid redundancy by letting use cases 'share' sub-flows.

A uses association from one use case, A, to another, B, shows that an instance of A can perform all of the courses of events that are described for B. The uses association is used when you want to show that descriptions of transactions are shared by several use cases.

In the description of A, you describe the transactions in B that are to be performed. In B, you describe how the transaction finishes and returns to the associating use case's description.

Example
Uses association between use cases. In the use cases Eating Dinner and Eating Lunch, ordering and paying procedures are to be carried out. Since these procedures are identical at both dinner and lunch, the flow of events has been extracted to constitute a use case of its own, which is used by both Eating Dinner and Eating Lunch (Figure 5.20).

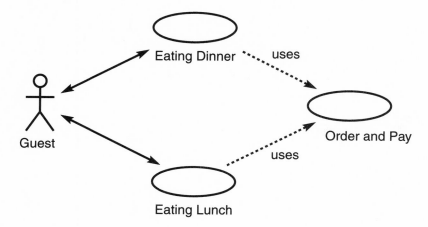

Figure 5.20 *Use cases in the restaurant.*

Uses associations are similar to inheritance associations in that both represent reuse of a description. A use case can have uses relationships with several other use cases — compare this with multiple inheritance.

5.7.3 Uses versus extends associations

Just like uses associations, extends associations can be viewed as a kind of inheritance. Let us explain the difference between uses and extends by means of the following example.

Example

Eating a Starter, Eating Dessert and Candlelight Dinner have extends associations to Eating Dinner. Only the use case Eating Dinner is instantiated, but this instance can, during some period in its life cycle, follow the description of Eating a Starter, Eating Dessert and/or Candlelight Dinner. However, this will only happen if certain conditions are met, that is, if the guest asks for one or more of these extensions. Thus, Eating a Starter, Eating Dessert and Candlelight Dinner are never instantiated on their own in this model (Figure 5.21).

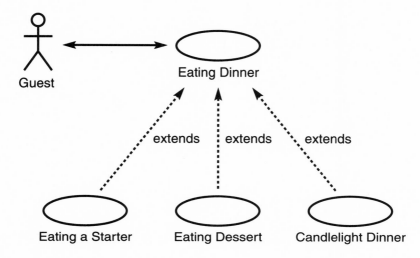

Figure 5.21 *The extends association to Eating Dinner from the other use cases means that only the use case Eating Dinner will be instantiated independently.*

What happens, then, if we choose a uses association instead of an extends association? There are two alternatives:

(1)   Eating Dinner uses Eating a Starter, Eating Dessert and Candlelight Dinner (Figure 5.22). Thus Eating Dinner has references to the extensions, which means that one of the purposes of extension has not been fulfilled, namely, that Eating Dinner be understood and developed independently of Eating a Starter, Eating Dessert and Candlelight Dinner. The advantage of this is that we can make different types of changes in the course of events of the basic use case without having to take into account whether the extended courses of events will be affected.

(2)   Eating a Starter, Eating Dessert and Candlelight Dinner use Eating Dinner. In this case, the model we get will not be the equivalent of that in Figure 5.22, because the restaurant in this model can only offer a limited number of variants of dinner – a main course and a starter, a main course with dessert or a candlelight dinner with only a main course. In order to get the same functionality as in Figure 5.22, we need use cases for different combinations of eating a main course, a starter, a dessert and having a candlelight dinner.

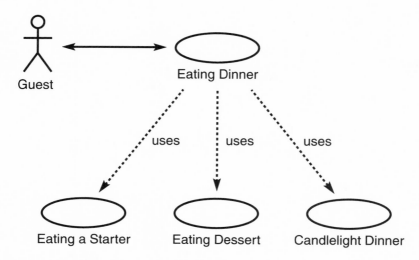

Figure 5.22 *Uses instead of extends association.*

In most cases, the choice between uses and extends is easy. Uses can be found by extracting shared sequences in several use cases, whereas extends is found when you add new sub-courses of events.

5.8 More about use cases

The purpose of the use-case model is to give what we call an *external view* of the system. This means that it is primarily directed towards the purchasers and users of the system, not its implementors. Use cases should express what the business will do, while an object model shows how the business is run. We usually say that the use-case model is a 'what model', in contrast to the object model, which is a 'how model'. To make this possible, we have made a few decisions about what should or should not be shown in the use-case model:

(1) Communication between courses of events in the system is not shown in the model. Thus, instances of the use case cannot communicate with each other, otherwise we would have to describe the interfaces between them.

(2) Instances of use cases of the same class or different classes will obviously affect one another in the business; the use-case model

offers no possibilities of showing this. Of course, relations of this kind are very important, but they would show details of the inner workings of the business that are of no interest to the people who need the use-case model. Therefore, we express these effects in the object model instead.

(3)   We do not express parallel courses of events in the use-case model. We assume that the use cases interpret a single instance and a single transaction at a time. Therefore, we describe the transactions of the use cases as if they were atomic and serial.

(4)   Owing to the above, we only show class associations in the use-case model.

One of the most important questions is whether use cases – instances or classes – are allowed to communicate with each other. It is obvious that they are dependent on one another; for example, various instances of the same use case can use the same resources in a business. This leads us to a solution in which we must regard the use-case instances as instances of behaviour and permit them to manipulate a global status area – a database. There are two good reasons for not choosing such a solution:

• It will result in a function/data model (a structured model). This is not an attractive way of describing things, since the picture that it gives of the business more resembles a task performed by a computer than work carried out by real people.

• The picture given of the business is not just the external view, since a model of the database must be regarded as a detailed picture of the inner workings of the business.

Thus, we obtain a use-case model that can be used to understand the requirements of the business, as well as a way of ensuring that everyone who uses the system or works with it can agree on how the model will look. In many cases, it can be a good idea to simulate courses of events in the business at an early stage in the modelling work. The use-case model cannot be used for this purpose; therefore, we suggest that the object model is used instead. Using the object model, you see more plainly how to solve the problem posed by certain things being handled in several courses of events.

What does a use-case model mean? What should it contain, and how should it be interpreted? It is important that there are clear definitions of this, both for those who develop the model and for those who interpret it. You must, for instance, be certain of the difference between a class and an instance of a use case, as well as knowing what the various relations between actors and use cases mean in reality.

However, a model that is so unambiguous that it can only be interpreted in a single way would have to be so formally and correctly expressed that it would – in all probability – be difficult to get an overall view of it, and it would also cost too much to construct. Therefore, we prefer to content ourselves with a model that can be interpreted with 'sufficient' correctness, by which we mean that the risk of the model being misinterpreted either by those who are familiar with the business or by those who are its customers is, while not negligible, at least very small.

5.9 Subsystems

It is necessary to divide large businesses into smaller ones, sub-businesses, before you can begin to describe courses of events in detail. In a large business, you will find many different competences. Since these competences will need different kinds of support, development and treatment, it would be wise to separate them. We call this identifying the business's high-level architecture. The architectural concept we use to describe this is the subsystem. If the business is very large, there may even be good reason to identify several levels of sub-businesses. Note that the hierarchies we are talking about here are on a much larger scale than the 'old-fashioned' functional hierarchies consisting of, for example, groups within the sales department, the finance department and so on.

Subsystems can be found by, for instance, looking at the areas of responsibility found in the organization. In an existing business, there is usually a functional hierarchy, or a division into groups that corresponds to the subsystems in the business: the finance department, the personnel department, the marketing department and so on.

What, then, is a subsystem? A subsystem is a package that contains functionally allied objects and/or subsystems. An object or a subsystem cannot belong to more than one subsystem.

Why do you make subsystem divisions? You should do this when the business is so large that you do not want to model everything in it at once, but one thing at a time. You might also divide it simply to make the model more understandable and easier to present. People who are involved in a particular part of the business will find it easier to understand the overall picture if the model expresses exactly how their part of it is affected by other parts.

You can also use subsystems to package objects into units of responsibility suitable for one person, who is responsible for one or more tasks as well as for the products and other things that carrying out the tasks will require. These tasks and things are represented by objects in the object model.

Example

The Checkered Tablecloth restaurant consists of a kitchen that is run by the chef, and a dining room where the head waiter is in charge. It is important to clarify how personnel in the dining room and kitchen communicate with each other and how their division of responsibility works. To show this clearly in the model, we can identify two subsystems in The Checkered Tablecloth restaurant – Dining Room and Kitchen (Figure 5.23).

We can show how these subsystems are dependent on each other by means of *dependsOn associations*. If an object in subsystem A has an association to an object in subsystem B, then subsystem A has a dependsOn association to subsystem B.

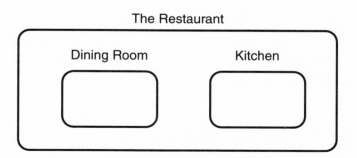

Figure 5.23 *Subsystems in the restaurant.*

Dining Room   Kitchen

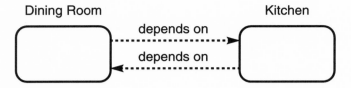

Figure 5.24 *Dependency between subsystems in the restaurant.*

Example
Since the objects in our model have associations in both
directions across the subsystem boundaries between
Dining Room and Kitchen, we have a dependsOn
association in both directions (Figure 5.24).

Use cases and subsystems
What is the difference between use cases and subsystems? Both
occurrences can be seen as a grouping of objects; however, use cases
primarily represent a description of the courses of events that will be
carried out by the business system. An object can belong to several use
cases, but only to one subsystem. In subsystems, the objects are grouped
according to their function. Conversely, a use case can be carried out by
objects from different subsystems. Thus, we can say that a use case runs
through several subsystems.

The Restaurant

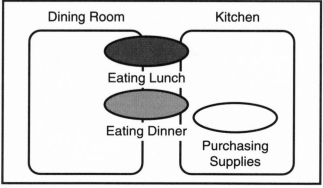

Figure 5.25 *Use cases can run through several subsystems.*

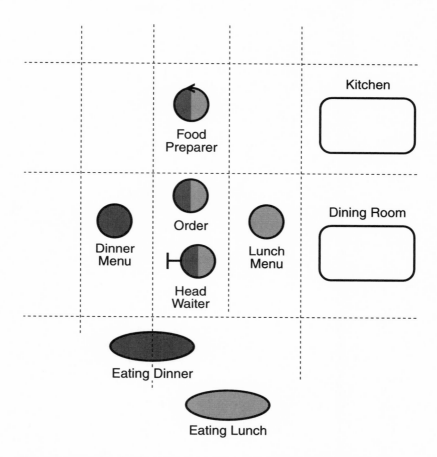

Figure 5.26 *An object can participate in several use cases, but only in one subsystem. To simplify the picture, we have only included two of the use cases and a few of the objects.*

Example

The use cases Eating Dinner and Eating Lunch have courses of events that are carried out partly in the subsystem Dining Room (ordering, serving, paying), and partly in the subsystem Kitchen (preparing the order). On the other hand, the use case Purchasing Supplies is performed entirely within the subsystem Kitchen (Figures 5.25 and 5.26).

5.10 Summary

In this chapter, we have discussed the architecture of the object-oriented business engineering method. We have defined the concepts that are used and the models that are developed when we follow the object-oriented business engineering methods.

Essentially, the work of describing a business in order to renovate it (that is, reengineer it) consists of two phases: describing the current situation, and describing the organization as you wish it to be. In both cases, we need to have an understanding of what the business is meant to accomplish, and for that we use the use-case model. To get an understanding of how the business is to work — what data flows and tasks will be involved — you can construct one or more object models.

The 'what' model — that is, the use-case model — consists of actors and use cases. An actor represents something that interacts with the business, whereas a use case specifies a flow of events that a particular actor wants performed in the business. The use-case model helps us to describe the business as its users wish to see it. The model should also be understood by users of the business, which means that the level of detail shown in it must not be too fine-grained (Figure 5.27).

When the use cases have been described, we are ready to make a complete object model of the business. To identify this ideal object model, we proceed from the use-case model, and to intensify the model's expressiveness, we use three types of objects: interface objects, control objects and entity objects. Interface objects and control objects generally represent tasks in the business, while entity objects represent products and other things that are handled in the courses of events (Figure 5.28).

In some cases, it may be useful to construct a model that shows how you have elected to realize the ideal object model — a real object model.

Which models you choose to construct depends on how detailed you want the descriptions to be and also on the purpose of the business description. Constructing a use-case model to show which processes are used in a business is a mandatory undertaking, whereas constructing more than one object model is optional. In the examples presented in the following chapter, we have decided to develop a use-case model that reflects the current system (a reverse model). To reflect the visionary system, we will develop both a use-case model and an ideal object model (a forward model).

Use-case model concepts

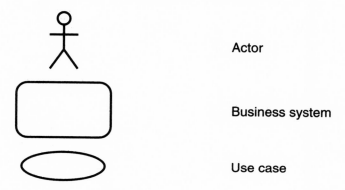

Actor

Business system

Use case

Use-case model associations

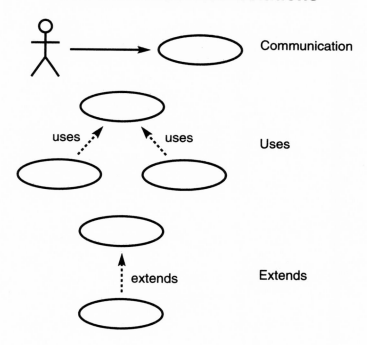

Communication

Uses

Extends

Figure 5.27 *Summary of the use-case model, its concepts and associations.*

Object model concepts

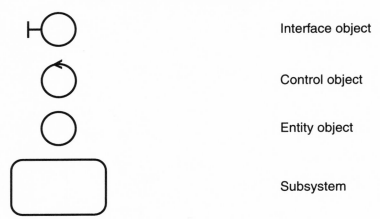

Interface object

Control object

Entity object

Subsystem

Object model associations

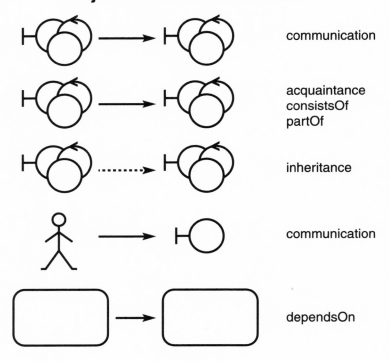

communication

acquaintance
consistsOf
partOf

inheritance

communication

dependsOn

Figure 5.28 *Summary of concepts and associations in the object models.*

5.11 References

Davenport T.H. (1993). *Process Innovation, Reengineering Work through Information Technology*. Boston, MA: Harvard Business School Press

Hammer M. and Champy J. (1993). *Reengineering the Corporation: A Manifesto for Business Revolution*. NY: HarperCollins

Jacobson I. (1987). Object-oriented development in an industrial environment. *Proceedings of OOPSLA '87. SIGPLAN Notices*, **22**(12), pp. 183–91

Jacobson I., Christerson M., Jonsson P., Övergaard G. (1992). *Object-Oriented System Engineering – A Use Case Driven Approach*. Reading, MA: Addison-Wesley; New York: ACM Press

Meyer B. (1988). *Object-Oriented Software Construction*. Englewood Cliffs, NJ: Prentice Hall

Shlaer S. and Mellor S.J. (1988). *Object-Oriented Systems Analysis*. Englewood Cliffs, NJ: Prentice Hall

Sudkamp T.A. (1988). *Languages and Machines: An Introduction to the Theory of Computer Science*. Reading, MA: Addison-Wesley

Wirfs-Brock R., Wilkerson B. and Wiener L. (1990). *Designing Object-Oriented Software*. Englewood Cliffs, NJ: Prentice Hall

chapter 6
Reversing the existing business

6.1 Introduction

During the envisioning work, you work with the reengineering directives to formulate an objective specification. This work requires an understanding of how today's businesses operate. In order to change something, you must know the current situation. We call this work reverse engineering. This involves designing a model of the existing company, which is then used as the basis for the modification work in forward engineering of the company.

Reverse engineering consists of two main activities:

- Use-case modelling: to produce and describe a process model of the existing business in terms of actors and use cases. We call this model an outside view of the company. The model is used as the basis for prioritizing the processes to be reengineered. The courses of events of the prioritized use cases are described. Metrics for each use case are produced and then used to make sure that the required objectives are achieved in the new business.

- Object modelling: to produce an object model of the existing business. This model is aimed at providing an inside view of how the existing business operates. To avoid becoming bogged down in modelling the existing business, you should only model the functional hierarchy and how the use cases are spread over the subsystems corresponding to the functional units.

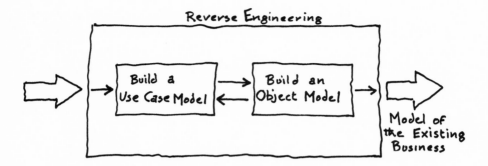

Figure 6.1 *Reverse engineering of the existing business consists of two activities.*

The envisioning activity produces a first sketch of the business processes that the reengineering work will aim to improve. The result is used as input to the reverse engineering work, in which the use-case construct is used to model business processes.

Use-case modelling and object modelling are dependent on each other. The main work flow starts with the use-case model and switches to object modelling when a stable use case model has been reached. In some cases, it may be possible to start identifying a number of obvious objects at the time the use-case modelling commences. It is worth noting, however, that to achieve a good result, it is necessary to work iteratively between the models (Figure 6.1).

The result of the reverse engineering work is a model of the current status of business, expressed in the form of a use-case model and an object model.

It is important to understand that a practical way of working in reengineering a business implies use of only a subset of all the tools that our modelling technique offers. Each company should use the tools that help them get the best possible result, leaving aside those that slow down the work without adding any value. In the following sections we give advice on how to go about using what is needed but no more.

6.2 Why reverse engineering?

It is not always the case that a company wishing to reengineer its processes already has a well-documented model of the existing business.

Even if such a model exists, it is unlikely to describe the business as it really is. It is even less likely to be understandable by those responsible for the business, those who perform the reengineering work and other employees who should be able to understand and have opinions on it. There are many reasons for this. People have enough to do running the business and there is usually a belief that not enough time is available either to produce an initial model or to update an existing one. Another common reason is that the business is far too complex and that there is no good way of describing it. The methods available to describe businesses can only be understood by those who have made the descriptions and not by the business entrepreneurs themselves; the method of description is not intuitive and obvious, and is often controlled by the techniques. See Section 2.5 for further information on traditional business modelling techniques.

Is it, in fact, wise to make a model of the existing business? Some writers state that it is better to start anew than to first try to understand the existing business. People are afraid that imperfect knowledge of how the company operates today could limit creativity and thus restrict the actual change. This is a classic problem. Can knowledge really be dangerous? We have another opinion. We assume that the people you select can free themselves from how the business looks today and instead think of how it should be able to operate tomorrow. They have realized that as long as they are prejudiced, they will not be able to perform the necessary changes that are required to enable the organization to be competitive in the market. You may choose to examine the business and propose changes to its organization before you have reverse engineered it, but we do believe that you need a good picture of your current organization before you can finally decide on the best way to change it. If the reengineers understand the business as it is today, they will be able to avoid making unfeasible change proposals. The reengineering team thus wins the confidence of both the employees and the managers, and are therefore trusted when they hand over their proposals. This makes the installation work simpler, because the staff's confidence in the changes will be easier to obtain. This last point is not to be taken lightly. Motivating the staff and getting them on your side is probably the most difficult job for an organization, because it involves drastic changes in their daily work.

It is possible to make simple, clear and general descriptions of a business. It is important that there are both general descriptions, which give overviews of the business as a whole, and detailed descriptions.

Each of the detailed descriptions delineates a part of the business or a part of its processes, but they can, when required, be put together to create a detailed description of the whole business. Thus there is continuity between the general descriptions and the detailed ones. This is important to enable everyone in an organization to contribute to business development. People may be interested in reviewing the business at different levels of detail, depending on the roles they play within the organization. The more general descriptions can be attractive for top management, who are not normally interested in having all of the details presented to them. Process managers, on the other hand, are interested in understanding the details of the flow of their own processes and possibly being able to look more closely at the surrounding processes on which they depend. You must at least understand the existing business with respect to those areas in which changes are to take place. There are many reasons for this:

- to enable the people who perform the reengineering work to obtain a common understanding of what is not working well in the business. With this basic knowledge, you can identify the areas that need to be changed.

- to understand how you must proceed in order to change the existing business so that it satisfies the new objectives and requirements.

- to enable you to describe to employees why the old working routines are inadequate and why they must adopt a new way of working.

- so that you can measure the use cases you wish to change. These measurements are used later to evaluate the benefits of the proposed changes.

6.3 Overview

By identifying and describing the processes that have the greatest scope for improvements, you can later focus the reengineering work. Thereafter, measurements are carried out on these prioritized processes. The resulting values are used to confirm that the new processes will really lead to the desired dramatic changes.

It is normally appropriate to start by making a survey map of the entire business, not just the prioritized processes. The advantage of having a survey map is that you can save a lot of time if people in the reengineering project are in agreement on a general picture of how the business operates. Producing such a model can be very frustrating, however, especially when dealing with the first reengineering project, so you may have to compromise and describe only the highest priority processes, setting aside the remaining processes.

One of the greatest challenges in describing a business is finding just the right level of detail. You do not want to model just for the sake of modelling: the models should help, not hinder! It is important that the method used for modelling the business offers an architecture that captures the business, both at a high level of abstraction and, where required, in detail. As a rule, it is often sufficient to identify the processes and produce a high-level description, without needing to describe them in detail. If you also show how the prioritized processes are spread throughout the existing functional units in the business, you will obtain a sufficiently good understanding to be able to proceed with modelling the new business. Normally, it is wise to restrict the development time for a current-status model of a medium-sized company to weeks rather than months.

6.4 Building a use-case model

Start by making a general use-case model to outline the whole business, prioritize the use cases in the model, then use the general model to make a more detailed use-case model. In this way, you will generate an overall picture of the business which can be communicated to everyone in the organization and discussed with the company management. It is unusual for the whole company to be reengineered. The most acute use cases are prioritized, and complete models and descriptions are constructed for them. The work of producing a use-case model often starts with a 'brainstorming' session, in which the reengineering team sketches out an initial idea of the actors and use cases of the existing business.

In this chapter, we describe how to produce a complete use-case model, irrespective of whether it is to be a general one or more detailed.

6.4.1 Finding actors

We recommend that the first step should be to try to identify the actors in the business. The most important actors are normally found by looking at the different types of customers. It is, of course, primarily the customers that you want to please with the way the business works and the result that it produces. Other typical actors can be partners, suppliers, authorities and subsidiaries. If you opt to model only one part of the company, the other parts will be regarded as actors. This means that even individuals within other departments of the company will become actors. The criteria for something to be an actor are that it lies outside the part of the business being modelled, that it interacts with the business in some way and that typical instances of it can be found. Instances of human actors are realized by actual people.

A hint on how to verify that all of the actors in the business have been found is to study a set of examples of real people with whom the company has contact. Group those people according to the role they play *vis-à-vis* the company. Each such group will correspond to an actor that should be included in the model.

6.4.2 Finding use cases

When everyone in the group is in agreement on a first attempt at identifying actors, you can attempt to identify the use cases in the business. Begin with the customer actors. At this stage it is easy to become bogged down in too much detail. Remember that use cases model complete courses of events and that these must have a measurable value for the customer.

In the early phase of the modelling procedure, you can iterate with different variants of the model and feel your way to a model that everyone is content with. To verify that all of the responsibilities of the business are actually included in the use-case model, you should make sure that for each responsibility it is always possible to point to at least one use case in the model.

Finding good use cases can be difficult. The boundaries between the functional units can sometimes seem to be unsurmountable obstacles, and it may not be quite clear how the use cases cross them. You should not

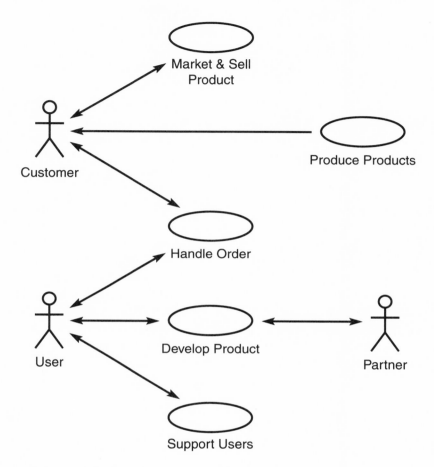

Figure 6.2 *A use-case model of an existing business.*

divide up the use cases in the business too much. It is normal to have 10–20 use cases in a business. If you identify more than 30 use cases, you should suspect that too much detail has been put into the model; perhaps you have forgotten that use cases are to be complete courses of events.

Let us look more closely at an example of common use cases in a business (Figure 6.2).

In many companies, the following actors may be identified: Customer, which models individuals that have or may develop an interest in buying the product; User, which models the people for whom the product is actually produced; and Partner, which models any company that is helping with development of the product. The use cases are also very general: Market and Sell Product, which broadcasts information about the product to the market; Handle Order, which registers and processes incoming orders; Develop Product, which handles the development of the product; Support Users, which helps the user with questions concerning the product; and Produce Products, which deals with manufacturing the product.

If you look critically at the result of the identified use cases, you will probably discover some uncertainties. It may be the case that a number of identified use cases are not connected to any actor. It is, however, a little strange if no one is affected by or interested in the result of these use cases. So do these use cases exist? It may be that these use cases are courses of events in the business whose contents are heavily dependent on how the business is implemented. They may also consist of activities that need to be performed for the organization to run smoothly, typically flows of events that handle the infrastructure of the company. If this is the case, you can instead choose to model such use cases in an underlying layer that shows just how the implementation will be performed. The example in Chapter 8 contains such a layering. Such use cases may also be sub-flows in the business that you represent in this way because they 'always' have been considered as stand-alone flows of events, even though they are actually part of a larger use case. A typical sub-flow consists of planning activities.

You should not waste a lot of time in trying to find the perfect picture of how the business operates; be satisfied with a model that states all of the important flows within the business and proceed from this.

Structuring use cases
Our modelling technique (see Chapter 5) allows you to structure use cases via uses and extends associations. However, in the model of the existing business, you should not waste too much time in doing this. We describe how this is performed in the modelling of the new business in Chapter 7.

6.4.3 Prioritizing use cases

A first result is thus a preliminary model of actors and use cases in the business. Based on this model, you must prioritize the use cases that are appropriate for starting the renovation work. The business processes that, for various reasons, are seen as the most critical for the reengineering team to deal with are given priority. There are a number of different ways to prioritize use cases:

- Identify those that have the greatest effect on customers of the business.

- Identify those that have the greatest potential for radical improvement.

- Identify those that seem to have the most problems.

- Identify those that can be improved simply and quickly.

- Identify those where improvements would have the greatest effect internally in the business.

The handling of the prioritization of use cases is done in terms of ranking. The rank denotes the importance of a use case – the use cases that perform the main tasks of the system have the highest ranks. Rank the use cases and let the rankings guide the further modelling in increments. In the first increment, the use cases of the first rank are modelled; the next increment comprises the second rank, and so on. Eventually, the entire business has been modelled. In Figure 6.3, we illustrate how a business may be reengineered using the ranking technique.

Work can now be focused on the prioritized use cases. The other use cases can be left after being described very briefly.

6.4.4 Describing use cases

Each prioritized use case in the model should now be fully described. Each use case may be described at this stage either informally or in a more structured way. You should not be too formal in these descriptions. Actors of the use cases are described at the same time, so that the interface between them and the use cases can be specified clearly.

When you have described the basic course of events of a use case, you should go through this description to identify important alternative or optional courses of events and exceptions. During this session you should look for circumstances that may lead to an interruption of the basic course of events and another series of events taking over. Taken

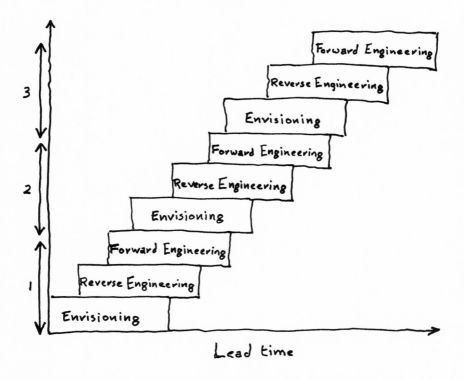

Figure 6.3 *A business may be reengineered incrementally by ranking the use cases. The use cases of a specific rank are then developed together. (Note that the relation between the activity boxes' sizes and the time axis should only be seen as an example.)*

together, these alternative courses of events usually demand more extensive activities than the basic course of events. Therefore, it is of the utmost importance that they are planned for and dealt with in a practical way in order for the reengineering effort to be successful.

It is easy to become bogged down in the use-case descriptions and to add too many details. Be aware of this and try to maintain a relatively high, abstract viewpoint when drawing up these descriptions. The work must not be allowed to take too long or take away the enthusiasm for the important job remaining, namely the actual reengineering work.

A use-case description should only include the areas of responsibility that are carried out within the business combined with the interaction with the actors with whom it communicates. It should not include the behaviour that the actors may need to perform on their side.

Describing the use cases may therefore be a difficult task, if the system boundary is unclear; that is, if you have not adequately defined what lies inside and what lies outside the business' areas of responsibility. Finding this boundary is one of the most important results that use-case modelling should achieve: if you are not quite sure about the business' responsibilities, how can it be reengineered?

6.4.5 Selecting metrics

Metrics are the key to improving a use case, since they help you to understand what the goals of reengineering really are. As Harrington (1991) put it, 'Measurements are key. If you cannot measure it, you cannot control it. If you cannot control it, you cannot manage it. If you cannot manage it, you cannot improve it. It is as simple as that.'

The selection of metrics is not always easy. The metrics that are interesting depend on the use case being evaluated. A good combination of metrics usually contains a number of time metrics, cost metrics and quality metrics. From experience, focusing on optimizing time parameters – for example, lead time – in a use case usually leads automatically to improvements in both the cost and quality parameters.

In selecting metrics, you must not forget what is actually important: the customer's awareness and appreciation of the improvements. Start, therefore, from the customer's perspective and make sure that the metrics selected can actually be measured. For example, the following metrics might be interesting in the Handle Order use case:

- cost per entered order

- lead time from received order to entered order

- percentage of rejected orders

6.4.6 Reviewing

When the use-case descriptions have reached a relatively stable state, a review meeting should be held. It is important that all of the parties involved agree that the use cases are correctly stated. The following list represents a number of suggestions for review points for each use case:

- Is the communication to and/or from actor(s) correct?

- Is the course of events described at a suitable level of detail?

- Is the course of events correct and complete?

- Are important alternative courses of events described?

To be able to capture all of the errors at an early stage, it is important for representatives from the reengineering team, employees (who are carrying out the process), current process owners and current process leaders to take part in this review.

6.5 Building an object model

An object model is, as described in Chapter 5, a model of the business in terms of interacting objects. These objects are grouped in subsystems and the use cases run across the objects in these subsystems.

In the reverse engineering work, it is usually appropriate to start by capturing the subsystems and then to describe the use cases in terms of communicating subsystems. Eventually, if required, the subsystems are modelled in terms of objects.

6.5.1 Finding the subsystems

Most companies today are structured in a functional and hierarchical way. This structure is modelled by a subsystem for each functional unit. Each company has its own designation for these units; common names are division, department, section or group. Since such a unit can contain other smaller units, there are often (especially in larger companies) several levels of subsystems.

A typical business is shown in Figure 6.4. In this example, only the top-level subsystems are shown, but each of these can in turn consist of smaller subsystems. This type of relation is called a *consistsOf-association*.

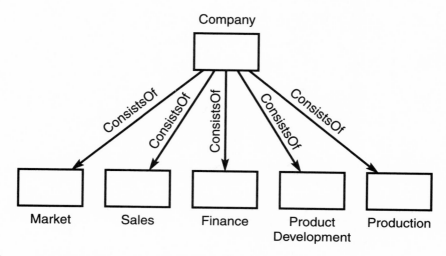

Figure 6.4 *A common subsystem hierarchy in a company.*

The number of levels in a model may vary from company to company; however, the objective is to reach a deep understanding of the use cases.

The responsibility of each of the business functions is described in the text, so that the interface between the different participating organizational units is clear.

6.5.2 Describing the use cases in relation to subsystems

Having identified the subsystems, you describe each use case again, but this time in terms of communicating subsystems. It should be possible to see which subsystems participate in the course of events of a use case. This further clarifies the interface between the different subsystems and shows which subsystems need to work together to fulfil a particular use case.

How a use case is realized in terms of participating subsystems can be described by use-case interaction diagrams, as presented in Section 5.6.2. However, in most cases this is not necessary; it would result in too much detail. Instead, a simple diagram like the one in Figure 6.5 is enough. In this diagram, you can see that the use case Market & Sell Product is realized by the subsystems Market, Sales and Product Development.

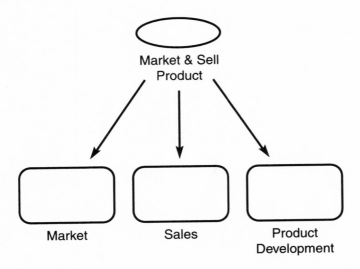

Figure 6.5 *A use case is normally performed by several interacting subsystems.*

6.5.3 Finding the objects

In most cases, it is enough to identify subsystems and to describe the use cases in terms of these communicating subsystems. There are, of course, situations where it is necessary to go into more detail, but this should be weighed up against the negative consequences of further modelling. Such consequences are, for example:

- the project is delayed as a result of this fixation on detail.

- both the renovation group members and other personnel lose their drive and their belief that a positive change is in progress, because of the amount of time taken.

- the assumptions for the renovation work have time to change before you have even started to look at ways of improving the business.

If it is still thought necessary to have more details of the business before proceeding with the modelling of the new business, you can, based on the use cases, identify objects and show how the use cases are realized in more detail as object interactions. In this case, a view is drawn of the participating objects for each use case, which shows how the participating objects work together to realize the use case. You can also use interaction diagrams to show how the participating objects cooperate. More information on how to find objects based on use cases and the technique of drawing interaction diagrams is given in Chapter 7.

6.6 Analysing the result

When the reengineering team have reached agreement on the way the courses of events run in the prioritized use cases, an evaluation of each of these use cases should be carried out. You should now understand in depth what you have. How far you proceed with this analysis is a matter of judgement, but the following steps should be taken:

- Perform measurements of the existing use cases according to the defined metrics. These values will later be compared with the values in the modified use cases. If shorter lead times is an objective for a new use case, it is important to be able to verify that this objective has been satisfied.

- 'Walk through' one use case at a time and look critically at the course of events. Classify each individual activity within a use case as value added (VA) or not value added (NVA). A VA activity gives, from the customer's perspective, an increased value to the final product. A NVA activity can be eliminated without the customer noticing whether the value of the product has been reduced. Each NVA activity is then further reviewed to identify the actual reason for it being performed, and information on the cost of performing it is produced. You can look at the possibility of eliminating the NVA activities and, of course, even of minimizing the costs of performing the VA activities. Certain NVA activities cannot be eliminated; for example, if a law exists stating that an activity must be performed. However, these actions can produce a good basis for optimization.

- Based on the metrics values of the existing use cases, you can now identify their problems and limitations. To produce this information, it may be useful to interview the personnel affected by the prioritized use cases. The aim is to obtain insights into problems with the existing use cases and to elicit suggestions for improvements. If you succeed in motivating personnel to be interested in the renovation work, you may find that they respond by contributing enlightening information and creative ideas.

- Investigate short-term rationalization improvements of the existing use cases. To be able to evaluate the more radical rationalization suggestions, you should first understand what can be done simply to improve the existing business. It is also important that the personnel see that progress is being made at an early stage in the renovation work. It keeps them motivated. These actions must be simple to implement and should produce the desired result quickly. From the perspective of the staff, even small changes in the daily routine can be regarded as something very positive.

- Determine the existing computer support, with respect to both software and machines. One way of modelling computer support is to assign a subsystem for each element of IT support used in the existing use cases. (For more information on how to handle the connection between models of businesses and models of computer support, refer to Chapter 9.) Identify use cases where computer support is used. Describe how computer support optimizes the work and discuss both the advantages and disadvantages of its use. Investigate whether greater effectiveness can be achieved by expanding or modifying the parts of the use cases that are implemented using computer support. For example, tasks that used to be carried out manually might instead be carried out using computer support. It is important to be aware that old information systems risk making organizations permanently hierarchical. Sometimes, it is simply impossible to reengineer a business without constructing completely new computer support. At the same time, it is important to realize that it can also be impossible, in one step, to throw out everything that the business has invested a great deal of money in. Along with prioritizing processes in the business, you may be forced to prioritize processes in computer support development. Jacobson and Lindström (1991) describe the reengineering of computer systems using object-oriented techniques.

- Make an inventory of knowledge and special competence areas. This is important in order to understand the additional competence that will be required by the personnel of the new business. It can be useful to look at the roles that key personnel have in the existing business, and to be able to spread this knowledge and possibly divide the work tasks among a number of people. All companies have 'key' people — that is, individuals who drive the development of the company, or have unique knowledge about the company's products. But it is dangerous to be too dependent on a few individuals. The company cannot in any way guarantee the availability of these people in the capacity required. Key people falling ill or leaving the company could lead to a catastrophe.

- Try to determine the requirements for future changes in the use cases that might arise from the environment. This can result in changes in existing use cases, but may also show that the business must be able to offer completely new use cases, whose requirement has not previously been envisaged. The competitive situation may require this; either because competitors are already offering certain services that customers are now demanding or because the company has identified a new way of increasing its competitiveness. In the first case, it means launching something that is seen as being at least as good as the competitors' products. In the second case, the company is in a much better position, being one step ahead of the competition.

The result of this analysis is used as input to the objective specification work in the envisioning activity.

6.7 Summary

The result of the reverse engineering work is thus a model of the existing business. While we realize that it is vital to produce this model, we wish to emphasize the importance of not spending too much time on it. Identify a basic model of the actors and use cases and describe them briefly. Based on this model, prioritize the use cases that are most critical and focus further work on these use cases. It is also useful to identify a subsystem model that describes the functional hierarchy in the existing business. To understand how the use cases are realized in terms of subsystems, you should describe the subsystems that participate in each use case. This will be critical information for the work of describing the interfaces, and thus the division of responsibility, between the different subsystems. You can describe in more detail how the use cases are performed by objects, if required, in order to achieve a sufficient level of understanding of how the use cases are handled in the business. Here, however, you should be careful not to create models that are too detailed.

Once the models have been reviewed and approved, you should try to analyse how, in the best possible way, you can achieve a more effective utilization of the business. The existing use cases are measured to obtain metrics values that can be compared with corresponding metrics from the use cases in the new business. Problems and limitations in the use cases are identified, and existing knowledge and computer support in the business are considered. Rationalization improvements that can be implemented simply are introduced at an early stage to achieve a high level of staff motivation. Managers must clearly show their enthusiasm for the project in order to stimulate their staff. The key to success is making individual employees believe that the changes will affect them positively.

6.8 References

Harrington J. (1991). *Business Process Improvement*. NY: McGraw-Hill
Jacobson I. and Lindström F. (1991). Reengineering of old systems to an object-oriented architecture. In *Proceedings of OOPSLA*, Phoenix AZ, October 1991, pp. 240–50

chapter 7
Forward business engineering

7.1 Introduction

During the envisioning activity, the existing processes that need to be reengineered are identified. The objectives for the new business are expressed in terms of these processes in the objective specification. Management has made a decision to perform a reengineering project based on this specification. The organization of the development work has been determined and everyone is prepared to support this work. Thus, the real development work can commence.

This is the time to discover how the new objectives will affect the existing business and to determine the best way of improving and optimizing the prioritized processes.

Engineering the new business comprises five main activities:

- Build a use-case model: this is an 'outside' view of the new company. Use cases capture processes in the new business.

- Build an ideal model: this is an 'inside' view of the new company. It describes the company in terms of communicating objects and captures how these objects interact in order to realize use cases.

- Build a real model: this involves adapting the ideal model to the restrictions found in the business, and building a real object model of the business.

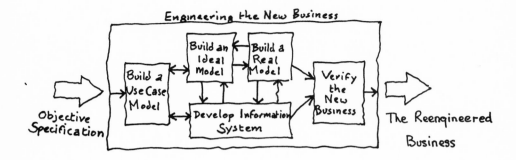

Figure 7.1 *Engineering the new business comprises five activities.*

- Develop an information system: this involves creating IT support for the processes in the new business. It can be quite extensive.

- Verify the new business: before full-scale models are installed in the business, they must be tested on a smaller scale.

Because these activities are dependent on each other, the work should be performed largely in parallel. It will be necessary to work iteratively in order to achieve the best possible result. The principal flow in the work procedure, however, is from left to right in Figure 7.1.

The envisioning activity involved sketching out how the processes in the existing business need to be changed to incorporate the new strategic objectives. The next major step is aimed at producing models illustrating how the modification proposal from the envisioning activity will be handled in the business. Use-case models and one or two object models describing the new business are produced. These main activities are described in Sections 7.2–7.4. The work also involves testing, in parallel with the actual modelling work, the proposed changes on a smaller scale in parts of the business. This is described in more detail in Section 7.6.

7.2 Building a use-case model

The use-case model is the same type as the one presented in Chapter 6. The results from the envisioning activity (the objective specification) and from the reverse engineering activity (the model/models of the existing business) form the initial material.

7.2.1 Finding actors

Based on the actor model of the existing business, you proceed through the objective specification to find out how the new requirements may affect this model.

For each actor, check whether its role remains unchanged in relation to the objectives for the new business and whether its associations with use cases will still be the same.

It may, indeed, be possible to remove an actor that was incorporated in the model of the existing business, as a result of changes in the new business. For example, the business may no longer need to use a supplier to produce a component of the product, but will instead produce this component itself.

In this work, it is usual to find entirely new actors. This can arise if the business decides not to perform a certain task itself, but instead employs a company specialized in this type of service.

It is also common for an actor included in the existing business to have a completely different role in the new business — certain tasks that the actor performed previously are perhaps now performed by the company or vice versa.

There are, of course, actors that are not affected at all by the changes in the business.

7.2.2 Describing actors

Changes in the actor model also affect the descriptions of the actors. New actors should be described and the descriptions of the actors whose role *vis-à-vis* the business has been modified must be updated.

Normally, actors are described very briefly. What is essential is that the actor's role is clearly expressed. Actors are, as mentioned before, supposed to define where the boundaries of the business lie. It can often be rather difficult at the start of modelling to define exactly where the boundaries are; that is, to identify what is inside/outside the system's framework. During the work, these boundaries become progressively clearer, which means that the actors' descriptions will need to be updated several times. It is important to be aware of the advantages of well-defined actors, because if this boundary is not clearly defined, it will be impossible to describe the use cases correctly.

This description should also contain information about which use cases the actors interact with and the way in which they interact.

7.2.3 Finding use cases

The effects of the requirements in the objective specification, which are expressed in terms of processes, on the existing use-case model are investigated. Each dramatic change probably means that you have come to a new overall understanding of the use cases.

These types of changes in the business also involve iterating between different possible use-case models to find the one that reflects the new objectives in the best way. This work is normally carried out during brainstorming sessions and, if possible, with the help of prototypes (Section 7.6). The normal situation is for radical changes to occur within the framework of the existing use cases, but it may well be that a requirement is so radical that an entirely new use case is needed.

During the modification of the use-case model, it is useful to work as a group. In this activity, it is helpful to involve members of the reengineering team and representatives from the affected parts of the business. It may also be appropriate to involve someone with experience of other reengineering projects. If this experience cannot be found within the company, it may be necessary to contact a reengineering consultant. The responsibility for the use-case model, however, remains with the management of the actual reengineering team.

What is a good use case?
One of the most important characteristics of use cases is their ability to capture good business processes. The use-case concept is more precise than the process concept. It has a definition that clearly indicates that it is a question of processes that capture the business in the way the user of the business wishes to see it, not primarily as participants in the business

wish to structure it. In Chapter 5 there is a more formal definition of the use case. We now give some further guidelines for what is considered to be a good use case.

Certain reengineering teams feel that they need detailed models and many small use cases to be able to satisfy their requirements. There are examples where it has been felt necessary to capture businesses with hundreds of use cases. Others teams believe that there should really only be two or, at most, three use cases in a model. Rockart and Short (1988) identified three major processes: developing new products, delivering products to customers and managing customer relationships. Finding the right number of use cases means weighing up the advantages of obtaining a simple and easily understandable picture of the business against having difficulties in understanding, measuring and modifying an individual use case. The larger the use cases, the simpler it is to view the whole business. Unfortunately, the consequence of this is that each individual use case becomes very abstract and difficult to substantiate.

A compromise is often made. Most businesses can be described at a good level of detail with perhaps 15 core use cases. The use cases are sufficiently small to be understood, handled and modified. The model as a whole contains just enough use cases to enable a comprehensive picture of how the business operates to be obtained. Davenport (1993) also suggests that between 10 and 20 business processes should be used, and that this rule should be used together with Harrington's (1993) technique of allowing each member of the company management to put forward a proposal for those use cases that they are responsible for and, from these, to construct an entire picture.

Some general characteristics of a good use case are:

- It must be clear and easy to understand. When the business receives a stimulus to start a course of events, it is important that you can easily interpret which use-case description to follow.

- A goal is that as few people as possible should be involved when an instance of a use case is performed. Most importantly, the interface towards the customer should be as uncomplicated as possible. Thus, if the use case is relatively small the tasks within it will, as far as possible, be capable of being performed by a single person. Hammer and Champy (1993) call this individual a case worker. This reduces the number of handovers, which only result in delays and thus extended lead time.

- All steps within a use case should (where possible) contribute to increased value for the customer.

- The people who perform the tasks within a use case will have total responsibility, and will thus be able to ensure that any problems are solved so that the work continues to run in an effective way. Instead of having to obtain approval from their managers each time something unexpected happens, which often results in delays, they will have the authority to make decisions themselves.

- It should be easy to adapt the use case to any restrictions in your own business. A use case, or really its class, can exist as several variants. A multinational company may, for instance, have a similar sales process in all countries, but with important differences in each individual country. Different companies may have similar development processes, but these will differ in essential respects depending on the size of the development business, type of products, level of maturity of its employees, and so on.

Structuring use cases

After initial identification of the use cases, it is time to consider how to structure the use-case model. There are different techniques available to accomplish this:

- One way is to use the uses association. When two or more concrete use cases contain enough substantial common behaviour, you should take it out and place it in a separate use case to which the concrete use cases have a uses association. This means that the common behaviour is only described in one place, which simplifies future changes.

- The other way is through use of the extends association. In the following cases, we believe that it is appropriate to extract the description of a course of events to an individual use case that has an extends association to the original use case:

  - When a sub-course of events (in the cases it actually runs through) is considered to be very important and substantial. In this way, the course of events becomes clearly visible in a map of all of the use cases.

  - When the behaviour in a sub-course of events differs considerably from the behaviour of the basic course of events; that is, the behaviour involves an entirely different type of work and respons-ibility than is represented by the basic course of events. (An example of this type of basic course of events can be seen in the use case Product Procurement. Here, the basic flow of events is the current development of the product, but you could extract the tasks related to long-term development and product research.) Another reason for extracting a sub-course of events might be that the sub-course has a different time cycle to the basic course of events.

— When a sub-course of events occurs in a number of use cases. Instead of describing it as an alternative course of events in a number of use-case descriptions, you only need to describe the course of events in one place. (You could have used the uses association here, but if you use the extends association, the original use case need not know where and when the extracted use case will be inserted.)

You describe when the extracted use case will be inserted in the original use case as a condition linked to the extends association.

- The types of use cases that can be created by the use of uses and extends associations should be substantial enough in themselves to justify this action. However, there are normally one or several alternative courses of events in each use case. These should be described by structuring the description of the use case and not by creating new use cases. This implies that these courses of events are not explicitly visible in the use-case model.

  — We have said that a use case has a basic course of events, which should be described. However, it is normal for a use case to have not just one basic course of events, but several equally common alternative courses of events. This is especially true in a reengi-neered process organization, where the customer should be offered tailored processes. The first communication between a customer and a process involves finding out which basic course of events the process should follow in order to serve the customer effectively. Thereafter, the process offers alternative ways through the business, which is expressed by offering alternative courses of events in the corresponding use case.

  — Simple exceptions or simple optional courses of events are described in the basic course of events itself.

We now give an example of these different ways of structuring use cases. Let us look more closely at how you could structure the use case Selling. If the customer is an individual wishing to buy a standard product, Selling looks entirely different to when it is a question of a company wishing to buy a tailored product. The individual customer interested in buying a standard product should not need to be dealt with in an unnecessarily complex way; his/her product should be delivered quickly. This can be modelled in several ways, as described above. The alternative selected depends on the requirements of the model. We start by looking at the consequences of selecting uses associations (Figure 7.2).

This alternative means that the customer initiates either Off-the-shelf Selling or Tailored Selling. Off-the-shelf Selling may be initiated if a customer comes to the company and buys a product directly 'off the shelf' or via mail order. Tailored Selling, however, is initiated when a representative of a company contacts the sales department to discuss a potentially large order of customized products. Off-the-shelf Selling and Tailored Selling contain a number of common parts, such as invoicing routines. To avoid describing the common parts in the descriptions of both use cases, we have created the abstract use case Common Sales. An advantage of this approach is that you do not need to make future changes of the common behaviour in both of the concrete use cases. Making the change in the abstract use case is sufficient. The disadvantage with this approach is that it implies that the customer has to know in advance which use case should be used.

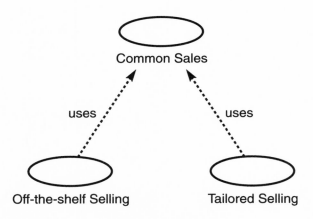

Figure 7.2 *Use of uses to structure the use case Selling.*

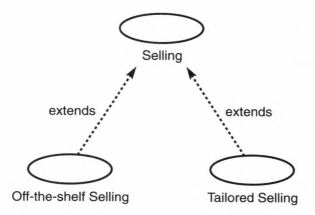

Figure 7.3 *Use of extends to structure the use case Selling.*

If, on the other hand, you decided to use extends associations between use cases, the interpretation would be somewhat different (Figure 7.3).

Here, the course of events in the use case Selling is started, which means that the customer does not have to know in advance which of the use cases, Off-the-shelf Selling or Tailored Selling, to initiate. The first thing that happens in Selling is getting to know the type of customer you are dealing with. There is perhaps no obvious way, as in the above mentioned case, of knowing whether you can handle a certain customer in a simpler way, or whether a more comprehensive sales routine is required. As soon as this is determined, either Off-the-Shelf Selling or Tailored Selling is built on to the use case Selling. These use cases contain the entire subsequent course of events and it is not until the operations are completed that you eventually return to the original use case Selling. In this alternative, therefore, we have not taken into consideration the fact that there may be common parts in the two variants of the course of events (which is the reason for the name change between the two figures, from Common Sales to Selling).

If you consider that this type of structuring does not need to be shown at model level, and instead believe that it is sufficient to structure only within the use case Selling, there are two variants of how this can be done. You either describe the whole of it as one basic course of events and define a number of alternative courses of events associated with this basic one, or you can write two entirely separate basic courses of events. If a large part of the courses of events are the same, you would use the uses association, whereas if the courses of events are either substantially different or you see that the value of having two complete course of event descriptions is greater than the value of reusing common parts, you would use the extends association.

7.2.4 Describing use cases

When the reengineering team, management and other people affected have accepted the model, it is time to divide up the responsibility for describing the individual use cases. It is a good idea to give one person the task of describing a use case. The use case's defined process owner then approves the result.

Use cases are best described using simple language to facilitate understanding. They are described in episodic, narrative form. The results of interviews conducted during the envisioning work will now be put to good use. It may well be necessary to interview again the employees who are now performing the old process in order to complement and clarify the new processes. These interviews should be informal, and should recognize that the interviewees are important. The aim of consultation is to determine how the new processes should operate in a practical and effective way.

Use cases will represent a complete course of events in the business, which means that they will contain well-defined start and end states.

The starting point is a description of the basic course of events, or the alternative courses of events, within each use case. Thereafter, all exceptions or optional courses of events are identified and described. It is important that only one team member is assigned the responsibility to complete and describe an individual use case. The rightful owner, that is, the defined business process owner for the use case, will thereafter validate each use case's compliance with the established corporate objectives.

7.2.5 Documentation

The use-case model is documented in the form of an overview document for the whole model and a description for each use case.

The overview document contains brief descriptions of all actors, use cases and relations between them. The document aims at providing an overview of the model as a whole. If, thereafter, you want to obtain more information on a particular use case, you can turn to the description for this use case. To further increase understanding of the model, it is useful to look at a diagram that graphically illustrates the relations between the actors and the use cases. Such diagrams are provided as appendices to the overview document.

A use-case description should contain the following information:

- A list of associations to actors.

- A list of associations to other use cases.

- A detailed description of the use case's basic and possible alternative courses of events.

- A detailed description of all of the use case's exceptions and optional courses of events.

7.2.6 Reviewing

The reviewing job is divided into two sub-activities: reviewing the model and reviewing the individual use cases.

Reviewing the use-case model means checking that the correct actors and use cases are identified and that the model is structured in a sensible way. Reviewing also involves reaching agreement on the brief descriptions of all actors and use cases in the overview document. The review is normally performed by the reengineering team together with the executive management.

Reviewing an individual use case occurs when the person responsible feels satisfied with their description and arranges a review meeting. The number of people who will review a certain use case and who should be selected varies depending on the nature of both the business and the use case. Representatives from the following groups should be selected:

- The reengineering team.

- Personnel who are to be used as resources to realize the corresponding processes and are thus directly affected by how the course of events in the use case operates.

- Those responsible for other use cases that depend on how the course of events in the described use case operates.

- Developers of computer support linked to the use case.

Use-case descriptions should be distributed in good time so that all reviewers have enough time to read through and properly prepare themselves for the review meeting. A number of points that should be considered before reviewing are as follows:

- Is communication to and/or from actor(s) correct?

- Is the course of events described at a suitable level of detail?

- Is the course of events correct and complete?

- Is it possible to simplify and speed up the course of events?

- Are all alternative courses of events described?

7.3 Object modelling

There are essentially two different types of object model that can be produced to describe *how* the business will implement the use cases: an ideal-object model and a real-object model. These models have different purposes and thus there are different reasons for producing them – if, indeed, they are produced at all. Both the ideal model and the real model are object models in the sense we discussed in Chapters 3 and 5.

Both of these models use three object types: interface objects, control objects and entity objects. When you commence work with the ideal-object model, you base the work on the use cases, but with the real-object model, the work is based on the ideal-object model in order to see the modifications required. The procedure of identifying the objects in the two models is therefore different. The real-object model will normally give you a better starting position because you can reuse large parts of the result obtained from the ideal-object model.

We start this section by describing the differences between an ideal- and a real-object model, and then go on to discuss the advantages and disadvantages of producing both of these models. The next section describes how to find objects and how to document the result.

7.3.1 Differences between ideal- and real-object models

The use-case model of a business aims to provide a description of *what* the new business should offer the environment. It is an outside view of the company because it describes what the company does as seen from its environment. Object models describe *how* the new business will offer use cases to the environment. An ideal-object model contains only those objects required to perform the use cases. The ideal objects describe how the business would operate in the best possible way. In a real-object model, the restrictions on the business are taken into consideration. This may mean that certain tasks cannot be performed in the most effective way, as described in the ideal-object model, but must be adapted to the restrictions. In the real model, the following issues, which do not need to be considered in the ideal model, are taken into account:

- Whether the business is geographically spread or centralized. A business that is distributed faces much tougher requirements than a centralized one. This does not contradict the requirement that the business should be able to become distributed if it expands. This is, of course, important, and this expansion should be prepared for in every possible way. However, it is impossible to cater entirely for these costs before the requirement really exists.

- In the ideal model, it is assumed that the employees have a certain competence to be able to perform the tasks required. This competence may not exist in today's business, and it may be much too expensive initially to make sure that it does. It could, in fact, require mass training of a greater part of the company's personnel, which could be impossible with respect to both the cost and the time required.

- Implementing the business in terms of both techniques and people. It may, for example, be necessary to continue to use partially out-of-date IT support for processes for several years. Replacing all computer support at the same time would be far too costly.

- You may perhaps have a working business that you do not wish to change at present. There are many political reasons, unfortunately, that can delay the time it takes to obtain the full effect of a reengineering project.

These restrictions might be seen in the real model in that:

- An object is added that was not required in the ideal model.

- Several objects are combined to form one object.

- An object is divided into several objects (for example, when distributing the work of a process).

- Certain objects are replaced by a completely new object.

- Changes are made to certain object descriptions.

The ideal model is normally much easier to understand than the real one. The latter can easily be regarded as being complex, because restrictions in the business must be modelled. It is perhaps not always obvious why these limitations exist and why the real model thus appears as it does. The real model also often becomes more complex because the descriptions contain more detail than the descriptions of the ideal model. The real model is the one that will be implemented, therefore more detail is required.

In brief, the ideal model shows the direction, while the real model shows how far one has actually had the opportunity to travel. If the ideal model is retained, the objective will also be kept in view; otherwise it is easy to lose sight of this.

7.3.2 Should you make two object models?

The reengineering team will need to decide which models to produce and must therefore discuss the advantages and disadvantages of the various ways of modelling the business. The team is confronted with the decision of whether to produce:

- only an ideal-object model

- only a real-object model

- both an ideal- and a real-object model

Only an ideal-object model

In most reengineering projects, this alternative is seen to be most suitable. The reengineering team obtain a clear picture of how tasks are related to products and deliverables, without needing to go into too much detail. The ideal model describes the objects that are to implement the use-case model in the business in a simple and not too detailed way.

In order to be able to install the new structure in the business, you must produce work flow descriptions (see Section 7.3.8) that describe in detail how the work will be performed in practice. Before you can do this, you must consider how the realization of the ideal model will affect the organization. You avoid the real-object model, going directly to the work flow descriptions. These descriptions will therefore operate as a means of communicating the new organization to the majority of the employees.

The advantages of this model are that it is easy to communicate, simple to update with new changes in the organization and should not take a long time to produce.

A disadvantage with only producing this model is that you will still find yourself at a relatively abstract level in comparison to the actual state of the business.

Only a real-object model

The difference between this and the previous alternative is that the real-object model describes how restrictions in the business affect the implementation of the model. In this case, you start by finding the ideal objects and then successively replace them with real objects as you introduce the restrictions in the business. The ideal-object model can be envisaged as only a working model, which is modified to a real model that shows how it will operate in practice.

The disadvantage of making a real model is that it takes longer to produce and it is questionable how much is gained by doing this. Based on the resulting object model, you will still need to produce work flow descriptions (see Section 7.3.8), which must be given to, and understood by, the employees.

Both an ideal- and a real-object model

In those cases where it is decided to produce both an ideal- and a real-object model, there are consequences for future versions of the business model. In the first version, the ideal model is used as a starting point, and the changes made relative to it in the real-object model are considered carefully. The ideal-object model is then seen as a desired objective, showing the direction the business should be taking. When the objective is later modified, the ideal model is used as a source for making the desired changes before they are included in the real model. To justify making more than one object model of the business, the extra value must exceed the costs that a further object model would incur. It can, therefore, be difficult to argue in favour of producing two models.

A major problem with two different models is coping with the updating. This can be very difficult to achieve even with one model, and it is more than twice as difficult with two models. The relations between the models must also be dealt with. A change in one of the models can require changes in the other; if the change is made to the ideal model, this is nearly always the case, but not necessarily so the other way around. It must also be possible to handle and update the traceability between the two models.

We recommend, therefore, primarily the building of an ideal-object model, even if it is up to the reengineering team to decide in each individual case what is best for their business modelling. It is, however, important, irrespective of the combination of models chosen, that the IT support developed is well adapted to the business. This must be firmly established at an early stage (see Section 7.6).

In the rest of this chapter we will assume that an ideal-object model is built, and will not discuss further the factors that need to be considered when building a real-object model.

7.3.3 Finding objects

Finding objects, and especially good objects, is an art that often seems quite difficult to master when you first become acquainted with the object-oriented way of thinking. Here, we describe a method that has been proved to give very good results.

It is often the case that you already know a number of occurrences that could be put forward directly as suggestions for entity objects. Examples of this type of 'obvious' object are products, deliverables, documents and actions that have to be carried out as part of the daily work or that are required by regulatory authorities.

When you have a first proposal for the most obvious entity objects, you continue to work with the use cases. You identify objects by traversing one use-case description at a time to ensure that there is an object responsible for each part of the use case's course of events. For each actor/use case pair, you can assign an interface object. This object handles all communication with the actor and as much as possible of the internal course of events. In those cases where there is no reason for, or possibility of, the same resource performing an internal course of events, a control object (or possibly even several) is assigned. When you work through the use case's course of events in this way, it is probable that you will identify further object entities.

The course of events description of the use case is therefore divided into:

- Behaviour that is directly related to the tasks involving contact with actors. The interface object is responsible for this type of behaviour.

- Well-defined tasks that lie inside the business and do not involve interaction with actors; for example, qualified specialist work. The control object is responsible for this type of behaviour.

- Occurrences in the business that are handled by the use case. These can be products, documents, contracts, and so on. These become entity objects.

The process way of thinking has the objective of one resource being able to perform as much of the process as possible. Ideally, therefore, all work connected to a use case should be performed by an interface object (or if the use case involves more than one actor, possibly by several interface objects). If the tasks within a use case are divided into several objects, there is a risk that the implementation of the use case will spread over several resources. This would mean handovers between resources, which only increase the risk of long lead times within a use case. By assigning one object the responsibility for these related tasks, the mapping to a single resource in the implementation of the business is simpler.

In those cases where there is no possibility of integrating the tasks related to a use case to one and the same resource, perhaps because the use case is too complicated or because certain tasks require specialist competence, it is appropriate to designate a resource to be responsible for the customers. The tasks involving communication with customers are thus modelled using an interface object. The other tasks, which are internal to the business, are modelled as control objects. The interface object will operate as a buffer between the customer and the rest of the business. In order to be able to handle the customer's questions and problems, the resource that implements the interface object will need to have access to the resources that implement control objects and possibly to the IT support that these objects utilize. Hammer and Champy (1993) call this type of interface-object resource a case manager.

Let us look at how the two variants of the sales process, off-the-shelf and tailored, would be described using objects. In both cases, you can see immediately that an interface object Seller is required to handle the contact with the customer. When we have identified objects for the use case Off-the-shelf Selling, there is no reason why the work should be split across more than one resource. The interface object Seller checks that the product exists and that the customers receive their goods. If the product has to be sent to the customer address, you can regard the actual ordering of the delivery as a separate work task, thus producing an extra interface object, Delivery Orderer (Figure 7.4).

In the above example we have modelled the actual product as an entity object. This object is required because you will need to hold information such as model, colour, price and inventory on the product.

When we have identified objects for the use case Tailored Selling, the result is not quite so simple (Figure 7.5).

Since the work of handling the actual sales process is more complicated, we choose to divide up the responsibility into two different well-defined objects, instead of collecting it together in the interface object Seller. Seller is now responsible for customer contact and order handling, and the control object Product Designer handles the actual

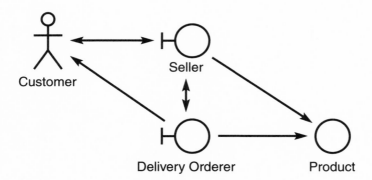

Figure 7.4 *The participating objects of the use case Off-the-shelf Selling.*

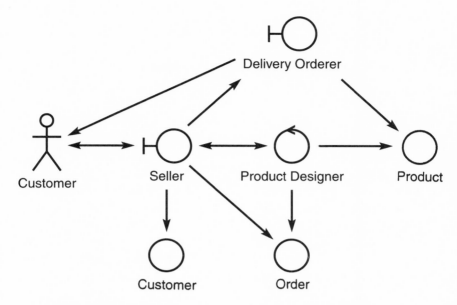

Figure 7.5 *The participating objects of the use case Tailored Selling.*

tailoring of the product according to customer demands. With large orders, you can be quite certain that the products will be sent to the customer. Therefore, even in this case, we have an interface object Delivery Orderer that orders the delivery of a product to the customer.

We have also added the entity objects Customer and Order in this view. The first represents data you need to hold about the customer, while the latter represents the specific order entered by the customer. These objects were not needed for the use case Off-the-Shelf Selling. There, the customer directly received the products requested. If a specific product was not available, the customer would simply have to come back later to ask for it.

It is always difficult to know the level of detail to use. You do not want to have objects that are too small; this results in models that are difficult to understand and overview. Neither do you want objects that are too large. The tasks that are modelled by an object must be related to each other in a sensible way. It should be possible to guess the tasks of an object just from its name. If a number of unrelated work tasks are collected together into an object, it will be difficult to know what the object is really responsible for. This complicates the updating of the model as a whole. This effect is similar to what in a structured approach would be called cohesion in a module or a subroutine. In the object-oriented world, this is translated to object cohesion (see Yourdon and Constantine, 1978).

Finding associations between objects
The dynamic associations between objects, communication associations, are found when the individual use cases are investigated to identify the objects required to perform the use case and how these objects interact.

When it applies to the static associations, acquaintance, consistsOf and inheritance, identification is normally performed at a later stage when the object model as a whole is reviewed. Acquaintance associations between objects that need to know about each other are identified, as are consistsOf associations to illustrate that an object contains other objects and inheritance structures, in order to reuse common properties between objects. See Chapter 5 for definitions and examples of these associations.

7.3.4 Describing objects

Each identified object is given a brief description. A use case places demands on the participating objects to perform together the course of events in the use case. Each object that participates in a use case can be considered to play a certain role in that use case. Each such role is described in terms of operations and even, in certain situations, attributes. You should not go into too much detail in this work, but should restrict yourself to the abstract level. The essential thing is that all of the roles that use cases in the business expect a certain object to play are briefly described for the object.

It can be difficult not to become too detailed. Remember that the aim of documenting is not just to fill up a specified number of sides of paper or shelf area: what is written should be of interest to a well-defined target group of readers.

7.3.5 Subsystem modelling

Important activities and responsibilities can just as easily become lost in a purely process organization as in a purely functional one. Therefore, it is important to model and describe the functional units even in the model of the new business. You use subsystems to model functional units. See Chapter 5 for a full definition of subsystems. These subsystems describe competence responsibility: a subsystem is realized by personnel with similar competence. The person who is responsible for a function is also responsible for the development of the personnel within that function. Compare this with a process owner, who is responsible for the operation of the process. This is carried through with the assistance of the people who have been obtained from different functions.

The procedure for producing and describing the functional hierarchy and how the processes in the business operate through the functional units is the same for modelling both the existing business and the new business. We therefore refer you to Section 6.5.1 for more information.

When you have identified and described objects in the forward engineering work, additional work is required to divide the objects into different functional units.

7.3.6 Documentation

The object model is described with the help of three different types of document:

- An overview document listing all of the subsystems and objects in the model, along with a brief description of each of them.

- Descriptions of each use case, describing how the participating objects perform the use case.

- Descriptions of each object, describing the roles of each object.

As you know, it is often said that a picture says more than a thousand words, which is one reason why you should produce a diagram to show the objects and their relations.

A very useful type of diagram is a use-case view of the participating objects. The aim of this type of diagram, called Views of Participating Objects, is to illustrate how objects interact to realize courses of events in a use case. These diagrams are used both during identification of objects, based on individual use cases, and as an aid to understanding how each individual use case is related to the object model. See Chapter 5 for more information on these diagrams.

You may also want to see the entire picture of how objects in the model are dependent on each other. If the object model is very large, this diagram may be divided into a number of smaller diagrams, one for each subsystem. We call this type of diagram Global Object Views.

In certain circumstances, for example if a certain object is very complicated, it may even be of interest to produce a diagram to show this object with all of its relations to/from other objects. This type of diagram illustrates very clearly the objects that a specific object is dependent on (all objects it is associated to) and all objects that are dependent on it (all objects that have associations to it). This type of diagram is called Local Object Views.

7.3.7 Reviewing

You divide up the work of reviewing objects into three different types of review: reviewing the object model as a whole, reviewing a use case's participating objects and reviewing the individual objects. In all three cases, the reviewers are normally people in the reengineering team. It is unusual to communicate the object models to the employees in general, which means that the only people who are really involved and competent to review these models are in the reengineering team. Within the reengineering team, however, are people whom the employees in general know and trust. These people should at least have a basic understanding of object orientation.

Reviewing the object model involves checking that the model as a whole is sound, by ensuring that good objects have been identified (according to previous recommendations), that several objects do not occur that really have the same responsibility, that all objects have unique names and that the inheritance structures and containment hierarchies are correct.

Reviewing a use case's participating objects involves checking that the use case's course of events can be realized with the selected objects, and that all the behaviour and responsibility required is distributed between and described for these objects. The reviewer must have access to the use-case description, its view of the participating objects and the participating object's descriptions. The reviewer's objective is to ensure that all sub-courses of events (even the alternative and optional courses of events and the exceptions) in the use case's description are taken care of by the participating objects in an appropriate way. By reviewing the view of the participating objects together with the use-case description, the reviewer ensures that both the required objects and the required associations between them are included. Thereafter the participating objects' descriptions are reviewed to ensure that they contain descriptions of the required responsibilities.

Reviewing the individual objects involves checking that the objects' descriptions are consistent and homogeneous. The different use cases that the object participates in place different demands on the object, and these demands should not conflict in any way.

7.3.8 Work flow descriptions

When it is required to distribute information about the new business to personnel, the object models are not sufficient. Instead, it is normal to complement these object descriptions with work flow descriptions that are specially adapted for this purpose. It is not good salesmanship to place only an object model in the hands of an employee, where his/her tasks are described in terms of objects with operations. The object model is used primarily to enable the reengineering team to produce a good model of how the business operates and, from this, the necessary work flow descriptions are used to communicate the details in an informative way to the employees. These can appear in many different forms (see Johansson, 1993).

It is not really so strange there are completely different descriptions of the business for those who work with modelling it and those who use the result. Compare this with system development. You might compare your object models and their documentation with the design documentation of the code that system developers write. Furthermore, the work flow descriptions can be compared with the user manuals for a system, which describe the system in a manner that is useful to the user. By analogy, the work flow descriptions describe the organization in a way that its personnel can understand.

7.4 Interaction diagrams

One of the most important techniques for identifying and clarifying the roles an object plays, and thus its responsibility, is to draw an interaction diagram. Interaction diagrams are also very useful to people who are trying to understand how the use case's course of events interacts with the participating objects. In Chapter 5, we described the interaction diagram in technical terms. In this section, however, we discuss how and when you can use this technique for distributing responsibility to objects (Figure 7.6).

On the left of the diagram, there are descriptions of the use cases Off-the-Shelf Selling and Tailored Selling as they appear in the use-case model. The descriptions in this example are not in any way comprehensive – or even, perhaps, complete – but are there to illustrate how the use cases place demands on the participating objects and how this can be shown in the interaction diagram. On the right of the diagram, you can see how the descriptions of these use cases appear in the object model.

Since a use case often comprises a number of alternative courses of events, it is usual, for practical reasons, to divide up these descriptions into a number of interaction diagrams. Each interaction diagram is designated a unique name for each use case. The basic course of events is described in one interaction diagram and all alternative courses of events in other, separate diagrams. This is done for ease of understanding – alternative courses of events that are described along with the basic course of events will be much more difficult to understand.

It is only after you have drawn interaction diagrams for all courses of events in all use cases that you can be certain that you have found all of the roles that the system requires each object to play and, thus, the responsibilities of each object. In Figure 7.7 we show how the requirements from the interaction diagram in Figure 7.6 affect the Seller object.

Difficulties can easily arise in the distribution of responsibility between the people responsible for the development of a use case and those responsible for the development of objects that participate in the use case. An interaction diagram is part of the documentation of a use case, which means that the person responsible for the use case should produce it. When an interaction diagram is produced, the use case's course of events is distributed to the participating objects. This means that the person responsible for the use case thereby places demands or responsibilities on these participating objects. All such demands on an object are collected into a document called an object specification. The person responsible for the objects then formulates these demands into an object description.

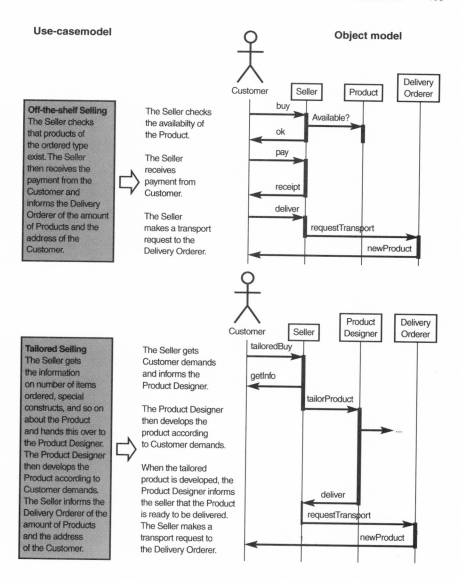

Figure 7.6 *The flow of events in a use case is described by communicating objects in one or more interaction diagrams.*

There is a risk of going into too much detail when using this technique: it is not necessary to delve too deeply in the description of the object's responsibility. Identifying all operations that represent the object's responsibilities, and the parameters of these operations, is in most cases delving too deep. It is, of course, possible to go into more

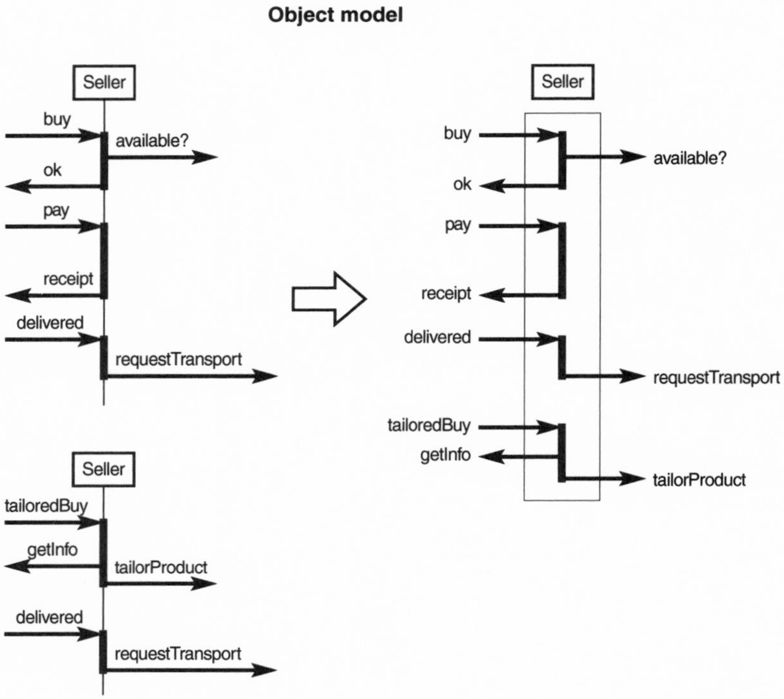

Object model

Figure 7.7 *The responsibilities of an object may be found from all of the interaction diagrams where the object plays a role.*

detail in these descriptions, but this should only be done when there are good reasons for doing so.

7.5 Information system development

Part of the work of designing the new company is developing the supporting information system. The new business cannot be installed until this is in place. Object models of the business benefit if the work begins with models of the information system.

The work of building the information system and the work of building models of the business is initially an iterative process with great mutual dependency. Later on, these activities can proceed mainly in parallel. The final object models of the company and the information system to support the processes in the company will be completed at approximately the same time. Because they are so dependent on one another, one cannot be completed before the other.

From this, it should be emphasized that it is extremely important that the models of both the company and the information system are very easy to communicate between both groups of people taking part in the reengineering team – the builders of the business and the builders of the information system. In our proposal (see Chapter 9) we use the same (or nearly the same) modelling language in both activities.

7.6 Verifying the new business

It is very important to ensure that the models produced are well verified at an early stage. If a reengineered business, with its integrated support system, is not checked regularly it is in principle absolutely impossible to forecast how it will operate. It is also very unlikely that a perfect result will be obtained after testing on just one occasion. A number of iterations between development and tests are required. At each test, you learn from the results and fine-tune the models of the business.

Davenport (1993) describes a technique for testing, which he calls *organizational prototyping*. He defines it as 'a small-scale, quasi-operational version of a new process that can be used to test various aspects of its design'. According to Davenport, there are different levels of prototyping: computer simulation (simulation at an early stage of the new processes using computers), paper process test (information test of processes with pen and paper), stand-alone process prototype (isolated process prototypes), prototype with interfaces (process prototypes with interface to other processes and IT support) and prototype with full enablers (final integration test). Different types of test are suitable for different stages of modelling. The first tests help to trace any errors and miscalculations at an early stage, although they are less exact than the later tests. You usually divide this verification work into the following cases:

- Simulating the business in the ideal-object model, where it has not yet been decided what is to be performed by people, machines or computer support.

- Making a prototype to show how the computer support will operate.

- Carrying out a trial installation of the model of the whole new business, but in an isolated part of the organization.

Simulating the ideal model

Once a first proposal for the ideal model has been produced, the new processes are simulated with the help of software. This simulation is done before deciding exactly how the processes are to be implemented in the business; that is, which parts will be performed by human resources, IT support or machines.

Simulation helps to verify that the different steps in the processes are reasonable. By assigning these steps different values, it is possible to measure the simulated business and obtain an estimation of how it operates.

Simulation tools are available in the market and, in certain cases, it may well be cheaper to buy such an application than to try to develop an individual simulation program. The disadvantage is that commercial products are seldom easily adapted to the special requirements of a particular business. Also, it is quite easy to produce a simulation program based on the object model already produced. By allowing each object in the model to be directly represented in the software, and implementing each object in an effective language (such as Smalltalk), you can quickly achieve the required result.

A complementary technique, which may be used if you do not have access to an effective and well-adapted simulation tool, is to execute the processes manually, using pen and paper. This old-fashioned 'desk check' type of simulation can actually be just as effective as a simulation tool.

Making a prototype of the IT support

In collaboration with the developers of the IT support, the parts of the processes that are to be implemented with IT support are decided. When the requirements for the IT support have been determined, a use-case model is produced and the user interface is sketched out. After discussing the proposal, a prototype is made.

The aim of such a prototype is to give the users of the IT support a feel of how it will operate and thus enable them to suggest any improvements at an early stage. You should also be able to measure how much more effective the new IT support will really make the business.

Using prototypes of the IT support, you can even experiment with whether the effectiveness of a process increases by extending those parts of the process that are handled by IT support.

Carrying out a trial installation
Once the information system has been built and tested integration tests are performed in an environment in which representatives of the real users participate. One trial installs the processes with the information system in an individual small business and simulates the interaction with customers and suppliers. In this way, the simple processes are systematically tested, one at a time, then several processes that do not have mutual relations are tested simultaneously. Thereafter, a number of parallel processes with mutual relations are tested.

The result of these tests will highlight any problems and limitations, which must be fed back to the models and the work of building the information system. After a number of iterations of this type, you will be ready to install the new business in the actual organization.

7.7 Summary

The result from reengineering the existing business provides a good foundation when the objective specification is received from the envisioning activity. Based on the resulting models and analyses of these models, the forward engineering activity commences. The work starts by identifying how the objectives of the new business affect the use-case model of the existing business. This can mean major modifications, such as adding or deleting entire use cases or modifying the basic course of events of a use case. You continue to work with the details in the descriptions of the use cases' courses of events, and modify the use cases' courses of events by eliminating all non value adding (NVA) activities identified and optimizing all value adding (VA) activities.

When the use-case model and use-case descriptions are reviewed and approved, the participating objects in each use case are identified. An overall view of these objects and their interactions is produced for each use case. For more complicated courses of events, interaction diagrams are drawn to help in allocating behaviour and responsibilities to the participating objects and to illustrate in more detail how these objects cooperate to realize a use case. The demands from all use cases on a specific object are collected together, and the object's behaviour and responsibilities are described in terms of operations and, sometimes, attributes.

At the same time, prototypes should be produced to check how the modification proposal may appear in the business. Cooperation with the support system development should also begin. A support system that is as integrated as possible with the work in the new business should be built. The new support system will affect how people work in the business, so the earlier this cooperation starts the better.

During the development of the models, you should continually verify that the new ideas will really lead to effective and implementable solutions. This work normally results in the feeding back of important improvements to the models and requires a number of iterations before the new business is good enough for full-scale installation.

7.8 References

Davenport T.H. (1993). *Business Innovation, Reengineering Work through Informa-tion Technology*. Boston MA: Harvard Business School Press

Hammer M. and Champy J. (1993). *Reengineering the Corporation: A Manifesto for Business Revolution*. NY: HarperCollins

Harrington J. (1993). *Business Process Improvement*. NY: McGraw-Hill

Johansson H.J. (1993). *Business Process Reengineering — Breakpoint Strategies for Market Dominance*. Chichester: John Wiley & Sons

Rockhart J.F. and Short J.E. (1988). Information Technology and the New Organization: Towards More Effective Management of Interdependence. *Working Paper CISR 180*, MIT Sloan School of Management, Center for Information Systems Research

Yourdon E. and Constantine L. (1978). *Structured Design*. Englewood Cliffs NJ: Prentice Hall

chapter 8
An example

8.1 Introduction

We decided to use ourselves (Objectory AB) as guinea-pigs to obtain an example of how a business model expressed in object-oriented business engineering terms would look.

Objectory AB was founded in 1987 by Dr Ivar Jacobson to market the technique of systems engineering that he had developed during his 20 years at Ericsson and while writing his thesis. The thesis described a method for object-based design. During the first two years of the company, a first version of a method for object-oriented system engineering, called Objectory, was developed. The first companies to test this product were BT Industrier in Linköping and Nokia Data in Stockholm. During a three-year period, Objectory AB grew to approximately 40 employees. It was a very expansive period, during which the first version of a computer-based modelling tool was developed. In 1993, our company experienced a rapidly growing, international interest in our products, and, in early 1994, reached a size of about 55 employees, with offices in Sweden, Germany and the US.

To meet the demands of an organization of up to 200 people, we realized that we had to reorganize our enterprise. We therefore made the decision to rebuild ourselves to become process-managed. We have not performed what business-process reengineering experts would call a complete reengineering effort. The primary goal has been to change our organization from being hierarchically governed to process-managed.

In this chapter, for practical reasons, we only present part of the complete model: the whole model would only be more of the same. The models will probably change, since they have not yet been fully installed.

8.2 What do we want to change?

One of the most important things when starting a reengineering project is to agree on the purpose of the work. If you don't know what the goal is, all you see is obstacles. The list we produced is very general: it could work for many different kinds of enterprise:

- Always prioritize our customer's needs.

- Always be competent and professional in all of the things we do.

- Always work towards goals and results.

- We want more employees willing to take on responsibility.

- We want to give our younger employees more responsibility.

A company cannot survive unless its primary goal is to serve its customers. We believe that our internal problems will be solved by the fact that a process-managed organization gives individuals a better chance of taking on more responsibility and developing their own profiles within the company. Discussions of this kind gave us arguments in favour of building an organization that directs its energy towards solving its customer's problems, not its own.

It is also important to bear in mind the overall strategy of the company when developing a model of the enterprise. In our case, it looks something like the following:

Our vision and mission

- We want to help our customers to perform business process reengineering on their software development process, from whatever it is today to an industrial process for software development. We maintain that this can only occur if the process is based on object-oriented ideas and, in particular, on Objectory.

- We want to help our customers to perform business process reengineering by building object-oriented models of their organizations.

Our business idea
The product

- The Objectory product consists of two parts: the Objectory Development Process and the Objectory Support Environment.

- The Objectory Development Process is defined by a set of handbooks, or by a document 'source system', which describes the process in terms of configurable objects. The Objectory Development Process is normally customized to the user's exact needs by defining a specific 'Development Case'.

- The Objectory Support Environment is a software system consisting of a set of tools. Embedded in the tools are Objectory rules for the modelling, documentation and management of Objectory models. The Objectory Support Environment is normally integrated with a set of complementary tools to offer the customer a complete solution to his/her exact system development needs.

The services

- Objectory AB's services offer the knowledge transfer and help needed to make our customers successful in their use of the Objectory product. Our services consist of three parts: training, mentoring and consultancy. Depending on the customer's competence, experience, preparation time and time constraints on 'coming up to speed' with Objectory, the level of these services may vary. At the lowest level, we provide 'plain training'. The highest level may involve training, long-term mentoring and the services of several consultants, throughout the entire customer learning curve.

We believe that the company will need to grow substantially to be able to meet customers' demands. A requirement for the organization we build is, therefore, that it can grow. We identified the following 'cases for action':

- We must improve our training by a factor of two and mentoring by a factor of four (meaning that users will only need to spend 50% of today's training time in learning Objectory and that our method consultants will only need to spend 25% of the time currently spent on mentoring).

- We must prepare a platform for growth and internationalization.

- We need more people to take on greater responsibility than before.

- We must make it clearer how responsibilities are distributed within our company.

8.3 What kind of organization do we have now?

The company has reached a head count of about 55 employees (1994). Our top-level management consists of seven people. We have five departments: financial (3), implementation services (11), marketing and sales (4), product management (7) and product development (21). Implementation services and product development are divided into sub-departments (Figure 8.1).

As a means of educating and developing our staff, we have actively enforced what is sometimes called 'job-rotation'. In our case, this has been implemented in two ways:

- Employees change assignments and responsibilities, which means that they move between departments, particularly between implementation services and process development.

- Although a person belongs to one department, he/she might, for a limited period of time, work for another department.

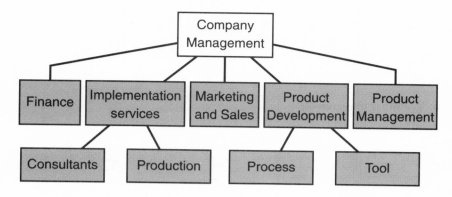

Figure 8.1 *A view of the hierarchical organization.*

An effect of the latter process is that the organization map does not really reflect the amount of time we put into different tasks, which can be confusing for both us and our customers.

We tried to identify the processes we had in the current organization and represented them as use cases (Figure 8.2). We did not go into any more detail in the description of the present organization.

As you can see, there is not simply one Customer actor in our model. We have identified different actors to show that different roles can be played towards our organization. We treat people according to these roles. For example, a Customer is someone with whom we negotiate to sell our products, while a User is someone who actually uses our products. It might be the case that one person acts in both of these roles, but this is seldom true. The level of detail you choose to have when identifying your actors is very much a question of judgement. There is no advantage to be gained in delving into too much detail. After all, it is not the business environment that we are to model. We only need enough knowledge to be able to identify and describe the right business processes.

Apart from the business processes, there are of course a number of supporting activities that must exist in an organization. The ones we identified were:

- Handling infrastructure: activities that concern everyone in the company, such as security, training, paying salaries, writing news-letters, and so on. Input to these activities comes from rules and regulations imposed on us by various authorities.

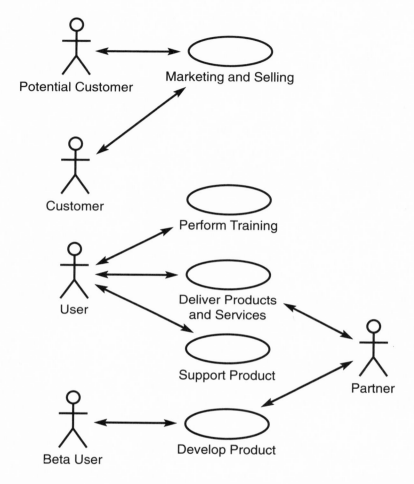

Figure 8.2 *Our view before redesigning the business processes. Brief descriptions of the actors and use cases in the figure can be found at the end of this section.*

- Develop business strategy: activities that concern strategic matters, such as long-term budget and resource planning. Input is information from market analysts. Output is a strategic plan for the development of our company.

We choose here to describe our company as consisting of two layers — a business process layer and a layer containing support activities (Figure 8.3). It is the business process that a customer is in direct contact

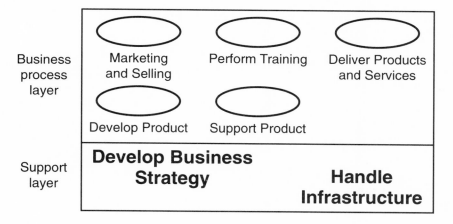

Figure 8.3 *The business process layer and support layer in our model of the old organization.*

with. The support activities must exist and function for the business processes to be able to work, and work effectively.

Why, then, did we make this layering? We found that the support activities are not unique in any way to our organization. They are not directly dependent on what product we are selling, and they do not produce anything of direct value to our customers. Every company needs something similar. The support layer is general in this respect. Another way of putting it is to say that the activities in the support layer do not characterize the company.

These general activities, however, should be considered as very important to describe and redesign. If they do not work, the business processes will not function efficiently. The activities in the support layer represent the grease that makes the process machinery run smoothly. This is especially true in an organization that expects to grow to 200 employees, as ours does.

To clarify the purpose of each actor and use case, we describe each of them briefly. The actor descriptions are one or two sentences long, while the use-case descriptions are three to five sentences.

Actors
Beta User: represents a user of a beta version of our product.

Customer: represents someone who has bought at least one product.

Potential Customer: represents an individual belonging to the market. An instance of this actor will belong to a segment of the market and/or regions of the market. It might also correspond to a reader of a certain magazine, an exhibition visitor or a reader of Jacobson *et al.* (1992).

Partner: represents a person at a company or an individual with whom we have a partnership agreement. The agreement might concern development of our products or delivery of services.

User: represents a user of our products.

Use cases

Develop Product: includes planning of product development, capturing requirements, implementation and testing. This work results in a production specification. Input is derived from the market. During the work, product plans, requirement specifications and roll-out plans for the development are produced. Output is a new product(s), in the form of printed and magnetic-media originals.

Deliver Products & Services: handles how products and services are delivered to a customer. It contains all of the actions from handling orders to giving method support to the user. Input to this process is an order from a customer. Output is Objectory products (Objectory Tool, Objectory Process) and services (training, mentoring, consultancy) to the customer.

Marketing & Selling: handles the dissemination of information about our products to the market. It also handles the process of coming to an agreement with a Potential Customer or a Customer. Input to this process is information about the current market situation. Output is information about our products that is of value to a potential customer in the evaluation process. Output could also be an agreement between us and a customer.

Perform Training: handles the planning and execution of training for a particular customer. Input to this process is information about the kind of training the customer requires, the level of knowledge that the project members have concerning system engineering methodologies, and also the application area of the project. Output is knowledge transfer to the customer.

Support Product: handles how operation reports from a particular customer are taken care of, and how the user is helped. Input to this process is one or several operation reports from the customer. Output is information to the customer on how we will handle the problem. This could be the delivery of a corrected product. It could also be information on the product release in which the problem will be fixed, or information on how the users can handle the problem themselves. This use case also handles answering questions from customers on how to find their way through the products, both Objectory Tool and Objectory Process.

8.4 New business processes

The reengineering team consisted of the authors of this book, augmented with the (former) members of the management group. They were interviewed individually to obtain an initial outline of the new processes. The authors acted as modelling experts.

Developing a model is an iterative process. As you work with the model, you will find new questions that need to be answered by the reengineering team. We (the authors) conducted three series of interviews to cover this need.

The result of the first series of interviews was two use-case models, showing our organization at two abstract levels. We found that developing two models is one way of solving the conflict that arises when trying to create a model that is easy to understand, but that also shows a level of detail that everyone is content with. A disadvantage is that it might be rather complex to explain what the relations between the two models mean.

As the discussions went on, we came to realize that it was not necessary to have two models. The difference between the two was so insignificant that it did not warrant the administration of two models. Consequently, after the second interview series we had a use-case model at one level only.

The aim of the third interview series was to further develop the textual descriptions of the use cases and actors.

8.4.1 Identification of use cases and actors

The model we finally produced included seven use cases and six actors (Figure 8.4). Marketing & Selling is considered as two separate use cases in this model. Perform Training is no longer a use case on its own; it is included in the Assist Customer Project use case, which handles everything that has to do with how we can help our customers in their use of our products. We found it wise to treat development of the methodology and development of our CASE tool as two separate use cases, since the two activities are performed by very different kinds of resources. We also identified a use case for handling development performed to correct flaws in our products that need to be fixed urgently. Such development is not induced by a release based product plan; it is something requested by current users of our products. The relationship to the actor is more direct in this case, compared to release based development. Thus, the old Develop Product use case was divided into three parts in this new model.

A brief description of all actors and use cases is given at the end of this section.

In this model, we have chosen not to use the word 'develop' in the names of use cases that concern how a new version of a product is generated. Instead, we use the word 'procure' to emphasize that we do not always carry out all of the development ourselves. The process leader might let another company (a development partner) perform parts of the development work, or may even choose to buy parts of the product 'off-the-shelf'.

Input to the processes for procuring our products consists of comments and requirements from all of our actors. With this as a basis, we develop a requirement specification for the next release, and then perform the development. The actors User, Customer, Potential Customer and Beta User all communicate with two procurement processes. This might not seem logical to the actor, so it is important to ensure that

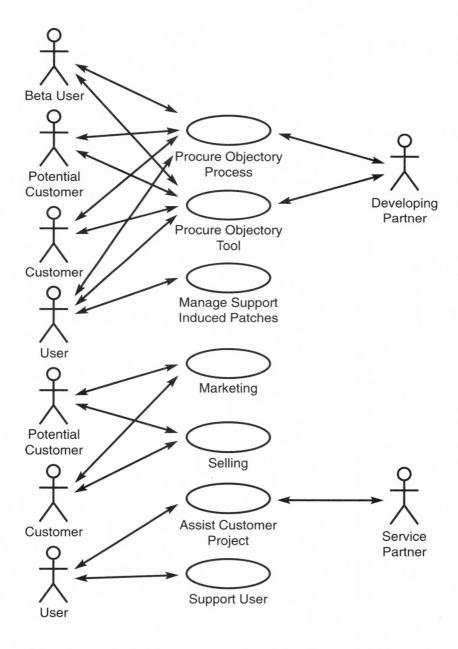

Figure 8.4 *The use cases and actors in our final model.*

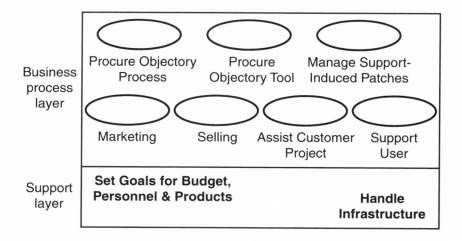

Figure 8.5 *The business process layer and support layer of our company.*

the interfaces of the two processes are the same. The result should be a new product, in the form of printed and magnetic-media originals.

In the use case Marketing, the market is supplied with information about our products. Potential Customers are contacted in the use case Selling. In this latter use case, product configurations are identified that satisfy the demands of the specific customer. Such a package might contain licences to use our product, support of the product, training and mentoring. When an order is accepted, the customer order is registered, and an invoice is delivered along with the ordered product.

Support activities were grouped into Set Goals for Budget, Personnel & Products and Handle Infrastructure (Figure 8.5).

Set Goals for Budget, Personnel & Products: handles long-term budget, personnel and product planning. This activity sets the objectives of the enterprise in marketing, financial and competence terms. Competence means not only what kind of people to employ, but also how to develop our resources. These activities also encompass maintaining and developing internal processes – that is, the business models of our company – which include quality work such as ISO9000. Long-term should, in this case, be interpreted as more than one year.

Handle Infrastructure: manages internal services of the office. Here, we describe how the 'resource owner' handles the development and maintenance of our staff. Other important aspects are short-term budgeting and financial forecasts (short-term should here be interpreted as one year). This activity also encompasses monitoring changes in legal requirements. As you might guess, this activity is rather complex and deserves a more extensive description. However, in our case, it is of no interest at this level of detail.

Actors
Beta User: represents a user of a beta version of our product.

Customer: represents an individual at a company that has bought services and one or more products.

Developing Partner: represents an individual at a company:

- that develops products we source into our products,

- from whom we buy components of our products,

- from whom we buy products and adapt them to be part of our products.

Potential Customer: represents an individual belonging to the market. An instance of this actor will belong to a segment of the market and/or regions of the market. It might also correspond to a reader of a certain magazine, an exhibition visitor or a reader of Jacobson *et al.* (1992).

Service Partner: represents an individual at an allied company that offers services to support our products.

User: represents a user of our products and/or services.

Use cases
Assist Customer Project: handles activities that concern the planning and administration of consultants for a particular customer, how the actual consultancy is performed for the customer and how feedback from the consultants is handled. This use case also handles activities that are performed when developing training material for a new version of the product, and giving a course to a particular customer. Input is information about the level of knowledge the customer has concerning system engineering

methodologies and also the application area of the project. Output is knowledge transfer to the customer.

Manage Support-Induced Patches: handles patch releases induced by customer demands. There are two main variants of flows in this use case: the first one is to develop a planned patch release to fix a certain number of reported faults; the second is to perform very urgent patch releases. Input is information about the customer's problems. Output is a new version of the product.

Marketing: handles communication with the market, for example, administration of exhibitions and user-group meetings. This use case also handles planning of marketing activities and development of marketing material. Input is information about the current market situation. Output is information about our products that is of value to future customers in their work.

Procure Objectory Process: handles the development of the Objectory Process. A sub-flow handles how to source parts of the products. Here, we also describe activities to acquire strategic knowledge. Activities might be: competition analysis, market studies, measurements of customer-satisfaction ratios, 'research' activities, developing and maintaining an 'intelligence network' of friends and contacts, and so on. Input is comments on our products from customers and other interested parties. Output is a new version of the Objectory Process, in the form of printed originals.

Procure Objectory Tool: handles the development of the Objectory Tool. A sub-flow handles how to source parts of the products. Here, we also describe activities to acquire strategic knowledge. Activities might be: competition analysis, market studies, measurements of customer-satisfaction ratios, 'research' activities, developing and maintaining an 'intelligence network' of friends and contacts, and so on. Input is comments on our products from customers and other interested parties. Output is a new version of the Objectory Tool, in the form of magnetic-media originals.

Selling: handles communication with a particular customer or prospect. Activities are concerned with reaching agreement with specific customers on how the products should be assembled to best suit their needs – that is, the configuration of the product, the type of services, and so forth. This use case also handles the order cycle for a particular customer. This includes assembling the products, delivering them to the customer, handling the invoice and evaluating the delivery. This use case also handles the production of 'configuration items', from which products can be assembled. Input is information about the current market situation. Output is products and services of value to the customer.

Support User: handles the activities that concern how operation reports from a particular user are taken care of, and how the user is helped. These reports are handled and given priority by a support council. The use case also handles the distribution of important information to users of our products. Input to this use case is one or several problem reports from the customer. Output is an agreement between us and the customer on how to handle the specific problem. This could be either the delivery of a corrected product or information on the product release in which the problem will be fixed. It could also be information on how the users can handle the problem themselves.

8.4.2 Description of the use cases

Some of our processes had already been described to some extent, which made us decide to keep the old descriptions where we thought they would work. For example, we already had an extensive description of product procurement, but we needed to adapt it to our new process model.

The use cases we have chosen to describe here are Marketing, Selling and Procure Objectory Tool. We have not described the flow in detail, but have chosen to keep the text at a level that is understandable to a layman in marketing, sales or the development of computer-based tools. Note, also, that we intend to make more than one description of each use case. This first one has the purpose of clarifying how the use case communicates with its actors and what it does. How things are performed in the business will be described in other use case descriptions. Later in this chapter we present a more detailed description of our use cases, in terms of how objects interact to perform the use cases. To limit the amount of text, we have not described all sub-flows in the use cases, but only indicated them. Furthermore, the descriptions do not contain any guidance as to how resources should be planned and distributed. This is something we will describe in the support layer.

Description of the use case marketing

Handle User-Group Meetings: this sub-flow describes how a user-group meeting is executed . . .

Handle Exhibitions: this sub-flow describes how an exhibition is executed . . .

Handle Advertising: this sub-flow describes how advertising is executed . . .

Develop Market Plan: an important sub-flow within the use case Marketing is the process of developing a marketing plan. This flow is initiated by the president, that is, from the support layer. The activities should be performed each year.

Before making a plan, you need an analysis of the market that shows a suitable structuring of it into a number of segments. Then, you need to decide what segments of the market to concentrate on. These decisions must conform to the company's strategic plan and budget, and should also depend on an analysis that shows how much input we can estimate from investments in a certain market segment. The information needed to make these decisions is either present as a result of work already performed within our supporting activities, or has to be assembled through contacts with our actors or through internal management meetings.

From this analysis, it has to be decided what marketing activities, such as exhibitions and conferences, we are to attend during the year, and how to conduct market communication and advertising. We also have to define our level of ambition – how many people, how much money and so forth. The available budget is a basis for this work.

If market segments – or our products – have changed, we need to decide whether to develop new marketing material and what resources to put into that work.

Another type of activity described within the marketing plan is how to handle user-group meetings. We must have a plan for interacting with the users and initiating the meetings.

The sub-flow ends when the marketing plan is approved by the president.

Develop Market Communication Material: this sub-flow describes how the development of market-communication material is executed...

Description of the use case selling

Communicate with Customer: this sub-flow describes how selling is executed towards a specific customer...

Develop Sales Plan: a sub-flow within this use case is planning the sales activities. This is something that should be done each year. The work is initiated by the president of the company, that is, from the support layer. To make a sales plan, you need information about the market, about the leads and prospects you have, and so forth. This information might be available from work done within the Marketing use case or from work performed within the support layer. The result of the work is documented in a sales plan for the period.

The sub-flow ends when the sales plan is approved by the president.

Description of the use case Procure Objectory Tool

Capture Requirements on our Products: within this sub-flow, we gather information from the market, from our customers, from our users, and from our 'intelligence network', about the most important things to change in our products. We maintain what could be called a 'wish list' for our products.

Develop Product Plan: the 'wish list' is analysed to obtain a list of requirements that can be prioritized and for which time estimates can be produced. With this information as a basis, we can develop a product plan. This product plan should be revised each year and should encompass three years. The product plan includes a release plan for our products.

Develop Requirement Specification: for each release, a requirement specification has to be developed. It should contain a detailed report on all of the requirements to be included in the release, together with rough time estimates.

Requirement Analysis: a requirement analysis activity is performed to ensure that the specification is consistent and that nothing has been overlooked. The result of the requirement analysis is a requirements model of the system to be built. A time and resource plan for the project must also be developed.

Development: the development of the new product is divided into a number of phases – ideal design (optional), real design, implementation and testing. For each of these phases, a model of the system is built. Before a project can be considered finished, beta testing of the system must take place, which involves a number of beta customers.

8.5 An object model of the new business

Before you can start identifying objects, you have to make sure that everyone working with the model has the same idea about the purpose of the model. The first thing you have to decide is whether the object model is something that is going to be discussed with everyone, or only within the reengineering team. We strongly recommend that you do not broadcast the object model to everyone. An object model is a rather technical thing, and it might easily be misunderstood or misinterpreted by those who are not used to working with object-oriented models.

Something that might be a problem is the fact that you will not see 'people' in the object model, only tasks and things. As a member of the organization, it is not always easy to accept being 'objectified'. Therefore, it is of vital importance that the members of the reengineering team have good knowledge of object orientation, and also that they understand the advantages of building abstract models of the real world. (In our organization this was never really a problem, since we are used to making object models of more or less everything.)

Since we wanted to clarify how to gather the information needed to develop a product plan and requirement specifications, we started looking at sub-flows of use cases that dealt with this matter. The danger of working like this is, however, that you can easily forget that it is the processes or flows you are supposed to describe, not groups of activities. If you do not look at whole use cases, you will not have the whole picture of what requirements the use cases put on the object model. You might fall into the trap of identifying the objects you assume you need. Remember that the only reason for having an object in the model is that it participates in at least one use case.

To give you an illustrative example of how a view of participating objects for a flow of events should appear, we have chosen to show the objects that may be identified for the use cases described previously. However, this object model has not been implemented in our organization, and we therefore expect it to change to some extent.

8.5.1 Identification of objects

The standard procedure is to start identifying objects for each individual use case. It is often the case, though, that several entity objects (representing products, deliverables, 'things') can be found without looking at the descriptions of the use cases. They represent things that we have always referred to when describing our company. Hopefully, the organization has a good picture of, for instance, the products it is dealing with.

To describe what we are selling, we identified the following entity objects: Objectory Tool (a magnetic tape or other media with a copy of the program on it), Objectory Process Description (copies of binders or books), Training, Mentoring and Consultancy. A Deliverable consists of a combination of these (Figure 8.6). Brief descriptions of the objects are given at the end of this section.

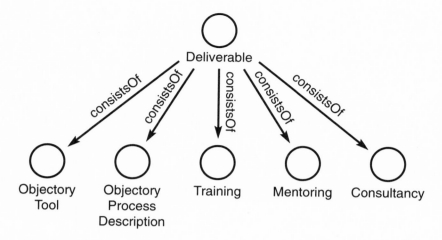

Figure 8.6 *General entity objects.*

We did not find it necessary to identify any detailed relations between the entity objects at this stage. Neither did we expand the level of detail in the model of our product objects to show how they could be grouped into different configurations.

The next step was to identify the objects needed to perform the flows of the use cases. To start with, let us take a look at the description we made of the Marketing use case. Even though the description was not complete, we could see that we needed a number of interface objects to handle interaction with the actors. We identified interface objects for each controlling activity that involved direct communication with an actor: the Advertiser, the Exhibition Handler and the User-Group Handler. We also saw that the task of developing and handling the market plan needed a specific competence. Therefore, we identified the control object Market Plan Handler. When communicating with the market, we need to have marketing material available, a task that requires a specific competence. We therefore identified the object Market Communication Handler to represent this task. Since the development of marketing material does not necessarily mean direct contact with our customers, Market Communication Handler is a control object.

What, then, are the entity objects we need? One obvious object would be a Market Plan, but we also need to access information about the market. For example, we need information about people or organizations outside the company that we interact with, and also the results of market analysis work. Therefore, we identified the entity object Market Research Data (Figure 8.7).

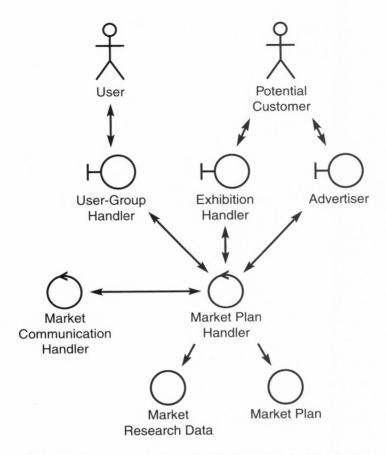

Figure 8.7 *A view of the objects that participate in the flow of events of the Marketing use case. The arrows indicate how the objects communicate.*

The objects shown in the figure are identified according to the description we made of the use case's flow of events. To clarify how we want the objects to take part in the flow of events, we made a new description of the use case, this time in terms of how the objects interact.

Description of the use case marketing
Handle User-Group Meetings: this sub-flow describes how a user-group meeting is executed...
    Handle Exhibition: this sub-flow describes how an exhibition is executed...

Handle Advertising: this sub-flow describes how advertising is executed . . .

Develop Market Plan: this sub-flow is initiated from the support layer by the president, and an instance of Market Plan Handler is initiated. The object represents the task of gathering information so that an instance of Market Plan can be created. To obtain this information, the object Market Research Data is accessed.

Another part of the task is to initiate (according to the Market Plan) and supervise the tasks represented by the objects Market Communication Handler, Advertiser, Exhibition Handler and User-Group Handler.

The sub-flow ends when the Market Plan is approved by the president.

Develop Market-Communication Material: this sub-flow describes how the development of market-communication material is executed . . .

The use case Selling is structurally very similar to Marketing. There is a 'planning' sub-flow and one for executing sales towards a customer. We identified the interface object Seller and the control object Sales Plan Handler (Figure 8.8).

What entity objects do we need? The person performing the Seller task will probably want to talk about Orders and Deliverables. It will need information about the saleable resources. We identified the Resource Object to represent this data.

We made a new description of the use case Selling, expressing its flow of events in terms of how the objects interact:

Description of the use case selling

Communicate with Customer: this sub-flow describes how selling is executed towards a specific customer . . .

Develop Sales Plan: this sub-flow is initiated from the support layer by the president, and an instance of Sales Plan Handler starts working to define a new instance of Sales Plan. To do this, the object needs access to data stored in Customer Object and in Market Research Data.

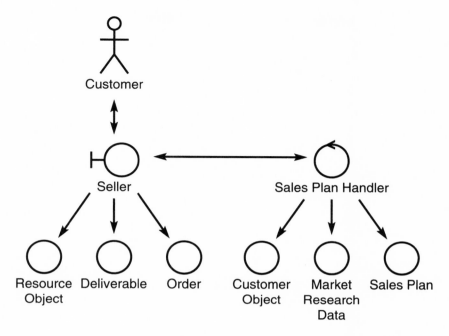

Figure 8.8 *Objects participating in the flow of events of the use case Selling.*

> The Sales Plan Handler initiates instances of Seller to perform sales activities according to the Sales Plan.
> The sub-flow ends when the sales plan is approved by the president.

We followed the same principle when identifying interface objects and control objects for the use case Procure Objectory Tool. In short:

- Interface objects for every activity that involves communication with an actor.

- Control objects for control of the more internal behaviour.

- Entity objects to represent things we deal with in the process.

Product procurement is a very complicated process. The descriptions and object views shown here are very simplified in comparison

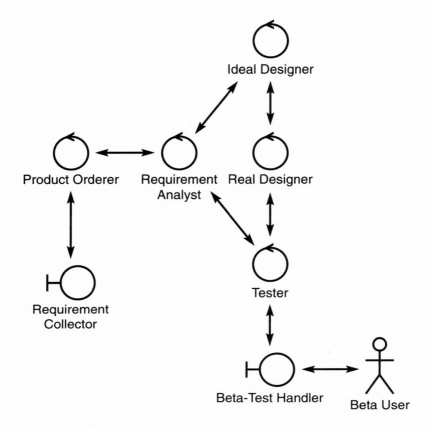

Figure 8.9 *Participating control and interface objects in the basic flow of Procure Objectory Tool.*

to how it will look in reality. We have minimized the number of objects and communication associations. For example, Real Designer will in reality be two objects: Real-Object Model Designer and Real-Object Designer.

To capture all requirements or comments our customers might have on our products, we identified the control object Product Orderer. This object needs an entity object Wish List for comments and requirements.

We found that the view became too complicated if we put all participating objects in it. Therefore, we first show a view of the control and interface objects, along with their communication paths (Figure 8.9). After this, there are a number of views that show how these control and interface objects access entity objects during different phases of the development work (Figures 8.10–8.13).

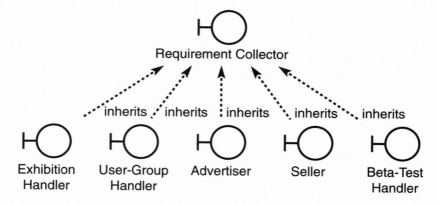

Figure 8.10 *The abstract interface object Requirement Collector is inherited by all other interface objects.*

To simplify Figure 8.9, we identified an abstract interface object Requirement Collector to represent the task of forwarding the information from the actors to the Product Orderer. The Requirement Collector is inherited by all other interface objects (Figure 8.10).

The reader might miss objects describing how a project is run. Such objects, however, form a generic set that will be described within the resource layer.

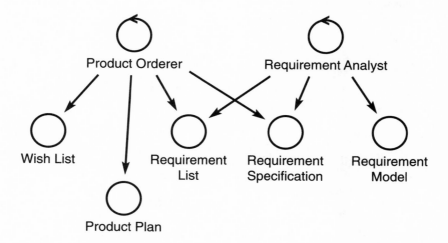

Figure 8.11 *Entity objects accessed when performing requirements capturing and requirement analysis.*

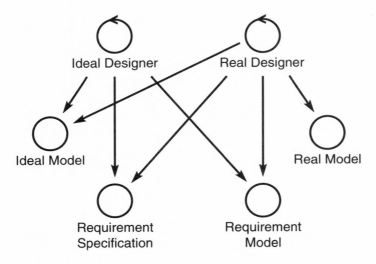

Figure 8.12 *Entity objects accessed when performing ideal design and real design.*

We made a new description of the use case Procure Objectory Tool, this time in terms of how the participating objects interact to perform the flow of events.

Description of the use case Procure Objectory Tool

Capture Requirements on our Products: information about what the market and our customers think about our product and how it should change is forwarded from the abstract interface object Requirement Collector to the object Product Orderer. The Product Orderer then stores the information in a Wish List. The Requirement Collector is inherited by all interface objects that interact with our actors.

Develop Product Plan: the basic flow of events for developing the Objectory tool is initiated once a year by the support layer. An instance of the Product Orderer object uses information gathered in the Wish List to develop new instances of Product Plan and Requirement List.

Develop Requirement Specification: an instance of Requirement Analyst is created. Its first task is to develop a Requirement Specification for the project.

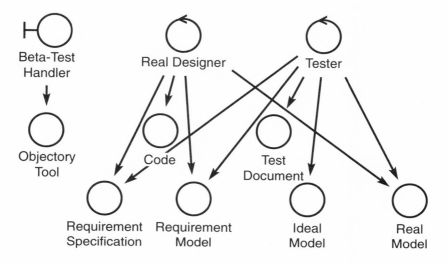

Figure 8.13 *Entity objects accessed when performing implementation, testing and beta testing.*

Requirement Analysis: according to the Project Plan, the Project Manager initiates and supervises Requirement Analysts to perform an analysis on the Requirement Specification. Output from this work is a Requirements Model. The Project Manager can now make a new version of the Project Plan.

Development: when requirement analysis has been performed, instances of Ideal Designers, Real Designers and Testers are initiated. They develop an Ideal Model, a Real Model, and Code and Test Documents, respectively. All control objects use the Requirement Specification and previously developed models as the basis for their work.

When a stable version of the system is available, a Beta-Test Handler is initiated, which interacts with a Beta User of the new Objectory Tool.

When all instances have approved the quality of the new version of the Objectory Tool, the development work is finished.

When you identify an object, you should at the same time write down a short description to clarify the purpose of it. All objects shown in Figures 8.9–8.13 are briefly described below.

Interface objects

Advertiser: handles direct advertising, such as advertisement campaigns in magazines or newspapers, and telemarketing.

Beta-Test Handler: represents the task of controlling beta-testing of the Objectory tool. Communicates with customers acting as beta-testers.

Exhibition Handler: responsible for the administration and execution of our participation in a conference. This task includes being responsible for the development of exhibition material.

Seller: responsible for handling sales contacts with specific customers.

Requirement Collector: an abstract object responsible for collecting comments on our products from all actors.

User-Group Handler: responsible for our contacts with the Objectory user-group.

Control objects

Real Designer: responsible for performing the work within the real design phase and the implementation phase of the development of a new release of the Objectory tool.

Market Communication Handler: has responsibility for the development and production of marketing material, such as brochures, business cards and other promotional items.

Market Plan Handler: develops a plan for how to proceed with the marketing activities.

Product Orderer: collects information about our product's position in the market and what our customers want to change. This information should be transformed to a product plan that shows how our product should change and develop.

Ideal Designer: responsible for performing the work within the ideal design phase of the development of a new release of the Objectory tool.

Requirement Analyst: responsible for performing the work within the requirement analysis phase of the development of a new release of the Objectory tool.

Sales Plan Handler: develops a plan for how to proceed with the sales activities.

Tester: responsible for performing the work within the testing phase of the development of a new release of the Objectory tool.

Entity objects

Code: represents a code unit.

Consultancy: represents expert consultancy that we sell to a customer. The knowledge should be sold in direct connection with the usage of our products.

Customer Object: information about one of our customers.

Deliverable: represents something that can be sold and delivered to a customer.

Ideal Model: an ideal-object model of the software system to be built. This model is developed during the ideal design phase of the software development work.

Market Research Data: information about the market.

Market Plan: a plan for how and when to perform certain marketing activities.

Mentoring: represents expert consultancy that we sell to a customer. The knowledge concerns the installation and usage of Objectory.

Objectory Tool: computer-based support tool for building models of a system.

Objectory Process Description: documentation of the Objectory process.

Order: represents an order from a specific customer.

Product Plan: represents a plan for how and when to develop our products.

Real Model: a real-object model of the software system to be built. This model is developed during the real design phase of the software development work.

Resource Object: information about our available resources, what competence they have and how they are scheduled.

Requirement List: a list of all requirements for our products. This list should be consistent and prioritized. The requirements should be described at a level of detail that makes it possible to give at least rough time estimations.

Requirement Model: a requirement model of the software system to be built.

Requirement Specification: a specification of all the requirements that are to be included when developing a new release of a product. The requirement specification consists of a subset of the items in the Requirement List, but further developed so that it can be used for project planning.

Sales Plan: a plan for how and when to perform sales activities.

Test Document: descriptions of how to test a new release of a product.

Training: represents a training package.

Wish List: an unprioritized list of all the different kinds of comments anyone has made about our products.

8.5.2 Description of objects

The level of detail chosen for your object model and for the object descriptions depends on how you have decided to use the model. Who is supposed to read and understand it? How is it going to be maintained?

We chose not to make any detailed descriptions of the objects we identified in the model. Some occurrences represented by objects have already been described, such as our products and deliverables, which correspond to entity objects in our model.

Why, then, did we not feel the need to describe our objects in terms of operations and attributes, as is suggested in Chapter 5? We found it was unnecessary for us to describe in detail the interaction between the objects – that is, what data was to be transferred and what specific actions were to be performed. It was enough to simply state the responsibilities that each object should have.

The work performed in describing an object is here illustrated by the Product Orderer object. This object takes part in the use cases Procure Objectory Tool and Procure Objectory Process. The responsibilities of the object in the model comprise the union of the responsibilities it has in both these use cases.

In order to visualize what the use cases expect the Product Orderer to be able to do, we produced interaction diagrams, one of which is reproduced in Figure 8.14, to depict the flow of events as it appears within the Procure Objectory Tool use case. The tasks the Product Orderer has in Procure Objectory Process are much the same.

The labelling on the stimuli-transmission arrows in the diagram is input to describing the object. The marginal text is very similar to that used for the description of the flow of the use cases in terms of their participating objects. This indicates that it might be wise to choose only one of the description types – either make a textual description of the flow of events in terms of objects or draw an interaction diagram. If a flow of events is quite simple (as is the one depicted in Figure 8.14), it might seem unnecessary to draw a diagram. On the other hand, if the flow of events is complicated, as in Figure 8.15, the more formal interaction diagram technique will help you to find all responsibilities and variants of flows that were missing in the less formal descriptions.

We made a view showing the Product Orderer, together with all of the objects with which it interacts (Figure 8.16). These are the objects that can send and/or receive stimuli to/from the Product Orderer. This kind of view could be called a local view of the Product Orderer.

Description of the control object Product Orderer

The Product Orderer is involved in the use cases Procure Objectory Tool and Procure Objectory Process. It captures all requirements on our products that come from all of our actors. All comments and requirements are categorized and put into a Wish List.

Initiated by the president, the Product Orderer develops a Product Plan that should encompass three years. The Wish List is used as the basis for this work. Another result of the work should be a Requirement List.

In the Product Plan, the Product Orderer defines when the next release of the Objectory Tool is to take place, and what requirements should be fulfilled.

The Product Orderer initiates the work with the next release of the product.

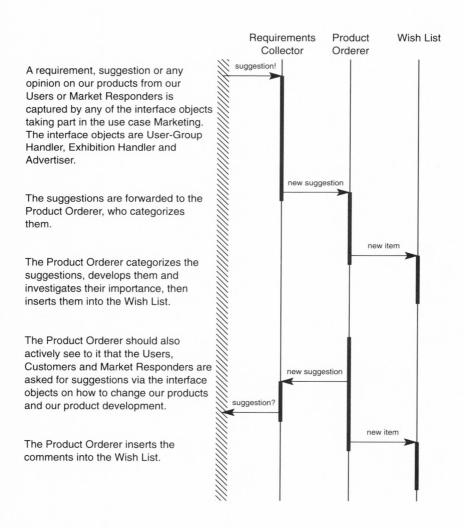

A requirement, suggestion or any opinion on our products from our Users or Market Responders is captured by any of the interface objects taking part in the use case Marketing. The interface objects are User-Group Handler, Exhibition Handler and Advertiser.

The suggestions are forwarded to the Product Orderer, who categorizes them.

The Product Orderer categorizes the suggestions, develops them and investigates their importance, then inserts them into the Wish List.

The Product Orderer should also actively see to it that the Users, Customers and Market Responders are asked for suggestions via the interface objects on how to change our products and our product development.

The Product Orderer inserts the comments into the Wish List.

Figure 8.14 *Requirements capturing within the use case Procure Objectory Tool.*

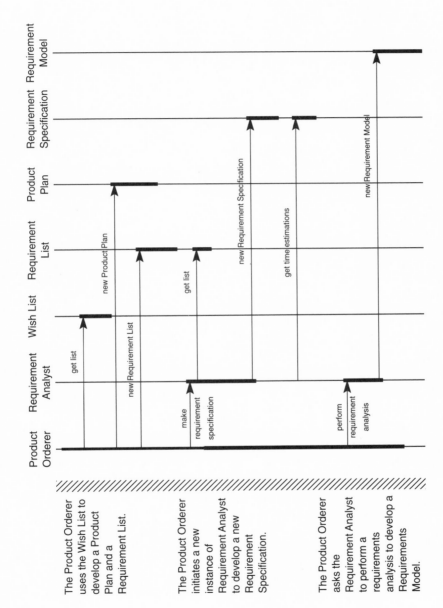

Figure 8.15 *Requirement analysis in the use case Procure Objectory Tool.*

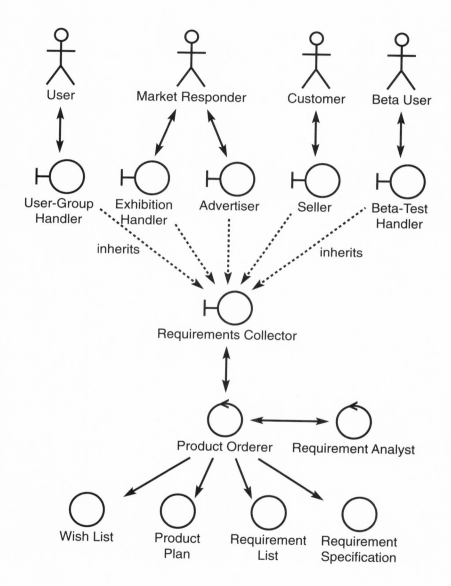

Figure 8.16 *A view showing the control object Product Orderer and all the objects with which it interacts.*

8.6 Work-flow descriptions

The object-oriented technique we propose helps a reengineering team to build consistent models of a new organization. But, just as a user of an information system needs a manual to understand how to use the system, the resources who work in a business need work-flow descriptions. The models you build of your business help those who work with reengineering or improvements of the organization. A person who works in the organization needs a description aimed at describing his/her day-to-day work procedures. Since people working at our company more or less live and breathe objects, such descriptions were not found to be necessary. This is, however, seldom the case.

We have chosen not to describe how work-flow descriptions should be written in this book; for information on this topic, see Johansson *et al.* (1993) and Harrington (1991). Producing such descriptions is not part of the modelling work, which is our main topic. It is, however, an important part of a reengineering project, in the same way as producing manuals is an important part of a software-development project.

8.7 Summary

We have developed models that describe the company Objectory AB in Sweden. The aim of the work was to turn ourselves into a process-managed organization.

The first thing we did was to develop a model of the existing business. We did not spend time on producing detailed descriptions at this stage; we only wanted to establish what responsibilities are held by the different parts of our company. You need a map of the organization you have to be able to discuss how you want to rebuild it. We produced the following documents to describe the existing organization:

- A block diagram to show the departments.

- A view of use cases and actors to show the processes we thought we had.

- A survey document, containing brief descriptions of each use case and actor.

We then identified use cases to represent the business processes we wanted to see in our new organization. The reengineering team consisted of the former management group, augmented with the authors of this book. The work was carried out as a series of interviews, where we (the authors) interviewed the rest of the reengineering team. We developed descriptions of the use cases to clarify what the actors expected each use case to do. The use-case model of the new organization was documented in:

- A view of use cases and actors.

- A survey document, containing brief descriptions of each use case and actor.

- A description of the flow of events of each use case.

To develop a more detailed understanding of how things are to be performed in our new organization, we produced an object model of the business. To achieve a better understanding of the responsibility of each object, we made new descriptions of the use cases, this time in terms of how objects interact to perform the flow of events. The object model of the new organization was documented in the following way:

- A view of participating objects for each use case.

- A description of each use case, in terms of how the participating objects interact.

- Interaction diagrams for some of the more complicated use cases, showing how the objects interact.

- A survey document, enumerating all objects and giving brief descriptions of them.

- A number of object views showing the static relations between the objects.

- For some of the objects, we produced description documents stating the responsibility of the object.

- For some objects, we drew diagrams showing the object itself and the other objects to which it had relations.

8.8 References

Harrington H.J. (1991). *Business Process Improvement*. New York: McGraw-Hill

Jacobson I., Christerson M., Jonsson P. and Övergaard G. (1992). *Object-Oriented Software Engineering — A Use Case Driven Approach*. Reading, MA: Addison-Wesley; New York: ACM Press

Johansson H.J., McHugh P., Pendlebury A.J., Wheeler III W.A. (1993). *Business Process Reengineering — Breakpoint Strategies for Market Dominance*. Chichester: John Wiley & Sons

chapter 9
Building the supporting information system

9.1 Introduction

Information technology (IT) is without doubt the most important enabler of business process reengineering. IT support has a decisive effect on how the business processes will operate. Used in the right way, IT support can make a business more effective, with dramatically improved results. The business processes will be affected and modified extensively. You should, therefore, envision what information systems you might use as early as possible. In that way you can see how it may affect your business processes.

But information technology alone is not enough. You need powerful technology to build the information systems: technology that can be used to support most – if not all – of your needs, including techniques for designing distributed systems, such as simple client–server applications or geographically distributed systems. You also need to build systems that are flexible and easy to change. Since the business will change continually, its information systems will also have to change. There is only one answer to this challenge: use object-oriented technology when building your information systems.

But object-oriented technology is no magic solution. Object-orientation should only be viewed as a basic technology (see Chapter 3), which must be extended with other techniques in a consistent manner to allow you to manage the complexity of real businesses. In this chapter we will introduce you to such a technique, called object-oriented software engineering (OOSE). What we present here, in Sections 9.2 and 9.3, is only an introduction to the subject; for a thorough description, see Jacobson *et al.* (1992).

Our technique for object-oriented business engineering is strongly coupled to object-oriented software engineering (OOSE). Apart from supporting their different usages, which of course is their most important task, they are both based on mature object-oriented techniques. The techniques are constructed so that, together, they support the work of reengineering a business. The use of object-oriented techniques in software engineering is increasing rapidly, because of its proven advantages compared to other techniques. Using the same type of technique for building both business-system models and information-system models makes it much easier to express the dependencies between the two.

How, then, can dependencies between models be expressed? We have chosen to use simple traceability relations between occurrences in the models. Given these traceability relations, it is easy to pass requirements from the business reengineering work over to the software development process. It will also help you to see how the new information system will affect the organization, which in turn will enable you to modify the original business processes. It is very important that you iterate between the business-system model and the information-system model at an early stage of the development; that is, before you go into too much detail in the descriptions of the two models. The different models will affect one another, which means that you will need to modify them. The more changes you find at an early stage, the cheaper it is to include them in the final result. To avoid misunderstandings, we have chosen to clearly spell out whether objects are in the business-system model of the information system. We hope that this does not make the text too cumbersome.

9.2 What is software development?

Software development is a business process in a corporation that develops software. It will thus be represented by a use case in a business model of that company. Actors to this business-system use case are the customers of the organization. In most cases you will find different types of customers, and thus different actors (see Chapter 8 for more discussion of this topic). Here, however, we simplify this by treating all these different actors as one (Figure 9.1). Input to the business-system use case

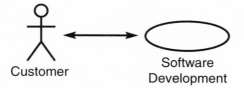

Customer

Software
Development

Figure 9.1 *Software development is a use case, interacting with the actor Customer.*

Software Development is requirements, or more accurately, changed requirements on the products produced. Output is a new version of the product(s), that is, a changed product.

Building information systems is a process of building different models that describe different aspects of an information system. Just as there are a number of handlers of the business (see Chapter 2), there are handlers of the information system. A handler may be an actor to the information system, but need not be. A handler is someone who is interested in understanding or proposing requirements of the information system. Since each one of them wants to see a different aspect of the system, we need to build different models to support that. Examples of handlers of an information system are depicted in Figure 9.2.

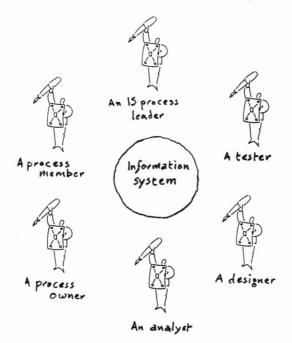

Figure 9.2 *Handlers of an information system.*

For each handler, models are built that describe the system (or business). Usually, each type of handler requires its own set of models. For the business system, some handlers are actors to it, like customers, and others are resources to it, like process owners and sales people. Typical handlers of an information system are its users, those who order it, process owners and those who develop it. As indicated in Figure 9.3, some people will act as handlers of both the business system and the information system. A person who is a member of a process in the business (a resource) will also be a user of the information system supporting the business (an actor). This is the reason why we argue that it is a great advantage if you can use the same technique when building models of your business as when you build models of your information system.

We now give a more detailed description of the handlers for which you are building your models, then we briefly describe the activities of software engineering resulting in those models, and what models are produced. In Section 9.3 we present a simplified business-object model of software development.

9.2.1 Handlers and models

The most important handlers of an information system are the orderers and users of it. As indicated in Figure 9.3, an orderer is, in this context, also an owner of a process in the business. Users of the information system are also process members in the business. When discussing the system with them, it is, in most cases, of no interest at all to discuss how the system is to be implemented. They are primarily interested in what the system will be able to do and how they can use it. For them, you will need to present different use scenarios of the system. These use scenarios can be represented by a use-case model of the information system. Actors to the information system are the different roles a process member/information system user can play.

Other handlers are the analysts. They want a model that helps to build a structure that is robust when faced with changed requirements. This model should not deal with details of the implementation. The important thing is to group functionalities in the system so that changes in the applications may occur without affecting the whole system. To meet these demands, we suggest that you build an ideal-object model of the information system; 'ideal' in the sense that it is independent of the implementation environment.

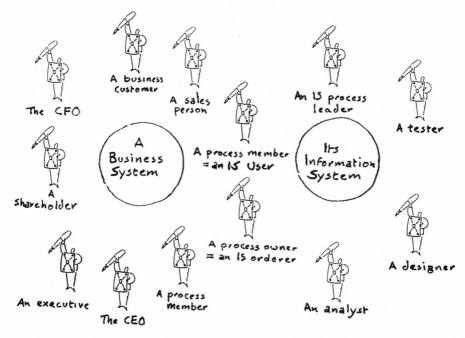

Figure 9.3 *Business systems and information systems have handlers in common.*

The designers of the system want models that can help them to express how to implement the system, solve different kinds of implementation problems and produce the code. When talking about object-oriented languages, code consists of classes only. It does not describe how these classes do something meaningful together. Therefore, designers need a description of how the classes should interact to realize the use cases. They want an abstraction of the code – a real-object model. The real-object model is also of help when you perform unit testing of the code. In the real-object model, you take the implementation environment (implementation language, capabilities, database handlers) and its problems and limitations into consideration. When the designers perform the actual implementation, they will produce the source code, which forms the implementation model of the system.

Lastly, we would like to mention the testers of the system. They want to see a model that expresses how they should proceed to test the information system, so that all requirements imposed on it are fulfilled. Their goal is to see to it that the users of the system can use it in the way they expect to. The use-case model of the information system will provide a basis for making specifications of the integration tests. Each possible instantiation of an information-system use case will correspond to one test case. These test case specifications form what we call a test model of the system.

9.2.2 Activities

Each of these models is developed and maintained by a number of business-system objects. Their task is to realize the software development process in the business-system model of the company. These business-system objects can be grouped into subsystems, where each subsystem corresponds to one of the models produced. Thus, we will have the subsystems Requirements Capturing, Requirements Analysis, Ideal Design, Real Design, Implementation and Testing (Figure 9.4). The business-system object model that we present in Section 9.3 is a simplified picture of software development. It does not include these subsystems, but introduces the object model directly.

How, then, should a description of the business-system use case Software Development look? This is something that is individual to each development organization. The final form of the description depends, among other things, on what type of information systems you are developing, what implementation language and techniques you are using, and how mature and large your development organization is. It is not even certain that you will choose to develop all of the information-system models suggested above; an ideal-object model, for example, is something that is often considered as optional.

We now describe briefly the activities that are performed to develop the information-system models needed by the handlers of the information system. The work steps to develop one model constitute a sub-flow of the total flow of events of the business-system use case Software Development. For comparison, see also the descriptions of the business-system use case Procure Objectory Tool in Chapter 8.

- *Requirements capturing*: here, you should collect all suggestions, ideas, requirements or demands your customers have on how your information systems should be developed and changed. An intermediate result of the work is a wish list, containing all of the information you can collect from your customers. This list is then further developed and the highest priority requirements are specified in detail to generate a list of requirements.

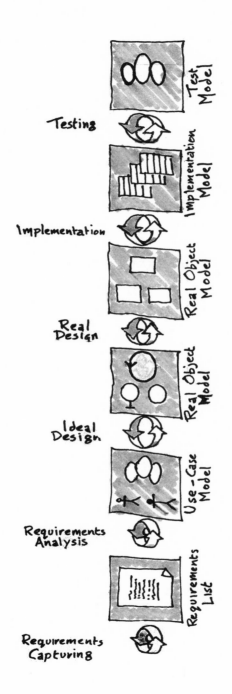

Figure 9.4 *The basic activities of Software Development.*

- *Requirements analysis*: the objective of this activity is to check that the requirements specification is consistent and that nothing is missing from it. The list of requirements is further developed to a requirements specification for the next release, then a use-case model of the information system is developed to validate the requirements. You will probably also develop a model, or prototype, of the graphical user interface at this stage. The result of this work is a use-case model of the information system, consisting of use cases, actors and descriptions of the user interface.

- *Ideal design*: find a structure for the information system that is robust when faced with changes. The result is an ideal-object model of the system.

- *Real design*: develop a model that can be used as a basis when implementing the information system. The result is a real-object model of the information system.

- *Implementation*: implement the information system – that is, produce the code.

- *Testing*: test that the information system fulfils all requirements placed on it. The result of this activity should be approved test cases.

Here, we only give a brief overview of OOSE; the explanations of the different concepts are only at an intuitive level. For a more thorough presentation, see Jacobson *et al.* (1992).

We have intentionally given corresponding concepts in business modelling and software modelling the same names. You will therefore recognize object types and association types, along with the way in which they are used. To separate business-system objects from objects in the information-system model, the latter are shaded in the figures.

9.2.3 The software development life cycle

All information systems will change during their life cycles. Changes constitute the main part of the total life-cycle cost of most systems. However, most existing development methods focus on new development, treating revision work only briefly. An industrial process should focus on system changes.

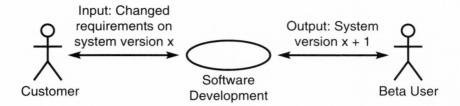

Figure 9.5 *All software development activities are performed for each new version. New development is only a special case – to develop version 1 of the system.*

It is a rule, rather than an exception, that the requirements of an information system are not fully known at the outset of the project. Knowledge of the system will grow as work progresses. When a first version of the information system is ready and in use within the business, new requirements will appear and old ones will change.

In some cases, it is probably best to develop the information system step by step, beginning with some of its highest ranked use cases. As better understanding of the system's role in the organization evolves, new use cases can be added. In this way, the information system is enlarged incrementally (see also Section 9.5).

An information system normally develops through the release of new versions of it. New development is, in that respect, only a special case – the first version of the system (Figure 9.5). Nevertheless, new development is a very important activity. Here, an architectural base must be established that can be expected to last for the whole lifetime of the information system.

When we describe this in business model terms, the orderer or customer of the business-system use case Software Development is a process owner within the business. The new version of the information system is delivered to a beta user, who is a carefully selected member of a process in the business.

A new version of the information system is a result of one pass through Software Development, but one specific change request need not affect all models of the information system. This implies that when you develop a new version of an information system, you need to go through all of the phases of software development, but one single change request does not necessarily require that you change all of the models. For example, a problem that often occurs is poor performance. To determine the reason why an information system is slow usually requires extensive analysis, but two common causes are inefficient code and inefficient user interfaces. Doing something about the first cause should only affect the real-object model and the implementation model of the information system, while the latter might in its worst case imply radical changes to all information system models.

9.2.4 The use-case model for an information system

In the use-case model, actors represent roles that users can play and use cases represent what the users should be able to do with the information system. Each information-system use case is a complete flow of events in the information system, as seen from the users' perspective. The symbols used to represent actors and use cases are shown in Figure 9.6.

Information-system use cases have two important roles:

(1)   They capture an information system's functional requirements. A use-case model defines a system through a set of use cases. The environment of the system is defined by describing the different actors. The actors then use the information system through a number of information-system use cases. A use-case model does not replace object models – one or more object models is developed to complement the description given by the use-case model. The use-case model is an external view of an information system; the object model is an internal view of the same information system.

(2)   They structure each object model into a manageable view. Although it is easy to build object models for 'toy' systems, object models for real information systems are unavoidably complex, as mentioned above. We have seen hundreds of examples of how object modelling can be applied to systems such as cruise control, conference management, home heating systems and so on. The problem with

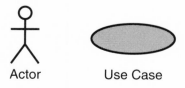

Figure 9.6 *The symbols used for the actors and use cases of an information system.*

all of these examples is that they do not reveal the complexity of real systems development such as applications for banking, insurance, defence and telecommunications. Methods that may seem to work well for simple applications do not necessarily scale up.

In order to manage the complexity of a real information system it is practical to present its object models as a number of different views. In our approach, one view is drawn for each information-system use case, and for each view we present only those objects that participate in that use case. A particular object may, of course, participate in several use cases. This means that a complete object model is seen through a set of object model views – one for each information-system use case. We can now find all of the responsibilities (Wirfs-Brock, 1990) of an object by looking through all use cases where this object has a role. Every role of an object means a responsibility for it. The total responsibility of an object is obtained by integrating all of its responsibilities.

The use-case model will govern the work with all of the other models. This model is central throughout the whole system development. It will be structured by the ideal-object model, realized by the real-object model, implemented by the code and used as a basis when developing test documents. The information-system use-case model also functions as a basis when writing operational instructions and manuals. Everything that the information system should be able to do is described here, from the user's perspective.

9.2.5 The ideal-object model for an information system

In this model, we use three different types of objects: interface objects, entity objects and control objects (Figure 9.7).

Interface objects handle communication between the information system and its surroundings. This involves transforming and translating

| Interface | Control | Entity |
| Object | Object | Object |

Figure 9.7 *The object types in the ideal-object model of an information system.*

events and (re)presentation from the system's internal representation to those of its surroundings, and vice versa. These information-system objects constitute the presentation-dependent part of the information system, whereas control and entity objects are surroundings-independent. Common interface objects are windows, communication protocols, sensors and printer interfaces.

Entity objects are in general long-lived occurrences in the information system, which means they live longer than the use-case instances in which they participate. They are used to represent attributes, associations and behaviour related to some occurrence, event or person. It is important to note that entity objects can have behaviour as complicated as that of other types of information-system objects. Entity objects often represent things that are dealt with in many of the information-system use cases. The value of their attributes is often entered by a user in a dialogue with an information-system use case. An entity object may also be needed for the internal tasks of the system. If business-system entity objects are handled by the information systems, they will be represented by business-system entity objects in the model of the information system.

Control objects are used to package use-case specific behaviour. Control objects often control other objects, thus they have behaviour of a coordinating kind. A control object offers behaviour that does not naturally belong to an entity or interface object. The behaviour is surroundings-independent because it should not be sensitive to how the surroundings communicate with the system, regardless of whether this occurs via electric signals, processor stops, keyboards, menu selections or procedure calls.

The reason for having three object types is that it gives a structure that is more adaptable to changes. The basic assumption is that all information systems will change. If you have a stable system, changes will be local. They will affect (preferably) only one information-system object. What kinds of changes, then, are common in an information system? Most common are changes with respect to user interface and functionality. Changes in the interface of the system affect only information-system interface objects. Changes in the flow of events of a use case affect information-system control objects. Changes of the entity objects in the business object model will affect entity objects in the model of the information system. Since the latter type of change occurs more rarely than the others, information-system entity objects are relatively stable.

9.2.6 The real-object model for an information system

In the real-object model, we have only one object type: the real object (Figure 9.8).

In the first outline of the real-object model, each real object will correspond to exactly one object in the ideal-object model. As you work with the real-object model, you might decide to split some real objects or add others. In the implementation, a real object will correspond to one or several classes. It is preferable for one of the classes to be public to classes realizing other real objects, and the others to be private. The public class is, among other things, the real object's interface to the world, while the other classes give the real object a sound implementation. The private classes show how you handle, for example, distributed architecture or persistent data to be stored in a relational database. Exactly what form the relationship should take between the objects in the real object model and the 'objects' in the implementation depends on what implementation language you are working with. Before you start working with the real-object model, you should decide how you want the relationship to look.

By interacting with one another, the real objects make it possible to perform the use cases in the information system. Each real object plays one or more roles in at least one of the information-system use cases.

What is considered to be a good real object very much depends on the implementation environment. The size of the individual real objects, for example, depends on what is generally accepted to be good style in the programming language in question. For example, what is considered to be right when using Ada might be wrong when using Smalltalk. Since the real objects should be mapped onto a particular construct in the language, you should structure them so that mapping results in 'good' code.

Even though the peculiarities of the implementation language influence the real-object model of the information system, it is important that you keep the object structure understandable and easily modifiable. You should design as if you had objects and encapsulation, even if the

Real Object

Figure 9.8 *The symbol for a real object in a model of an information system.*

implementation language in question (as, for example, COBOL) does not provide any support for this.

To manage the information system more abstractly, we use subsystems, which group several information-system objects together into a package according to some packaging criteria. They may be used in both the ideal-object model and the real-object model. Subsystems may include other subsystems; the construct is recursive. Thus, you may have a hierarchical structure for your information system, which is a means of managing complexity. The highest level in the hierarchy is the information system itself. The information system defines the borders of the application you are working with.

9.2.7 The implementation model for an information system

The implementation model consists of the annotated source code. The information space is the one that the programming language uses. We do not require an object-oriented programming language. All programming languages enable you to work with an object-oriented modelling technique, but an object-oriented programming language supports it. Using our modelling technique will enable you to obtain an object-oriented structure for your information system. An object-oriented programming language has the advantage of making it easier to map fundamental constructs in your model to language constructs.

9.2.8 The test model for an information system

The test model is the last model produced during software development. Simply stated, it describes the specifications and the results of the testing. Thus, the fundamental concepts in testing are the test specifications and the test result.

A test – like a use case – may be viewed as an object. By doing this, you can view the test specification as the test's class, and thus you can also inherit common parts or compose them from several test specifications. A test execution is, in this way, an instance of a test specification. The instance, quite clearly, has behaviour and also state. The outcome of a test execution is a test result.

9.3 The software-development business-system objects

The ideal business-system objects that participate in Software Development are depicted in Figure 9.9. What we show is a strongly simplified view. In reality there will be, for example, one business-system object to handle the whole information-system use-case model, and one business-system object to handle each individual information-system use case. A complete business-system object model for the basic software development process would consist of hundreds of object types. Of these, approximately 30% on average are interface and control objects; the rest are entity objects.

The Requirements Collector is an abstract business-system interface object. It is inherited by all interface objects in the business-system model that interact with any kind of customer to the business (compare also the object model presented in Chapter 8). The Beta-Test Handler interacts with the actor Beta User, which represents the most strategic users of the developed product. You can say that the Beta Users take part in the development work.

9.3.1 Requirements capturing

The purpose of requirements capturing is to capture a good picture of what requirements are imposed on the information system, built on what

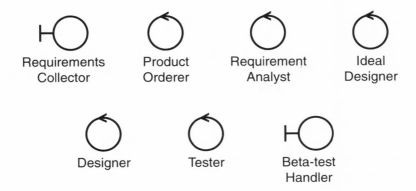

Figure 9.9 *The business-system interface and control objects participating in the business-system use case Software Development.*

customers want and what you yourself can accomplish. This knowledge should be used to identify the most important requirements, and to estimate roughly how much time would be needed to implement them. Thus, the result of the work performed here is a list of requirements.

A business-system model helps you find the functional requirements on the information system. You also need to find requirements of the more implementation-specific kind, like for example what hardware to use, what database handler to use, and so on.

Example

We have realized that we need to construct a system for handling automated-teller machines (ATMs) in our bank. Our customers want a system that enables them to:

- withdraw cash,

- transfer cash from one account to another,

- see the balance of an account,

- deposit funds.

This example should not be taken as an example of a requirements specification. Such a specification would probably consist of many pages, which we do not wish to bore our readers with. The requirements listed above are enough for you to understand what kind of system we are using in the example.

In the descriptions presented here, we have chosen to talk about the business-system objects in singular form. In reality, some of the classes will have several instances active in parallel.

The business-system objects that realize these activities are depicted in Figure 9.10. The interface object Requirements Collector is an abstract object that is inherited by all of the interface objects in the business-system model that interact with customers of the company. This means that every such interface object takes part in Software Development. All information collected by these business-system objects must be processed, which is done by the business-system control object Product Orderer. All suggestions from customers are stored in a Wish List. From

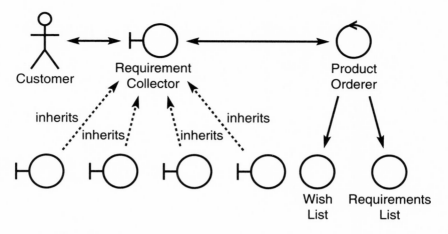

Figure 9.10 *Business objects taking part in requirements capturing. Unless otherwise stated, arrows indicate communication.*

this, a Requirements List is developed by the Product Orderer. This list contains requirements that have been prioritized, together with rough time estimates.

9.3.2 Requirements analysis

The purpose of requirements analysis is to delimit the information system and define the functionality that it should offer. The use-case model of the information system could function as a contract between the developer and the orderer of the information system.

If a business-system model exists, the work of developing a use-case model of the supporting information system can be performed in a straightforward way proceeding from the object model of the business to be supported (see Section 9.4). If no business-system model exists, you may find the use-case model through visualizing the information system to potential users of the system.

The use-case model of an information-system consists of use cases, actors and associated user-interface descriptions. Often, you first develop sketches of the user interface together with the users. Then, when both your and the user's knowledge about the information system has matured, you may build prototypes.

A prototype can serve as a means of communication between the developer and the prospective user. A written specification can never capture the dynamics of the information system in the same way as a

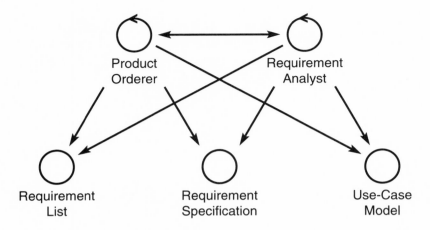

Figure 9.11 *The business-system objects participating in requirements analysis.*

working prototype. Prototyping differs from incremental development in that the aim is not to create a product, but to capture requirements and demonstrate certain properties of the intended information system.

Business-system objects taking part in requirements analysis are the Product Orderer, the Requirement Analyst, the Requirements List, the Requirement Specification and the Use-Case Model (Figure 9.11). The Product Orderer is responsible for initiating development work according to the Requirement List.

The work procedure in requirements analysis is iterative, and can be described briefly as follows:

- The Product Orderer initiates the Requirement Analyst to develop a Requirement Specification. The Requirements List is used as the basis for this.

- The Requirement Analyst uses knowledge about what resources will be available for the next development effort, together with the prioritizations given in the Requirement List, to develop a Requirement Specification for the next release.

- The Requirement Analyst starts by defining potential actors to the information system. To understand the information system, you must know for whom it is being built.

- The Requirement Analysts prepare a glossary of terms representing concepts that will be used when you describe the information-system use cases in the Use-Case Model.

- The Requirement Analyst identifies information-system use cases, based on the actors' needs and the Requirements Specification. If necessary, structure the use-case model by using uses and extends associations between the information-system use cases.

- The Requirement Analyst describes the information-system use cases in detail. This is the most time-consuming part of requirements analysis.

- The user interfaces of the information system are described in detail.

Example

We identified two actors for the ATM system. The Bank Customer is the primary actor; it is for this actor that we build the system in the first place. The ATM must communicate with a central system to get information about accounts and customers. This system is represented by the actor Financial System. We identified four use cases in the ATM system: Cash Withdrawal, Transfer Funds, Get Balance Request and Deposit Funds (Figures 9.12 and 9.13).

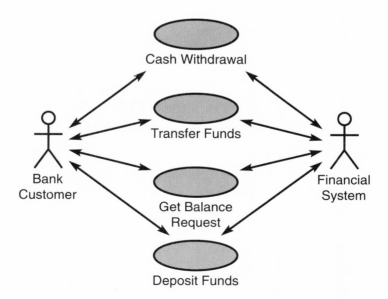

Figure 9.12 *A use-case model for the ATM system. Arrows indicate communication.*

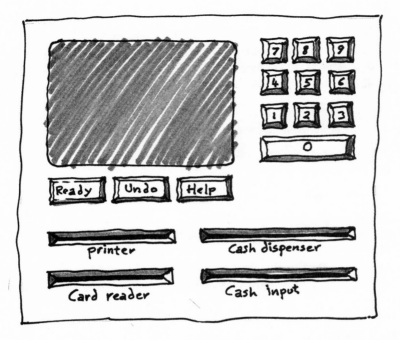

Figure 9.13 *A diagram to show the principle of the user interface of the ATM.*

Example
A description of the information-system use case Cash Withdrawal could look something like the following:

Initial Flow
Cash Withdrawal starts when the Bank Customer inserts a bank card. The system checks whether the card is valid or not. If the card is not valid, the use case terminates according to the Final Flow below.

Withdrawal
The system requests information about the account and the amount of money to be withdrawn from the Bank Customer. The system repeats this request until the given amount of money is a multiple of $20.

The system checks whether the requested amount of money is available in the ATM. If not, the use case terminates according to the Final Flow.

The system asks the Financial System whether there is enough money in the account in question. If not, the use case terminates according to the Final Flow.

If there is money, the system dispenses the cash and prints a receipt. The amount of money registered in the account is changed.

Final Flow
The ATM ejects the card; the use case is terminated.

9.3.3 Ideal design

The main purpose of ideal design is to show how the information system should be structured so that it will be easy to change if the functional requirements are changed. You will use the use-case model as a basis when building an ideal-object model of the system (Figure 9.14).

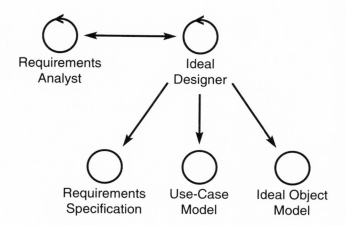

Figure 9.14 *The business-system objects that participate in ideal design.*

The sub-flow for ideal design can be briefly described as follows:

- When the Requirement Analyst has a first version of a Use-Case Model, the Ideal Designer is initiated. Input to the work is the Requirements Specification and the Use-Case Model.

- The Ideal Designer identifies information-system entity objects to represent things and occurrences that you can identify directly from the Use-Case Model.

- For each information-system use case, the Ideal Designer identifies objects needed to perform the flow of events of the use case. You should proceed from the actor initiating the use case when identifying objects. Thus, you will first find interface objects, then control objects. Additional entity objects will also be found.

- The Ideal Designer describes how each information-system use case is performed in terms of its participating information-system objects.

- Unify the object model by considering the model in its entirety. By unify, we mean, for example, that you must compare the information-system objects you have identified for the different information-system use cases in order to search for similar objects that should be merged. It also means working with the object model to ensure that it is made clear and logical and contains no inconsistencies. A simple rule is that there should be no synonyms and no homonyms among the object names.

- For each information-system object, find all information-system use cases in which the object has a role. The Ideal Designer integrates these roles to find all responsibilities of the object. The Ideal Designer then describes these responsibilities.

Example

For the information-system use case Cash Withdrawal we identified participating objects as shown in Figure 9.15. We also established communication associations between the objects to indicate how they interact to perform the use case.

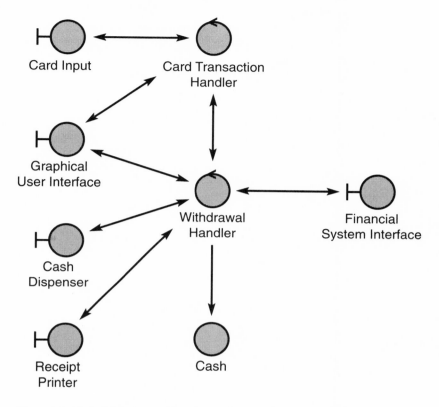

Figure 9.15 *Information-system objects that participate in the information-system use case Cash Withdrawal.*

Example

A description of how the information-system use case Cash Withdrawal is performed expressed in terms of the information-system objects that participate:

Initial Flow

The use case starts when an instance of Card Input notices that a bank card has been inserted. Card Input sends the identity and the code of the card to the Card Transaction Handler, which checks whether the card is valid.

If the card is not valid, the Graphical User Interface is notified so that it can give a message to the actor. The session is then ended according to the Final Flow.

If the card is valid, the Graphical User Interface is asked to request the actor to type in his/her PIN. When this has been done, the Card Transaction Handler reads the code and compares it with the code it received when the card was inserted. This is repeated until the code is correct. If repeated more than three times, the ATM will keep the bank card and terminate the session according to the Final Flow.

The Card Transaction Handler asks the Graphical User Interface to present a list of options to the actor. Card Transaction Handler gets the customer's choice in return.

Withdrawal

If the actor's choice is withdrawal, the Card Transaction Handler initiates the Withdrawal Handler, which starts by checking whether there is any Cash in the ATM.

If no Cash is available, the use case is terminated according to the Final Flow.

The Withdrawal Handler asks the Graphical User Interface to display information about withdrawal to the actor. The actor is requested to enter the account number and the amount of money to be drawn from the account. This information is returned to the Withdrawal Handler. This section is repeated until the amount of money is a multiple of $20.

If the amount of money requested is more than the amount available according to the Cash object, the use case is terminated according to the Final Flow.

The Withdrawal Handler requests the bank, via the Financial System Interface, to approve the withdrawal.

If the bank cannot approve the withdrawal, the Graphical User Interface is asked to display information about this to the actor.

If the withdrawal is approved, cash is dispensed via the Cash Dispenser object. The Cash object is updated. The Receipt Printer object is then asked to print out a receipt for the actor.

Final Flow

The bank card is ejected by the Card Input object; the use case is then terminated.

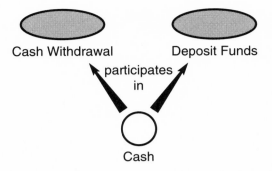

Figure 9.16 *The Cash object participates in two use cases.*

Example

The Cash object participates in the information-system use cases Cash Withdrawal and Deposit Funds (Figure 9.16). Its responsibility is to know how much money there is in the ATM. Other information-system objects can ask it to add or subtract an amount of money. If asked, it can inform other objects about how much money there is at the moment.

9.3.4 Real design

The main purpose of real design is to show how to realize the Use-Case Model in an effective way, given a certain implementation environment. It should perform, in that environment, the tasks and functions specified in the use-case descriptions written when the ideal-object model was developed. These descriptions, along with descriptions of the ideal-object model and a specification of the implementation environment, are used as the basis for real design of the information system (Figure 9.17).

The following is a brief summary of the work performed during real design:

- When the Ideal Designer has produced an Ideal-Object Model of the information system, the Real Designer may use it as a basis for developing a Real-Object Model. Other input to real design comes from the Requirements Specification and the Requirement Model.

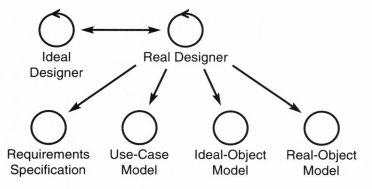

Figure 9.17 *The business-system objects that participate in real design.*

- The Real Designer starts by adapting the model to the implementation environment. If, for example, you intend to use an implementation language that does not include inheritance, you cannot use inheritance in your real-object model — you will have to find an alternative way of realizing it. You also have to decide how to incorporate things like databases and other existing software.

- The Real Designer distributes behaviour to real objects by developing interaction diagrams for each use case. This activity is known as use-case design, since you describe the use cases in terms of how the real objects interact to perform them.

- The Real Designer studies the interaction diagrams to identify operations and attributes for each real object.

Example

An example of when you need to adapt your ideal design to become a real design is if you use a relational database. When building your real-object model, you will realize that all real objects representing things that are stored in the database need operations describing how the data is accessed in the database. Thus, you need to define operations like 'create', 'modify' and 'delete'. It is wise to identify an abstract real object containing these operations. This real object can then be inherited by all other real objects that need the functionality (Figure 9.18).

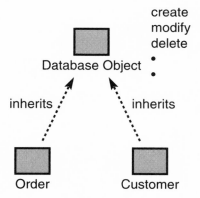

Figure 9.18 *To handle a relational database, you need to identify some extra objects in the real-object model, as compared to the ideal-object model.*

Example

To distribute behaviour over objects participating in the information-system use case Cash Withdrawal, we made interactions diagrams. To simplify the diagrams, we chose to make one diagram for each sub-flow (Figure 9.19).

Example

From the way in which the block Cash participates in the information-system use cases Cash Withdrawal and Deposit Funds, we find that we need to identify the following attributes and operations for the real object:

Attributes
Name: sum
Type: Integer
Brief Description: Holds current amount of cash in the machine.

Operations
Name: getSum
Parameters: OUT:currentSum
Brief Description: Gives current amount of cash in the machine.

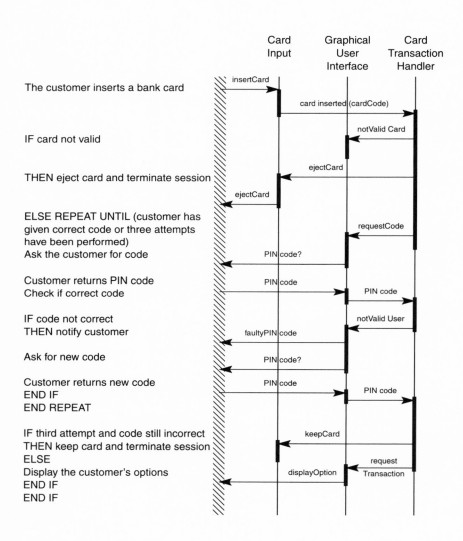

Figure 9.19 *Interaction diagram for the Initial Flow part of the information-system use case Withdrawal.*

Name: addSum
Parameters: IN:deltaSum
Brief Description: Increase current amount of cash with amount given as input.

Name: subtractSum
Parameters: IN: deltaSum
Brief Description: Decrease current amount of cash with amount given as input.

9.3.5 Implementation

The basis for implementation is the real-object model, in which you described the interfaces between the real objects and the behaviour expected behind the interfaces (Figure 9.20).

As we stated earlier, it is desirable to have an easy match between a real object and its implementation in the form of classes. If you have a very smooth implementation environment, typically an object-oriented one, this is easy to achieve. The real world, however, is not always cooperative in this respect. For example, object-oriented database handlers cannot always be regarded as suitable alternatives to relational database handlers. Therefore, you might want to know how to incorporate a relational database in an object-oriented design.

The ability to use components and whole frameworks is a very powerful implementation tool. Components are fully implemented parts

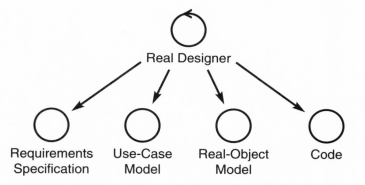

Figure 9.20 *The business-system objects participating in implementation.*

which enable you to build the information system using parts of a higher level of abstraction than the programming language can offer. Components can be regarded as ready-made building elements that are already placed in the implementation space, and that can be used directly in your real design. A framework is a subsystem designed to be reused and extended. Seen from the outside, a framework should look like a component or a pool of components. A framework imposes a style of collaboration between the components. Examples of frameworks are class libraries for graphical user interfaces, frameworks for implementing objects on relational databases, components for handling a distributed computer system and components for handling a particular communication protocol.

There are two main activities to be performed when implementing the real objects:

- Transforming the different real objects of the real-object model into code.

- Testing each implemented real object to verify that the specified behaviour and the internal structure are correct. You will test real objects; a process that is commonly called unit testing.

Implementation is always performed by the designer; in other words, the person who is responsible for the design of a real object will also implement it. This is why we have no Implementor object in this model. The Real Designer uses primarily the Real-Object Model, but also the Requirements Specification and the Use-Case Model, as a basis for its work to produce Code.

9.3.6 Testing

By testing we mean verification, which involves checking whether the system agrees with the specification. Testing takes time, perhaps 30–50% of the development cost. This figure is, however, in general lower when adopting a mature object-oriented development process. In this case, a more reasonable cost is 25% of the total development cost. Testing is a large part of the work and must be planned in the same way as other development activities.

In most software development projects, the typical situation is for testing to occur at the end of the project. However, most people agree

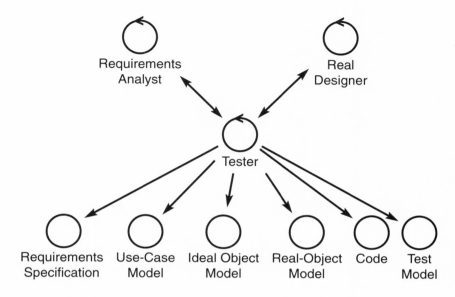

Figure 9.21 *The business-system objects participating in testing.*

that if you want to obtain high quality code, you need to assure high quality all the way through the development work.

The Tester develops Test Documents, using the use cases in the Use-Case Model as a basis. What the Tester tests is primarily the Code, but it needs access to all of the models of the information system that have been built. It has to be determined whether a fault originates from the real design work, the ideal design work, or even as early as the requirements analysis work. During its work, the Tester will communicate with the Requirements Analyst, and with the Real Designer (Figure 9.21).

9.3.7 Beta testing

A product cannot be considered ready until you have seen that 'real' customers are satisfied with it. To avoid unpleasant surprises, a product should be used by a carefully selected set of customers before it is released. The difference between this and ordinary testing is that the whole product is tested – that is, not only the information system but also a complete set of manuals. This way of ensuring the quality of the product is commonly called beta-testing.

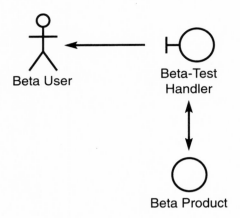

Figure 9.22 *The business-system objects participating in beta-testing.*

A mature software development process should guarantee that all requirements on the information system have been fulfilled. However, since it is imperfect human beings and not perfect machines that have developed the system, you need to validate and verify that you have produced the right product.

The Beta-Test Handler produces a beta-release of the product, that is, a Beta Product (Figure 9.22). The Beta Product consists of executable code and a complete set of manuals. The Beta-Test Handler delivers the Beta Product to the Beta Customer, and is then responsible for taking care of all comments the Beta User might make about the product. If you have worked according to a mature software development method and followed it correctly, you should have taken care of all requirements properly and have built a system of good quality. No serious problems should occur during beta-test.

9.3.8 Software development in summary

We have presented a description of the business-system use case Software Development. The description is written in terms of how the most interesting business-system objects that participate in Software Development interact (Figure 9.23). The Requirement Collector collects all kinds of remarks our Customer might make about the product. The

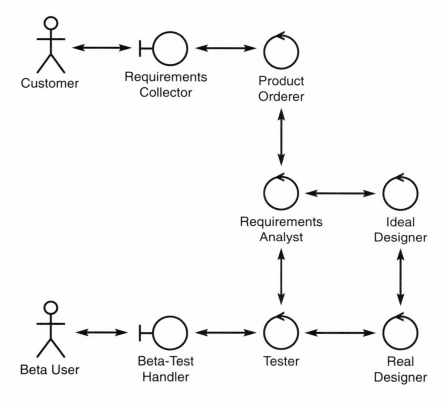

Figure 9.23 *All active business-system objects taking part in the business-system use case Software Development.*

Product Orderer analyses the remarks, lists the requirements that can be prioritized and gives rough time estimates. The Requirements Analyst details the requirements for the next release of the product and builds a use-case model of it. The Ideal Designer builds an ideal structure of the system, from which the Real Designer can build a real-object model. This model, in turn, can be used as a basis for implementation, then the Tester verifies the system. Finally, the Beta-Test Handler releases the product to Beta-Customers to verify that it fulfils all requirements and works as expected, and to get feedback from the Beta Users.

A goal when developing a new (version of a) product is that it should fulfil the needs and requirements of customers. This is the reason why it is important to let the customer take part in the development, not only as a source of requirements but also as a verifier of the complete product.

9.4 System development and business development

Let us briefly recapitulate what a business-system model is and what its different components represent. In a business system, the use-case model represents an outside view of the business processes in the company. The object models are more or less abstract views of the same company. The object model also shows how the use cases are performed by interacting objects.

An object may participate in several use cases; it plays a role in each of them. The total responsibility that the object must fulfil in the system is represented by the union of all of these roles. One instance of an object can participate in several use-case instances. This is how the use cases influence each other, but it also means that there are potential conflicts; it must be possible to eliminate these.

To understand how these conflicts can be eliminated, you need to investigate how the resources in your business will realize the object model. We have chosen to describe this as if the business system was structured in two layers: the business layer, where you find the business-system model, and the resource layer, where you find descriptions of how the resources realize the business-system model (Figure 9.24).

9.4.1 How is the business-system model realized by its resources?

In the object model of the business, there are three types of objects: interface objects, control objects and entity objects. Each of these captures a different type of occurrence in the business.

Business-system and control objects represent activities that should be performed by human resources, who may use different kinds of tools to help them. When identifying this kind of object, you should look for tasks that:

- one person can manage and enjoy. There should not be too much routine work; there must be a reasonable amount of challenge.

- logically belong together. They are best realized by one and the same kind of resource. For example, there are tasks that are best performed by someone who has sales competence.

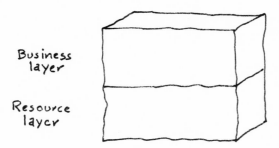

Figure 9.24 *The description of an organization is structured in two layers: the business layer and the resource layer.*

- should be performed by the same instance of a resource type. For example, it is appropriate to allow the same instance of a resource to be responsible for submitting an offer to a customer, ordering products for the customer, and following up to ensure that the customer receives what has been ordered and is satisfied.

Business-system entity objects represent things in the business. They can be implemented in many different ways. They may be physical things such as a car or a document, or abstract, such as knowledge about something.

The business-system model is thus implemented by the resources of the company. These resources are either human or inanimate (Figure 9.25).

Another way of putting it is to say that the business-system model has two layers: the business layer and the resource layer. In the resource layer you show how the people working in the organization interact and use information systems to perform the activities described in the business-system use cases.

In the resource layer, you will find different types of human resources, such as seller, designer, and developer. You will also find all technical support, such as information systems (Figure 9.26).

What kind of relationship is there between objects in the business layer and those in the resource layer? We could show that every object in the business layer consists of a number of objects from the resource layer – that is, there is a consists-of relation between objects in the two layers. This has, however, not turned out to be fruitful, because it is not important to connect the objects and show how they are structured. What is interesting to see is how objects in the resource layer cooperate to realize objects in the business layer. We have therefore chosen to use traceability relations to describe how business-system objects are

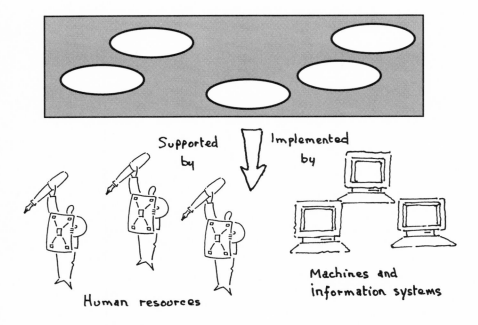

Figure 9.25 *A business is realized by its resources, both human resources and information systems.*

supported by use cases and objects in the resource layer. Thus, in an outside view of the information system you can describe how the business-system objects are supported by information-system use cases. This relation is less precise then a consists-of relation, but on the other hand it is more flexible and therefore also more powerful. A strict consists-of relation is limited in the sense that you can only express consists-of relations. It also implies that you should show *all* consists-of relations. A traceability relation only shows that there is a relation from one occurrence to another; there are no other implications as to what the

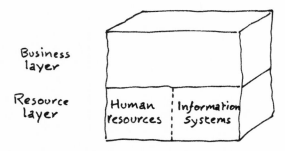

Figure 9.26 *Business layer and resource layer.*

relation between them is. Since you have not defined what types of relation you show, you are also free to leave relations out.

9.4.2 An algorithm for finding information-system use cases from the business model

When identifying the information-system use cases, you proceed from interface objects and control objects in the business-system object model. If you have developed a real-object model of the business, use that as a starting point, otherwise use the ideal-object model. To simplify the text, in the following we use the concept 'active object' to represent both interface objects and control objects. Thus, active object may be seen as a superclass of interface object and control object. We also talk about 'the information system', although in reality, there may be several information systems in use in an organization. Our term refers to the union of these systems.

For each active business-system object, perform the following work steps:

- Decide if the active business-system objects in the business layer will be realized by a resource type that is going to use the information system.

- If so, identify an actor to the information system in the resource layer. Give the actor the same name as the active business-system object.

- If the active business-system object has a responsibility that involves the use of information systems, identify an information-system use case in the resource layer for it. Give the information-system use case a name that reflects the identity of the responsibility it supports.

- If the responsibility is fragmented, you may identify several information-system use cases for it. By fragmented, we mean that the responsibility encompasses many different kinds of activities that are performed at different points in time and have no direct causal connection.

- Take a look at the names you have given your information-system use cases and actor in the resource layer. Ensure that they are meaningful in the context of the layered system, and also in the use-case model of the information system.

- Repeat these work steps for all active business-system objects in the business layer.

An entity object in the business layer will correspond to an entity object in the ideal-object model of the information system. In some cases, though, it might be suitable to let attributes in the business-system model correspond to entity objects in the information-system model as well. Entity objects in the business layer do not have any correspondence in the use-case model of the information system. An entity object in the business model may be accessed by several active business-system objects. Consequently, the corresponding entity object(s) in the information-system model may participate in several information-system use cases.

Example

In the business model, the active business-system object X has a number of responsibilities, here named A, B and C. We therefore identify an actor, which we call X, and use cases, which we call A, B, and C, in the information system's use-case model. When performing the responsibility named C, the active object X in the business model accesses the entity object Y. In the ideal-object model of the information system, this corresponds to the entity object Y participating in the use case C (Figure 9.27).

How should you interpret a communication association between active objects in the business model? The objects are communicating with each other, and you need to find out how this communication can be supported by the information system. You might be able to release the business-system object from the responsibility for taking the initiative for communication, if the communication can be performed automatically by an information system. Our belief, however, is that this is not a common case. It is more common for an information system to make it unnecessary to transport information between the business-system objects; the information is accessible in the information system.

What we have described so far is a systematic algorithm for finding an information-system model, using the object model of the business as the basis. This is, however, not enough: you cannot identify and detail a complete model of your information system using only a business object model as input. An object model of the business gives a far too abstract

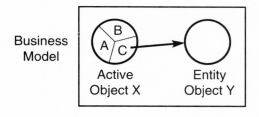

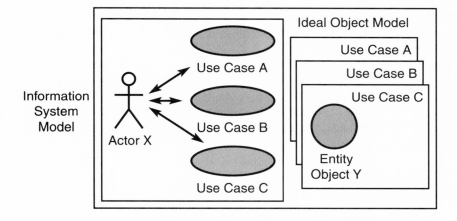

Figure 9.27 *Illustration of how objects in the business model correspond to actors, use cases and entity objects in the information-system model.*

view of how people in the organization want to use an information system. No algorithm in the world can help you to find a detailed description of how a human actor communicates with its information system, if you are using only a raw business-object model as a basis.

Building good user interfaces of information systems is a science in itself. Use-case modelling should be preceded by an envisioning activity, in which users participate to find the information-system use cases and the associated user interfaces. You may carry out the envisioning work as a series of workshops, in which user-interface designers are observers and users are the centre of interest. The users are observed in their workplace, they are interviewed and asked to describe in an episodic way different use scenarios; that is, use-case instances. As a means of achieving a better understanding of the users' needs, sketches of the user interface evolve and – when these have become stable and not before – prototypes can be developed. For more information about this see Jacobson (1994) and Constantine (1994).

9.4.3 An example

In a simplified business-system model of a bank, we find the actors Customer and Bank Information Bureau. The customer may initiate any of the use cases Loan, Manage Accounts and Invest (Figure 9.28). See also the descriptions of a bank business and its objects in Chapter 3.

In this simple model, there are three business-system use cases:

- The Loan use case represents what happens when a customer applies for a loan in the bank.

- The Invest use case shows how the bank can help a customer to invest money in a profitable way.

- The Manage Accounts use case shows how the bank can help a customer to manage his/her accounts in the bank, such as withdraw or deposit money.

The flow of events of the Loan use case is described in Chapter 3. There are two actors to this business-system use case, the Customer and

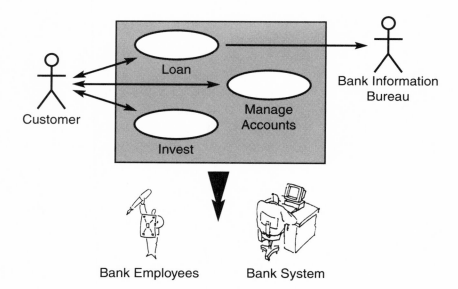

Figure 9.28 *The use cases in a bank are realized by Bank Employees and a Bank System.*

the Bank Information Bureau. You can identify two business-system interface objects: the Loan Handler and the Bank Information Bureau. The Loan Handler also holds the responsibility to control the flow of events of the business-system use case. What business-system entity objects can you find? First, you need to handle the Loan Application. Then you need to have information about what Loan Regulations there are. You also need to talk about things like Customers and Accounts in the bank (Figure 9.29). Note that the business-system entity object Customer is entirely different from the actor Customer. The business-system entity object Customer is needed since the business system we are building must hold knowledge about what customers are registered in the bank. To avoid confusion to the reader, we will explicitly state whether we are talking about the actor or the entity object.

The same type of reasoning leads you to identify the business-system interface object Investment Handler for the business-system use case Invest. There, you find the business-system entity objects Investment Plan, Market Knowledge, Customer and Account. You may also identify a business-system control object Market Analyst to represent the more long-term task of gathering Market Knowledge. For the business-system use case Manage Accounts, you find the business-system interface object Account Handler and the entity objects Saving Plan, Customer and Account.

However, many banks choose to implement a Loan Handler, an Investment Handler and an Account Handler with the same type of resource. We choose therefore to identify the business-system interface object Customer Handler to represent all three of these tasks (Figure 9.29).

Let us now take a look at what kind of information system you would need to support this business. To make it easier for the Market Analyst and the Customer Handler to keep consistent information and to perform their responsibilities, you may choose to include Market Knowledge, Customer and Account as entity objects in the information system. They represent data that is shared by several business-system objects. An information system should not only help you keep track of information, its most important task is to support you when performing the business processes. The system could, for example, help the Market Analyst to perform a market analysis by using already acquired Market Knowledge, and make investment calculations.

The requirements you have of your information system can be found by studying the business-system use cases and their participating

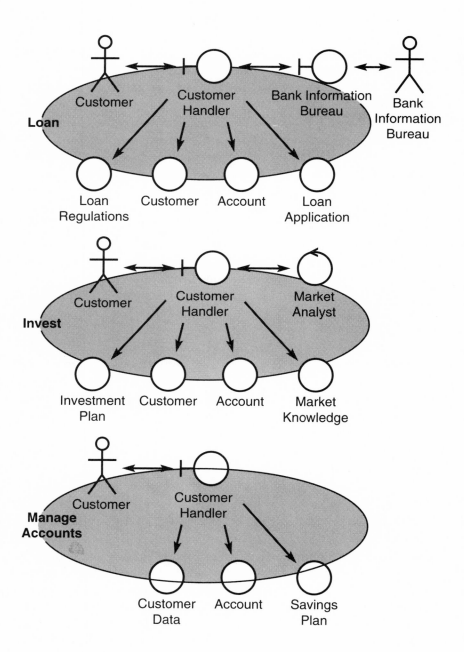

Figure 9.29 *Business-system objects participating in the business-system use cases Loan, Invest and Manage Accounts.*

objects one-by-one. The business-system interface object Customer Handler takes part in three business-system use cases, and therefore has at least three responsibilities to fulfil. To lend money out, the bank has to know how much money is requested, whether there is any security for the loan, and what capacity the customer has to pay back the loan. In other words, the bank needs to be able to set the risk for the loan in order to set the correct interest rate and to be able to ask for the right security guarantees. When money is to be invested, you have to be able to look at and analyze the different alternatives, such as stocks and bonds, and their associated risk levels. The analysis leads you to a suggested alternative with interest rates, expected revenue and so on. Therefore, the information-system actor Customer Handler and the two information system use cases Apply for Loan and Develop Investment Plan are identified. The business-system control object Market Analyst will lead us to identify the information-system actor Market Analyst and the information-system use case Analyze Market Knowledge.

Note that the complete views of participating objects also contain several other objects. We have only shown that the business-system entity object will, in this case, have corresponding information-system entity objects. Other objects will be found by working through the information-system use cases. Furthermore, note that we only show a small subset of the business-system objects, only one of the active objects of the business system is depicted. There will be correspondence relations between all business-system objects and objects in the information system as indicated in Figure 9.29.

The broken lines in Figure 9.30 represent traceability relations between occurrences in the business-system model and occurrences in the information-system model. The business-system interface object Customer Handler has two responsibilities, indicated by two different shades of grey. The responsibilities are each supported by a use case in the information system. In the use-case model of the information system, you will also find an actor that corresponds to Customer Handler. We have given the actor the same name as the business-system interface object. In the business-system model, the Customer Handler communicates with the business-system entity objects Account and Customer. They will both have corresponding entity objects in the model of the information system. Both of these information-system entity objects participate in the use cases Apply for Loan and Develop Investment Plan, and, therefore, you can see them in views of participating objects for the use cases in question.

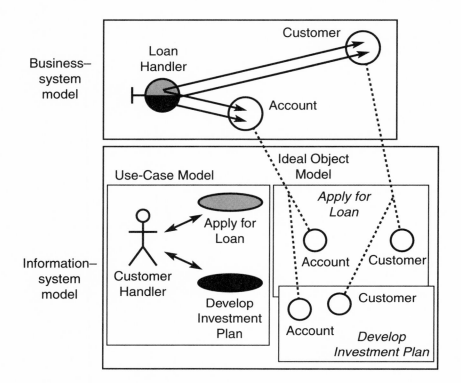

Figure 9.30 *The relationship between business-system models and information system models.*

What other kind of support does the Customer Handler need? When participating in the business-system use case Manage Accounts, the business system interface object needs to be able to control what money there is in a customer's accounts; that is, to withdraw cash from an account, transfer money between accounts, request balance on an account, deposit money on an account, and request market knowledge.

To fulfil the requirements you now have on the system, you could identify the additional information-system use cases Cash Withdrawal, Transfer Funds, Get Balance Request and Deposit Funds (Figure 9.31).

If you compare the use-case model for this Bank System with the one we developed for the ATM system above, you will find that they have use cases that from the bank customer's point of view have the same purpose. This is the result of the bank having two separate systems (the ATM and the Bank System) to serve the bank customer. The

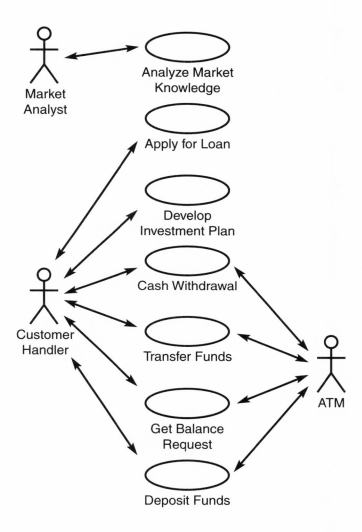

Figure 9.31 *The information-system use cases in the Bank System.*

functionality and implementation of the two systems are very different, though. The ATM communicates with the Bank System to manage accounts and customers, since it is the Bank System that is responsible for keeping this information. Thus, the Bank System is really an actor to the ATM, and vice versa. The bank customer can communicate directly with the ATM, while all communication with the Bank System goes via a bank clerk of some sort.

9.4.4 Iteration between models

The presentation we have given here implies that you first build your business-system model, and then your information-system models. This is, however, not quite true; it is a simplified view of reality. It is important to understand that the work must be done both iteratively and incrementally. This means that you will proceed step by step in your modelling work, and modify your models until you find something that can be agreed upon. Part of this work might be to build prototypes of the information system to avoid any major investment before you know what kind of system you want.

What we have described could be called a chain of models: business-system use-case model, business-system object model(s), information-system use-case model and information-system object model(s). As you develop your business and its information system, you will iterate between these models.

9.5 Procuring the new information-system support

What, then, is the best way of getting the right information-system support? We assume that you have developed a use-case model and an object model of your business. Using the business-system object model as a basis, you should develop a use-case model of the information system(s) needed. In this way, you will have a clear picture of the requirements you have on your information system.

Since all organizations are unique, you will not be able to purchase the perfect system 'off-the-shelf' and, thus, a conclusion would be that you need to develop everything yourself. But is this the right way to do it? Would it not, in some cases, be much more cost effective to purchase the information systems and adapt your new business processes instead?

You have to analyse your needs and costs and decide upon a combination of the following strategies:

- Buy 'off-the-shelf' support systems.

- Develop all support systems yourself.

- Reengineer and change existing systems.

If you decide to purchase your supporting information systems, you might, of course, have to adapt the use-case model of your information system to what you have decided to buy. A change in your information system's use-case model may eventually require a change in your business-system model. This may be acceptable if it helps you to achieve your business goals. Adaptation might also be necessary if you reengineer and change existing support systems.

A common opinion, often preached by BPR people, is that the best way of obtaining a new and well-functioning information system is to throw away the old system and install a completely new one. At first sight, this may be viewed as the most economical solution, but normally you get a much more stable and secure installation procedure if you keep the old system and change it step by step to meet the new requirements, rather than installing a new and unknown system. If reengineering and rebuilding the existing system cost twice or even ten times as much as installing a new one, it may still be more than worth it if the day-to-day work in the organization can proceed uninterrupted. For example, being able to continue using your existing database increases the reliability and availability of your new system. We will discuss more about what software reengineering involves in Section 9.5.1.

Another reason for not throwing the old information system away is that it takes a considerable effort to replace it, both in terms of man hours and money. In your existing organization, you have probably invested a lot in building information systems, an investment you should not just throw away. The only practical strategy is, therefore, to reengineer the existing information system, step by step. Here an important concept is the notion that the largest investment a company has made is not in its equipment and software, but in its data. Data is one of a company's most important assets.

The mere installation of IT support will not imply any revolutionary improvements to your business processes. To find the opportunities that the use of computers can provide, you should figure out the ways in which the use of IT support makes it possible to change how things are performed. As pointed out by Hammer and Champy (1993), the advantage of information technology is not primarily the fact that it helps you to perform things faster, but that it makes it possible for you to perform new things. They also say, as does Davenport (1993), that major business innovations can be achieved only if you proceed from technology and try to discover what opportunities it can give you.

To conclude, we would like to say that procurement in most cases means reengineering your old information system. You have made investments in your old information system that you should not throw away without strong cause. You should use your business-system models as a basis. But, if you really want to innovate, you should first try to find the opportunities that information technology can provide. Furthermore, to get a stable installation procedure, you should install your new information system step by step.

In the following sections we present some basic ideas and principles that are useful in the work of procuring the right IT support for your organization. You need to know how you can reengineer your old information system to meet the demands of the new business processes, how you can use information technology as an enabler of innovation, and what it means to install a system incrementally.

9.5.1 What is software reengineering?

Our approach to reengineering is that it is the process of creating an abstract model of the system to be reengineered, reasoning about the changes in that abstract model, then re-designing the system (Jacobson and Lindström, 1991). In most cases, it is not reasonable to replace the old information systems with completely new ones. You need to find a way of gradually replacing old parts with new (Figure 9.32). Furthermore, it might be possible to keep parts of the existing systems as they are, if you build new interfaces to them.

We divide the work performed when reengineering an information system into the following steps:

- Create a rough picture of what is to be changed.

- Identify the information-system use cases that belong to or will be affected by the change.

- Build an ideal-object model for these use cases.

- Find traceabilities between the objects in the ideal-object model and design units in the existing code.

- Define an interface between the old and new parts of the system.

- Implement and incorporate the changes.

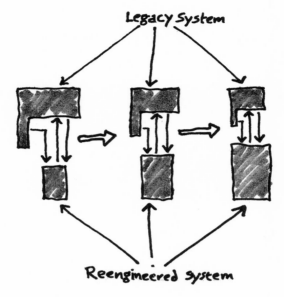

Figure 9.32 *The information system should be reengineered gradually.*

The first thing to do, then, is to see to it that you have a rough view of how you want to change your information systems (Figure 9.33). Input to this analysis comes from changes you want to make to your information-system use cases. This, in general, means changes in the functionality of the information system. There is another dimension of change – change in the implementation technique. This might be change from a centralized solution to a distributed one, or change to the graphical user interface. The implementation technique is often changed when the business is changed, but it might also be changed without change in the business processes.

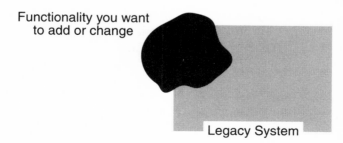

Figure 9.33 *Step 1 is to define roughly what functionality you want to add to or change in the old information system.*

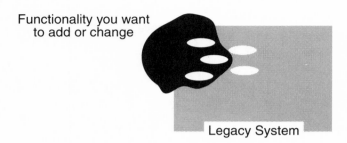

Functionality you want
to add or change

Legacy System

Figure 9.34 *Step 2 involves identifying use cases in the legacy system that belong to or will be affected by the change.*

Next, identify the information-system use cases in the old system that will be affected by the changes (Figure 9.34). This model is built using the existing documentation of your system as the basis: requirements specifications, user operation instructions, maintenance manuals, training manuals, test specifications and so on.

What this is all about is understanding the existing system. You cannot change something that you do not know anything about. Some people say reengineering can be automated. This is, however, not possible in more than minor parts of the total reengineering work. You can use simple tools to get a description of the code that is a little more abstract than the code itself. This has not been successful, unfortunately. Even though the descriptions obtained are abstractions, they are still very difficult to read and understand for people other than those who wrote the code in the first place. And these people would rather read the code anyway. What you need is an abstract description of what the legacy system is doing, not how it is doing it. Without doubt the best input to such work is the user manuals and/or test specifications. The test cases can help us to find the use cases of the information system; the user manuals help us to formulate descriptions of the use cases.

The next stage is to identify an ideal-object model that realizes the information-system use cases that belong to or will be affected by the change (Figure 9.35). During the preceding work step and this one, your view of the changes you want to make in your information system will become clearer. It will now be possible to define more accurately which parts of the old system you must replace, which new parts you must add and which parts you can keep as they are.

The models you have built so far still represent abstract views of the existing system. The next work step is to connect these models to existing implementation or design units (Figure 9.36). This means creating traceability relation items in your models and the design units. Input to

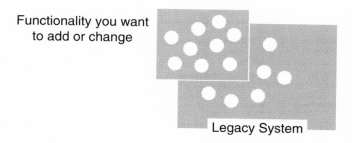

Functionality you want
to add or change

Legacy System

Figure 9.35 *Step 3 is to identify an ideal-object model. Your view of what must be changed will now become clearer.*

this work is, for example, documentation of the real design, source code files and database schema descriptions for the old system. This work cannot be performed without the help of people who know the code.

You now know enough about the old system to be able to identify the interface between the new system and the old, and to describe in more detail the interfaces between the parts you are to keep and the new parts of the system (Figure 9.37).

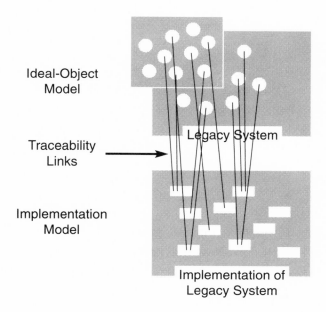

Ideal-Object
Model

Traceability
Links

Legacy System

Implementation
Model

Implementation of
Legacy System

Figure 9.36 *Step 4 involves creating traceability links between objects in the ideal-object model and design units in the implementation of the old information system.*

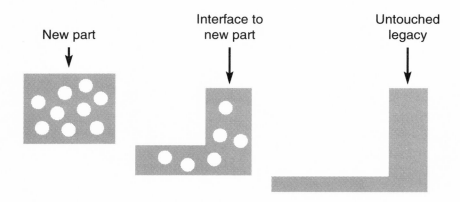

Figure 9.37 *Step 5 involves defining the interface between the old and new parts in the information system.*

You are now ready to implement the reengineered system. This means implementing the new object model and the interface, and introducing necessary changes to the existing system, all in parallel. This should encompass requirements analysis, ideal design and real design, as described in Section 9.3. The new information-system part is not necessarily tightly coupled to the old system by using the same software and hardware platform. It might be implemented using another implementation language, probably an object-oriented one. Legacy systems are often implemented using mainframes. You will now probably choose a simple distributed solution based on client–server architecture.

The interface we build between the legacy system and the new one must be able to translate between these techniques. It should let the new object-oriented system see the old one in terms of objects, but also let the old part see the new as if it were implemented using the old technique (Figures 9.38 and 9.39).

We have here described a general approach to reengineering. Reengineering of information systems is a consequence of reengineered business processes. What needs to be changed is primarily the parts that correspond to interface and control objects in an ideal-object model of the legacy system. The entity objects are more stable. They correspond to data elements (for example, data types or records) and program elements (parts of procedures or subroutines) that manipulate these data elements.

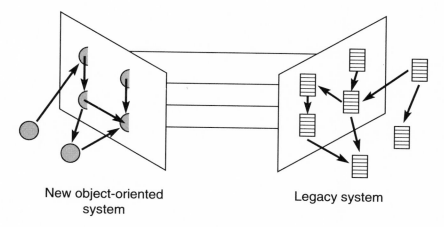

New object-oriented   Legacy system
system

Figure 9.38 *The interface between a new object-oriented system and a legacy system.*

Therefore, as a first attempt at reengineering the legacy system to make it support the new business, you should keep the data model you already have intact and make only necessary changes. Unless your legacy system is in a very bad shape, these changes should not require you to throw away all that you have. Normally, you should be able to keep most of your existing data model and consequently most of your valuable existing data. Instead, you should turn your interest to the interface objects and the control objects in your ideal-object model of

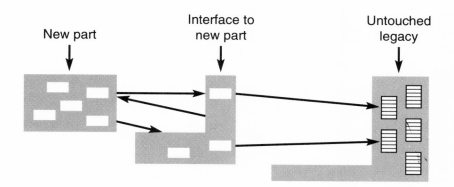

Figure 9.39 *Step 6 involves building and integrating the new part of the information system. The arrows indicate communication. The three parts — the old system, the new, and the interface between them — are developed, integrated and tested in parallel.*

the legacy system. This is probably where you must make most of the changes to adapt your information system to the new business, and it is here that you first reengineer your old software.

Later, the entity objects in the ideal-object model of the legacy system will be implemented as real objects – as classes in, for example, Smalltalk or C++. The classes can hide the implementation of persistent data, as described in Jacobson *et al.* (1992). Your data model can still be implemented on top of your existing database management system. Eventually, you might reengineer the database management system, too – that is, change it to a relational or an object-oriented database management system. This latter work should, however, be performed as a reengineering project of its own.

9.5.2 Information technology as a process innovation enabler

The work flow indicated in Section 9.5.1 does not, however, have the innovative touch we are also looking for. It will probably, in a convenient way, give you dramatic improvements in your business processes, but it will not necessarily lead you to the often more inconvenient, but fruitful, path of revolution.

Interestingly, if you study the impact IT has had so far on the productivity of businesses in general, the results are not very impressive. Davenport (1993) elaborates on this topic. He also points out that the likely cause of the failure is that companies have not taken full advantage of IT's capacity to change the way that work is done.

When performing business process reengineering, you should study how different types of IT support can be used innovatively to rebuild your business processes. You should find out how IT can radically *change* how things are done, not just *speed up* the processes. Furthermore, you need to ensure that the use of IT really improves the productivity of your business processes (Figure 9.40).

How can IT help you? We have, inspired by Davenport (1993) and Willoch (1994), identified three categories of change that IT can help with. The first one contains support to improve the lead times of your processes without necessarily changing what is done by whom. This kind of support does not imply any revolutionary changes to your business processes:

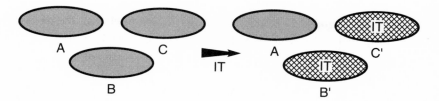

Figure 9.40 *IT should be used as an enabler to radical change of your business processes.*

- Automate work to eliminate human labour.
- Analyse data in a way that cannot practically be done by hand.

The second category encompasses support you need to be able to reorganize order or sequencing of the activities in a business process. The objective is to improve process-cycle times innovatively:

- Parallelize work or change sequencing of activities by using databases and networks.
- Distribute the organization by making it possible to access information from geographically different places.
- Move parts of processes outside the organization by giving your customers or suppliers access to your information systems.
- Help coordinate activities by supporting information exchange within the organization.
- Use expert systems to make it possible for non-experts to do specialized work.

The third category does not imply changes to your processes as such, but helps to control each process instance and detect where problems have occurred. Another important use of this type of IT support is to measure the business processes to find where improvements need to be made:

- Keep track of process status and performance.

This might seem like a long and complicated explanation for something rather simple and self-evident. But our experience is that only very mature organizations really know what they are doing and how much time they spend doing it. Very few organizations have reached the degree of maturity indicated by the fact that they actually use measurements of process performance as a tool when deciding how and what to reengineer (Humphrey, 1989).

9.5.3 Incremental installation

One way of making the installation procedure less turbulent is to introduce the new support systems into the organization incrementally. We now show a way of reengineering incrementally by using our modelling techniques. Let us assume that you have identified a use-case model for the ideal information system in your new organization (Figure 9.41). You have now realized that a major problem is that the model is based less on practice than on theory, since you have not had the opportunity to let prospective users test it. Because of this, you cannot be sure that the model describes what you really need.

A way to ensure that you will, in the end, arrive at the right solution is to install the new information system incrementally. Start by procuring a system that only fulfils a few of the use cases in your information-system model. You could, for example, choose to start with the information-system use cases that support activities in which most people in the organization are involved. Another criterion could be to choose information-system use cases that are expected to reduce the lead time for one of the business-system use cases dramatically. Using these criteria runs the risk of improving less important business-system use cases; that is, use cases of a lower rank in the business. If you do that, you might impose changes on your information system that turn out to be faulty or unnecessary when you start looking at the use cases of the

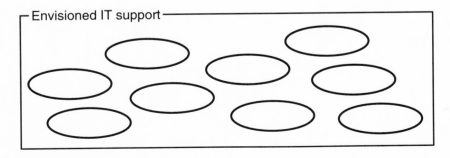

Figure 9.41 *The initial use-case model of the IT support system.*

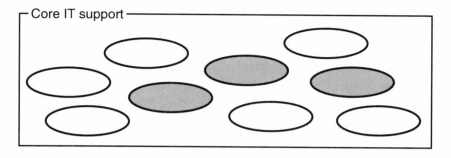

Figure 9.42 *The grey use cases are the ones that are procured first.*

highest rank. The best basis for future reengineering of your information system is achieved if you make sure that you select business-system use cases of the highest rank (Figure 9.42). It is, however, reasonable to assume that the information-system use cases of the highest rank are those that support the business-system use cases of the highest rank (see also the discussions about the concept of 'rank' in Chapter 6).

When you have procured and put into use the first increment of your new information system, you can start working with the next increment. As you gain more experience of the system in use, a new and, hopefully, more correct picture of the requirements you have on your information system will evolve. New ideas of how IT support could be used in your organization may arise, which could very well give reason to change your business-system use cases as well. The result is new, changed and even removed information-system use cases in your vision of the support system (Figure 9.43).

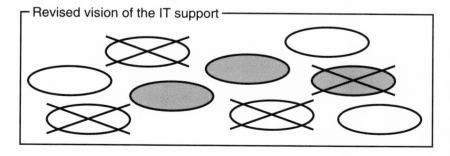

Figure 9.43 *When the first increment of the information system has been in use for a while, new and changed requirements on it will appear. Some use cases will be changed, some will be removed and some will be added.*

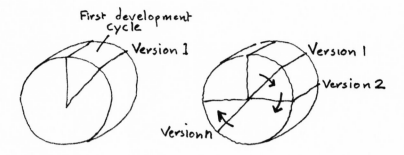

Figure 9.44 *The new information system is procured increment by increment.*

As indicated in Figure 9.44, the information systems are then installed incrementally into the organization. For each iteration, the vision of the ideal information system will change. In the ideal case of a relatively stable vision, what is installed will, for each increment, be closer to what was envisioned. It is important to realize, though, that the information systems will always need to be changed. This is the consequence of business processes changing as you continue to reengineer and improve them. Building information systems that can meet these constant demands for change can best be achieved by using object-oriented techniques. No other available technique gives you the possibility of keeping up with the fast changes required in modern business.

9.6 Summary

Our objective in this chapter was to show how elegantly use-case models and object models support each other in our approach. From the use-case model of the business you can find an object model for the same business. From the object model of the business, you can find use cases in the integral information system needed by the business. You will also find that some business-system entity objects will have corresponding information-system entity objects (Figure 9.45). The use cases of the information system, in turn, form the basis for the work of identifying object models of the information system.

Software development is a process of developing a number of models of an information system. Each model illustrates an aspect of the system. Different models are needed, since an information system has a

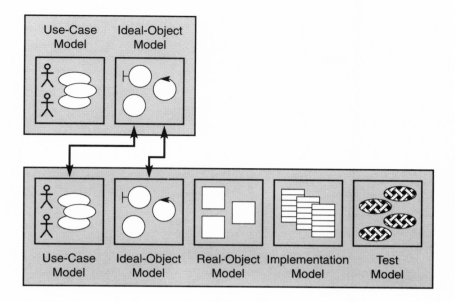

Figure 9.45 *The relationship between a business model and information-system models.*

number of different handlers, all wishing to see different views or levels of detail of the system. The information-system models discussed in this chapter are the following:

- The use-case model, consisting of use cases, actors and descriptions of the user interface of the information system. The use-case model serves as the basis for the development of the other models of the system.

- The ideal model, developed during ideal design with the aim of providing a system structure that is robust to changes. Information systems will have to change, since businesses change continually. You must, therefore, build a system that is robust when faced with changes in the requirements placed on it.

- The real model, used as the basis for the implementation work. It is also used for unit testing of the system.

- The implementation model, which simply consists of the code written for the information system. An object in the real model should correspond to one or more classes in, for example, Smalltalk or C++.

- The test model, which includes test documentation for the information system. The test model is considered ready when all tests have been performed and approved.

In this chapter we have described how to build IT support from scratch, given a good business-system model. We have also described how to successively reengineer an existing information system to support a reengineered business.

9.7 References

Constantine L.L. (1994). More than Just a Pretty Face: Designing for Usability. *Proceedings of Software Development, Spring Conference 1994*. San Jose, CA, March 1994, pp. 361–9

Davenport T.H. (1993). *Process Innovation, Reengineering Work through Information Technology*. Boston, MA: Harvard Business School Press

Hammer M. and Champy J. (1993). *Reengineering the Corporation: A Manifesto for Business Revolution*. NY: HarperCollins

Humphrey W.S. (1989). *Managing the Software Process*. Reading, MA: Addison-Wesley

Jacobson I., Christerson M., Jonsson P. and Övergaard G. (1992). *Object-Oriented Software Engineering – A Use Case Driven Approach*. Reading, MA: Addison-Wesley; New York: ACM Press

Jacobson I. and Lindström F. (1991). Reengineering of Old Systems to an Object-Oriented Architecture. *Proceedings of OOPSLA 1991*. Phoenix, AZ, October 1991, pp. 240–50

Jacobson I. (1994). Basic Use-Case Modeling. *Report on Object Analysis Design. SIGS Publications, Inc.* **1**(2), July–August 1994, in print

Wirfs-Brock R., Wilkerson B. and Wiener L. (1990). *Designing Object-Oriented Software*. Englewood Cliffs, NJ: Prentice Hall

chapter 10
Managing object-oriented business engineering

10.1 Introduction

In this chapter, we describe some of the activities of a reengineering project that will help you to achieve a successful result. We begin in Section 10.2 by describing how you should prepare the project in advance by tailoring the method to the project's needs. In this way the project runs smoothly from the outset.

In Section 10.3 we discuss how basic project management techniques can be applied to a reengineering project, then in Sections 10.4 and 10.5 we describe the different types of resources that are needed in such a project and in a process-managed organization.

Finally, we describe one of the most important success factors – the reviewing activity. We have already discussed where the reviews are performed in Chapters 6 and 7. In Section 10.6, we describe different types of reviews and how they are carried out.

A reengineering project is simply an instance of the Business Development process. Thus, in this context, when we refer to a project leader, we mean the process leader of the Business Development process. When we refer to activities and subactivities of the reengineering project, we are really referring to the subsystems or the objects participating in this process. However, to avoid unnecessary confusion, we will use the terms reengineering project, project leader, activities and subactivities in the rest of this chapter.

10.2 Tailoring the method

Reengineering projects differ in many ways:

- how familiar the project members are with the business itself,

- what level of experience of the method they have,

- how much (if any) reengineering experience they have,

- top management's level of commitment,

- how supportive the employees of the business are,

- the style of project management used,

- the type of customers the business has.

There is no method that fits every project, so every method has to be specialized. Each project has its own needs for a supporting method. For example, the demands of large projects (with perhaps 10–20 project members) are different to those of smaller projects (with, say, five project members). A method that works well for a small project will not necessarily scale up to a large project.

Object-oriented business engineering provides a set of techniques for making your project run smoothly. However, you should only use techniques that will actually aid your work, not delay or hinder it. Object-oriented business engineering should therefore be set up in such a way that it can be easily tailored to the needs of projects.

Starting from the complete set of techniques in object-oriented business engineering, you should define how your project should be carried through and draw up guidelines for what the result should look like. To achieve the best possible result, evaluate in advance the different object-oriented business engineering models, the architectural concepts, the documents and the work activities that are suggested in the method. Based on this evaluation, you should then decide how much and what parts of the method to use in your project. We call each specific way of using the method a *development case*.

Write a document – we can call it a development case description – stating the adjustments to the method that should be used in the project. This document should be produced by the method expert (see Section

10.4) in cooperation with the project leader and perhaps a reengineering expert. If too many people participate in this activity, it will probably turn out to be very time consuming. The idea is to save time by having these adjustments ready for the project members when they are about to start work. The document will typically cover the following deviations from the method:

- the models,

- the architectural concepts,

- the list of documents that should be produced (either as working documentation or final documentation),

- the list of contents of each document that should be produced,

- the work activities.

Find out which of the object-oriented business engineering models to use: for example, should you use the ideal-object model, the real-object model or a combination of the two in your project? Chapter 7 outlines some criteria to help you decide what to do in your specific project.

For each model, decide which architectural concepts to use. Many of these decisions come down to pros and cons. For example, if you use consistsOf associations between objects, the model will gain in clarity but at the same time you may need to allow more time for the developers to learn how to use the concept.

Decide which documents to use, as well as the content of each document.

Finally, you will need to adapt the work activities in the method, so that they are optimized to produce the specified result. This usually involves leaving out the work steps associated with the architectural concepts and documents that have been omitted.

You might also save a lot of time and energy by making templates of the documents that should be produced. A document template specifies the type of information that should be described in each section, and defines the level of detail in the descriptions. This is a way of ensuring that documents will be similar even if they are produced by different project members; that is, a more uniform result is achieved.

10.3 Project organization and management

There are many similarities between managing a software development project and managing a reengineering project. Therefore, the description in this chapter builds on the ideas described for software development in Jacobson *et al.* (1992).

Managing and organizing a reengineering development project requires a thorough understanding of the pitfalls of the trade. A necessary, but not sufficient, condition for successful reengineering is good project management. There is an abundance of literature on how to manage reengineering projects in general, so we will concentrate on the implications of object orientation and object-oriented business engineering on project management, and on what in particular project management should consider when working with this new technology.

In Figure 10.1 a project model, with generic activities, is shown for the overall management of a project. Each activity is delimited by a well-defined milestone.

The different activities can be described as follows:

- Pre-study: aims at defining the task by developing and evaluating different kinds of goals, needs and ideas to enable the technical and economic feasibility of the project to be assessed.

- Establishment: the project is organized and planned, and subjected to quality assurance. Detailed time and resource plans are developed.

- Execution: the project is executed in accordance with the plans developed previously.

- Conclusion: the project is completed, and proposals for improving the project and the development methods used are summarized.

Object-oriented business engineering will be used mainly during the pre-study and execution stages. The models developed are suitable for steering the project. All models have a well-defined result and it is appropriate to use them in combination with milestones; that is, to follow up the result at each milestone. Hence, the models can be mapped onto the generic project model. A mapping between the reengineering

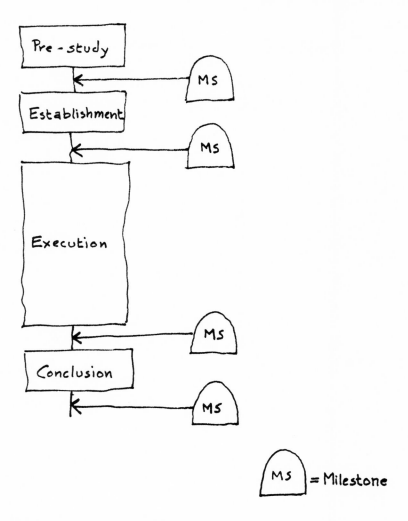

Figure 10.1 *The management part of a project.*

activities in object-oriented business engineering and a project model is shown in Figure 10.2.

The reverse engineering and envisioning activities are performed as part of the pre-study. (If the reengineering effort is substantial or if it requires a significant level of training in the new techniques, you may decide to view the reverse engineering activity itself as a project.) The forward engineering and installation activites are performed during the execution of the project.

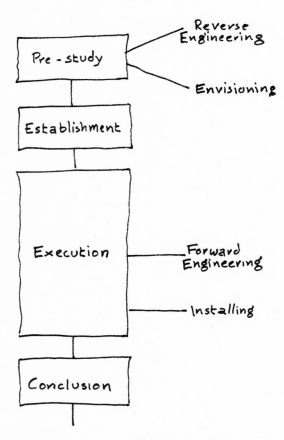

Figure 10.2 *A mapping between reengineering activities and the general project model.*

This ideal mapping gives a sense of an early waterfall model, in which the entire envisioning should be performed, reviewed and frozen before starting the work with the forward engineering activity. It is important to realize, though, that while working with one activity, you may very well find that certain aspects of the results from earlier activities need to be updated. In Figure 10.3, we illustrate how the work iterates between the different types of activities in a project. Even though the main flow starts with envisioning, moves on to reverse engineering and finishes with forward engineering, the work will iterate back and forth between these main activities, and also within them.

In addition to these iterations, you will also need to consider how the incremental work (see Chapter 6) will influence the project. It is

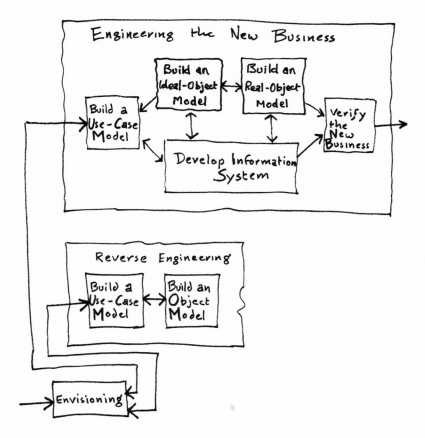

Figure 10.3 *A project iterates back and forth between the main activities and their subactivities.*

practical to view each increment as a project on its own, and handle the changes to the models by giving the result of each increment a version number.

A common way of working is to start with the envisioning activity and, after some initial work has been performed, initialize the reverse engineering activity in parallel. There will probably be some iterations back and forth between these two activities. When an adequate picture of the existing business has been formed, the forward engineering activity is initialized. After yet more iterations, the envisioning activity ends with the first version of the objective specification as the result. Based on the specified goals in the objective specification and the resulting models from the reverse engineering activity, the forward engineering activity is carried through.

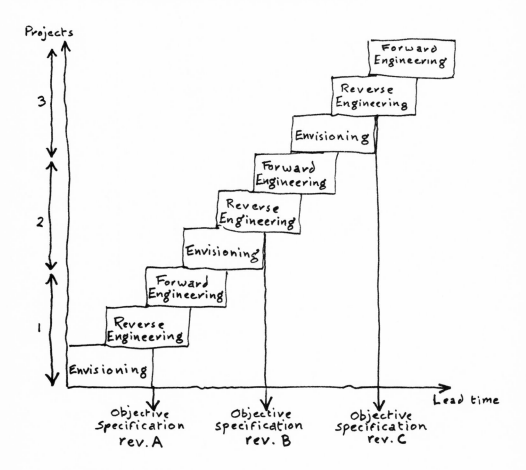

Figure 10.4 *Iterations and increments are handled by versioning the updated results from the different activities.*

Figure 10.4 shows how incremental development can be viewed in terms of projects. When the first project has been started, a second project can be initialized, so that it runs in parallel with the first. A new version of the objective specification is produced as the result of each envisioning activity. The objective specification, which should be approved by top management, contains a list of the goals of the system in terms of business processes. (There are additional goals that involve delivery date, resources and quality.)

The difference between objective specification rev. A and rev. B in Figure 10.4 may involve both clarification of and changes to earlier goals, as well as completely new goals (based on the next increment of processes).

The hardest part when defining the objective specification is to formulate it in such a way that top management can understand what will be delivered, and the reengineers have a complete and well-defined directive for the coming modelling work. There are three main reasons for modifying the objective specification during later activities:

- The goals are not distinct enough and need to be clarified.

- The project team realizes that the time or resources available will not be enough to fulfil all of the goals, and thus decides to omit some of them.

- Some of the goals are found to be unrealistic and not possible to install in the company as initially planned.

New or changed goals will inevitably generate new costs and may also delay the project. Furthermore, it becomes more expensive to add new goals the further you have progressed in the development cycle. A goal that was estimated to require 200 person-hours (of the reengineering team's resources) in the specification activity can very well cost 1000 person-hours if introduced late in the forward engineering activity.

10.4 Project staffing

In this section, we discuss briefly some typical ways of organizing an object-oriented business engineering project, assuming a medium sized project involving a reengineering team of around 10 people. (Staffing in activities other than the ones discussed in this book will not be covered.)

Assigning reengineering team members to a project comes down to manning the defined activities of the project. Besides the individuals who model the business, there may be a need for some special resources/ groups in the project. Examples of these are:

- Method expert: a person/group responsible for the method used, who should be expert in the method and should support the reengineering team in applying it. The method expert should understand the business area; that is, be able to explain the new techniques in terms of the business, which demands knowledge of the business area, the current organization of the company, the product structure and the competence of the rest of the reengineering team.

- Quality assurance (QA): people responsible for ensuring that both the business and the activities to develop the business are of high quality. This involves guaranteeing that the new business has a sound structure and that the documentation is consistent. Reviewing is a useful tool in this context; this is discussed in more detail later.

- Documentor: documentation of the business models should be made by the reengineering team. Work-flow descriptions, both for managers and employees in general, should be made by people with special skills. Planning for training in the new business must also be done. People who will need to be trained include process managers, process leaders, resources, customers and so on.

- Reuse coordinator: this resource/group is responsible for encouraging the reuse of already modelled infrastructure. In large businesses, or businesses with several subsidiaries, it ought to be possible to reuse the same infrastructure in several different places. The reuse coordinator should evaluate the extent to which the project is undertaking reuse, as well as investigate the reuse potential of the models developed. This person/group should work closely with the reengineering team. Reuse may not give payback in one specific project; the real gain comes in subsequent projects that reuse what has been developed in this one. Therefore, the cost of this function should not burden one project, but instead should be shared across several projects. Note that the coordination and management of the reuse library should be interproject.

- Prototyper: this resource investigates different solutions at an early stage to prepare for later development. Typically, customer interactions are worth prototyping in early activities.

- IT process owner/leader: this person is responsible for the development of the IT support, and functions as a coordinator between the business engineering development and the IT-support development.

- Staff: staff may be needed to help the project manager. One example is a special project administrator responsible for following up cost and time schedules. This is necessary in larger projects. Some of the above resources may be considered to be part of the staff.

It is effective for the people with these special skills to work with the actual modelling tasks as well. If this is the case, it is important to give them enough time to fulfil their double responsibilities.

10.5 Organization staffing

We now turn to a description of the staff needed in the new process organization. We have touched upon this subject several times in earlier chapters, but here we will try to give a more complete description of the different roles that are found in this type of organization. (In this chapter we use the term 'role' differently compared to how we have used it in earlier chapters, where we discussed the role of objects; here the term describes an employee's duty or responsibility within the organization.)

The long-term aim of the process organization is for each process to be a profit centre, which internally 'buys' resources, services and so on. This might not be implementable in the first reengineering project, since the new organization often needs to be 'tuned in', to establish a more powerful internal support system before it can work effectively. However, when the business has matured in its new setup, this provides for a dynamic organization. It is up to the process owners to ensure that their processes are considered to be worth belonging to, in order to attract the best people for the job. At the same time it is up to each individual to do a good job, so that the process owners are willing to buy their services.

In a business with a process organization, several different roles are needed to make it all work. An individual might play one or several of these roles. The individual's roles and process involvement are regulated by different types of agreements.

The president of the company appoints the resource owners and the process owners. There is one resource owner for each function in the organization, and one process owner for each process (Figure 10.5). (In a large company, there may also be executives responsible for different business areas, who are positioned between the president and the process owners/resource owners.)

The process owner has the operating responsibility for the resources allocated to his/her specific process, while the resource owner has long-term responsibility for all of the resources belonging to his/her specific function.

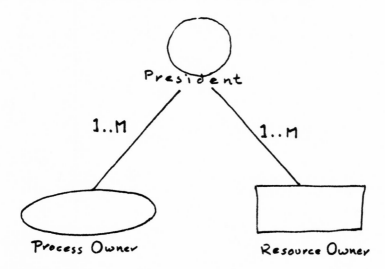

Figure 10.5 *The president appoints both the process owners and the resource owners.*

The process owner allocates human resources to his/her process by establishing agreements with the individual resources (the process operators). The actual negotiations are usually carried out as a three-party agreement between the process operator, the resource owner and the process owner. An agreement proposal is presented to the process operator and, if it is approved, is established and signed. Furthermore, the process owner appoints a process leader for each instance of his/her process. There is thus at least one process leader for each process, who has the operating responsibility for an instance of the process.

10.5.1 Roles and responsibilities

President
We are not going to define a president's responsibilities in general here; instead we list the typical responsibilities and tasks of a president in a process organization:

- The operational and long-term goals.

- The business strategies.

- The overall budget and financial control.

- Business and organizational development.

- Appointing the resource owner(s) and the process owner(s).

- Controlling the resource owner(s) and the process owner(s).

Resource owner
A resource owner has the following responsibilities and tasks:

- Making sure that the process operators are allocated to one or more processes in the business.

- Solving conflicts of resource allocation.

- Establishing agreements (that is, development plans) for individuals, so that they can clearly see their long-term personal development within the company. The resource owner is supportive in the personal development of his/her process operators and ensures that each individual has their own development plan, which is discussed each year.

- The total competence development of his/her personnel and current 'map of competence'.

- The long-term training budget and strategic training; this latter aspect cannot be assigned to any particular process.

- Recruitment of process operators, in cooperation with the process owners.

- Being supportive to all employees in negotiations, resource conflicts, personal development and so on.

Process owner
There is a process owner for each process in the business. The process owners' tasks are focused on the processes for which they are responsible, but their responsibilities must be defined in detail to avoid suboptimization. The process owner has the following responsibilities and tasks:

- Defining the process and ensuring that it is being developed in accordance with the strategic plan for the business.

- Determining the interface of the process by looking at the participating objects of the corresponding use case. If any of these objects also participate in other use cases, then they are part of the interface. The process owner needs to determine how these objects should handle their responsibilities towards the different use cases. This work is often performed in cooperation with the process owner(s) of the other process(es).

- Defining goals for the process and ensuring that they are achieved.

- Planning the budget for all of the instances of the process; thus, the process owner has responsibility for the total budget of the process.

- Appointing the process leader(s).

- Allocating resources to the process instances and establishing agreements (for example, process allocation) with each process operator.

- The short-term competence development of the process; the process owner therefore has a budget for this type of development.

- Participating in planning the long-term demand for resources, although the resource owner is responsible for carrying out this task.

- Developing and improving the quality of the process.

Process leader

The process leader has responsibility for an instance of a process, and may in many ways be compared with a project leader. In smaller businesses, an individual may be both a process owner and a process leader. The process leader may, if necessary, make adjustments to his/her process instance, for example in a subsidiary. The process leader has the following responsibilities and tasks:

- Running an instance of a process according to the budget.

- Interpreting the goals and plans for the process as well as implementing the process instance in an efficient manner.

- Agreeing possible adjustments or changes of the process with the process owner.

- Leading the resources and performing the short-term resource planning of the contracted process operators.

- Making sure that possible resource conflicts are noted and solved, in cooperation with the process operators, the process owner and the resource owner.

- Establishing agreements (that is, assignment agreements) with the allocated process operators.

Process operator
All of the individuals in the company are process operators. Some of these process operators are appointed by the president and by the process owners. These are the ones who have the special roles described above. A process operator performs the following tasks:

- Looks after his/her long-term personal development.

- Finds suitable tasks in one or more processes.

- Requires that agreements (of all the different types) are drawn up and followed.

- Makes his/her own detailed time plan in cooperation with the appropriate process leader(s).

- Performs the process tasks.

10.5.2 Different types of agreements

We have tested the establishment of agreements on a small scale, and the results are encouraging. We therefore want to share this way of working with you because we believe that it will help you to establish an effective organization, although it has not yet been attempted on a large scale.

The commitment and development of each individual within the company may be regulated through different types of agreement, three of which are:

- The individual development plan, which describes the more long-term courses that the process operator should participate in, as well as his or her possible advancement within the company, during a timeframe of 1–3 years.

- The process allocation plan, which allocates the percentage of time to be spent on different processes by a process operator during the year.

- The assignment agreement, which defines the terms under which a process operator agrees to fulfil a specified job. This type of agreement is used mainly with external consultants, who are brought into the project temporarily.

Since the individual development plan and the assignment agreement are not in any way specific to reengineering projects or process organizations, we will only describe the process allocation plan in more detail.

Process allocation plan

This agreement has a timeframe of one year and is renegotiated annually when the individual reviews his/her process allocation. In most cases, it is the resource owner who handles (in agreement with the process operator) the actual negotiations with the process owner(s). Eventually, the process operator, the resource owner and the process owner(s) sign the agreement. If possible, it should be stated how the allocation is distributed over time. If this cannot be done when the agreement is established, a supplement should be added as soon as this information is known. If there are intentions of commitments longer than one year, this may be stated as well.

The agreement should also include information about how a possible cancellation should be handled.

Figure 10.6 shows an example of the content of a typical process allocation plan.

Process	Share (%)	Main task	Process owner

Figure 10.6 *A typical process allocation plan.*

10.6 Reviews

Reviewing is the primary tool for quality assurance. Here we discuss very briefly the integration of reviews in object-oriented business engineering. First, some terminology: a *formal* review's objective is to decide whether or not to proceed to the next phase. This type of review is held at every major project milestone, and involves a fairly large review team, as well as customers or orderers. The purpose of an *informal* review is to discover errors. These reviews can be held at any time during development, for example when something is completed that ought to be checked before continuing the development process. Informal reviews often have quite limited participation, typically some of the developers and possibly also someone from quality assurance.

Where to use the different kinds of review when working with object-oriented business engineering depends on the size of the reengineering project. In a small to medium sized reengineering project, formal review points are typically between the main activities, that is, when each model has reached its first version. Informal reviews may be used after each subactivity, possibly with several subactivities being grouped together under one review.

Different kinds of review have also been defined by IEEE (1983) in a standard glossary. The following three types of review are based on the IEEE standard, but we have transformed them somewhat to make them applicable to object-oriented business engineering:

- Review: primarily a meeting to check out results and to make decisions. Reviews are held in order to ensure that all of the results produced so far in the reengineering project are complete and consistent. This is the only method of evaluation in which top management should participate. If they participate in the other evaluation meetings, the evaluation can easily become a judgement of the reengineer rather than of the document. The review looks at the total outcome of the reengineering project and authorizes the start of the next development activity. Top management needs to make this decision. At the review, the status of each document is controlled. The status is checked by finding out what types of evaluation have been applied to the document, and the number and severity of the errors detected. Participants should be project leaders, members of the reengineering team and process owners. The participants will check the inspection records and the documents created during the development activity. If the problems detected are considered to have too much of an impact on the following activities, corrections will have to be done before entering the next activity.

- Inspection: the most powerful of all the methods of evaluation. It is a formal evaluation technique and the result has to be recorded. This leads to good control of the reengineering project and the product status. It might also give valuable information for the future. The inspection involves well-defined inspection roles:

  - the *moderator*, who chairs the meeting and is reponsible for keeping it creative and making sure that the focus is on finding errors,

  - the *recorder*, who notes every error found during the meeting and its priority and severity class,

  - the *inspectors*, who are the participants responsible for commenting on errors or possible errors,

  - the *author*, or the reengineer, who explains things, if necessary.

Before the moderator ends the meeting it has to be decided whether or not the document should be approved without changes, approved after correcting detected errors or updated for a new inspection. The inspection meeting should not exceed two hours and the number of participants should be no more than eight.

- Walkthrough: a method of evaluation in which the reengineer leads one or more project members of the reengineering team through a segment of the model that he or she has written. The other members make comments on style, technique, possible errors, violation of reengineering standards and other problems. The reengineer starts by explaining the contents for the participants, then goes into more detail by reading through and explaining each chapter in turn. All errors that are found during the walkthrough have to be recorded by the reengineer for his/her own use. However, no formal record or report of the meeting is required: it is up to the reengineer to correct his/her work. The participants do not have to be prepared before the meeting, which means that it might be difficult for them to find errors. Nevertheless, it is a good information-spreading exercise.

Reviews may by characterized as formal, while inspections and walkthroughs are informal. Although every review is unique and focuses on a specific model or object, they have some points in common. Here, we do not give exhaustive lists of what to review in the object-oriented business engineering models, but simply highlight some examples.

Common to all reviews is checking of aspects like completeness of the model, redundancy, structure, naming, correct associations, understandability, versioning of documents, standards, views and so on. How these aspects are reviewed largely depends on the purpose of the review.

When reviewing each model, there are specific things to focus on. The following are some examples of points to review in the use-case model:

- Is the business delimitation appropriate?

- Do the use cases match the objective specification?

- Has the objective specification been updated?

- Is it possible to understand the use cases?

- Are all roles that interact with the business identified as actors?

- Do all actors have the right set of use cases?

- Are the interfaces described in a satisfactory way?

- Are the use-case flows correct and complete?

- Have enough alternative flows been described?

Of course, the actual questions may vary from time to time, but the intention should be clear from the above. When reviewing the other models the intention should be the same; to find errors made early in the development process and to guarantee high quality in the product.

When performing the review, different methods and techniques can be used. A systematic approach is necessary, to achieve high quality in the delivered system. Methods and techniques for this are described by Weinberg and Freedman (1982), Myers (1987) and Yourdon (1989).

When conducting reviews, management has an important role to play. It is important for management to show commitment to the method (in our case object-oriented business engineering) and results, and also to budget time for performing reviews. About 5% of the overall development time is not unusual. Likewise, it is important to use competent people as reviewers, to guarantee high product quality and high confidence in the review process from the development staff.

To achieve good discipline, and a high level of awareness, an independent quality group responsible for quality assurance is needed. This group can do reviews of how well the project members follow the given method of development and can also assess the project's chances of achieving its goals and highlight potential risks. However, the QA group should not function as a 'police force'; it should – in cooperation with the reengineering team – increase the quality of what is being done.

The key to a good quality product is to review the work thoroughly. Reviews are time consuming, but they may be a life-saver if they are used correctly. It is very important for the reviewers to get a fair chance to understand the material that they need to read. We strongly recommend that all reviewers have some organized knowledge about the method before the reviewing process begins. It is extremely difficult for reviewers to produce any intelligent feedback if they do not really understand the material.

10.7 Summary

Before you can start a business engineering project, you have to decide how your specific business development process should be configured. Things you need to decide on are:

- What models should be developed.

- What architectural concepts should be used.

- How the work should be documented.

You should adapt the work activities according to the above decisions and make document templates to ensure that all documents have similar contents and a uniform style.

You also need to decide how object-oriented business engineering should fit into your project model. You will need to consider all other aspects that are not supported by object-oriented business engineering but that have to be done in the project, for example how to install the new company. When this is done, you may staff the project.

When the project is in its execution phase, you will need to review the work done. We have described three reviewing techniques: formal review, inspection and walkthrough.

In the new process-managed organization, new roles will need to be defined or existing ones changed. The ones we have discussed in this chapter are the president, the resource owner, the process owner, the process leader and the process operator.

10.8 References

IEEE (1983). *IEEE STD 729-1983. Standard Glossary of Software Engineering Terminology.* New York: IEEE

Jacobson I., Christerson M., Jonsson P. and Övergaard G. (1992). *Object-Oriented Software Engineering – A Use Case Driven Approach.* Reading MA: Addison-Wesley; New York: ACM Press

Myers, G.J. (1987). *Software Reliability: Principles and Practices.* New York: John Wiley & Sons

Weinberg G.M. and Freedman D.P. (1982). *Handbook of Walkthroughs, Inspections, and Technical Reviews.* Boston: Little, Brown Computer Systems

Yourdon E. (1989). *Structured Walkthroughs* 4th edn. Englewood Cliffs NJ: Prentice Hall/Yourdon Press

chapter 11
Scaling up to large businesses

11.1 Introduction

It is easy to understand that a large company such as IBM, Xerox, Ericsson or ABB is much more complex to model than a smaller company such as Objectory AB. But what actually is the difference? What is meant by a large business?

The difference between large and small businesses is really only that there are many more occurrences, so that it is easy to drown in details and lose the overall picture. You need to be able to scale up your modelling techniques so that they can handle businesses that are more complicated, businesses that are geographically distributed – both nationally and internationally – and businesses whose infrastructure is so extensive and so specialized that even it must be modelled. Here we describe a number of techniques for supporting such an increase in scale. These different techniques can be applied independently of each other or in various combinations.

- We start by describing how you can use several use-case models, for different handlers at different abstraction levels, to describe a business.

- We then proceed by showing how to describe companies with several independent business areas which together serve a common customer.

- Finally, we show how, by layering your models of the company, you can differentiate the business parts that are generic and reusable from those that are specific to the company.

Our experience of applying these techniques is very limited. This can be seen from the often schematic examples shown; the examples that we used when we clarified our ideas. We present our experience here to show that our work is capable of being scaled up, and to offer others the opportunity of extending it.

11.2 Two use-case models at different abstraction levels

Use-case modelling is our instrument for modelling a company's business processes. Both the company's executive management and the process owners are interested in their company's use-case model — the management in order to work with the company's strategic objectives, and the process owners and process leaders in order to have a detailed picture of how their individual processes should be performed. Management needs a more comprehensive picture of use cases than the process owners and process leaders. This can be achieved by producing use-case models at different abstraction levels.

A use-case model uses actors to represent customers or partners and use cases to represent business processes. The level of abstraction and amount of detail in the model is chosen by selecting suitable actors and use cases. For example, in a use-case model for the company's executive management, the actor Market can be a suitable counterpart to the use case Marketing, but this would be much too abstract for the Marketing process owner. He/she may want to differentiate between various types of actors. Marketing is perhaps carried out in totally different ways, depending on the product, the market's geographical area, the expected characteristics of the buyer, and so on.

If the difference between the requirements of the executives and the process managers is too great, you should satisfy the various handlers with different, but related, models.

Let us consider an example. When we modelled Objectory AB, we started by producing a use-case model overview, which was later refined

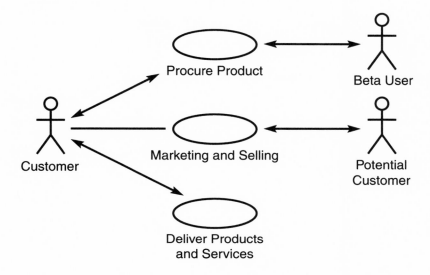

Figure 11.1 *The Objectory AB use-case model overview.*

into a more detailed use-case model, that eventually replaced the overview model. In this case, because of the company's size and the management's experience, it was appropriate to stay with just one use-case model. In a larger company, you would be able to keep the simpler model alongside a more detailed one. Figures 11.1 and 11.2 show two different use-case models of Objectory AB.

The models are created to serve different handlers. The model overview is intended for the executives, while the more concrete model is intended for the process managers. Instead of the term 'intended for', we use the term 'own'. The fact that a model is owned by a handler category means that this category has control over it; they can determine how it should appear, modify it and use it as a mutual communication instrument. This does not mean that other categories cannot use the model in some other way, for example to produce an individual model with different objectives. This is, in fact, quite common when several models of the same thing are constructed, for example models of a company or an information system. The relation between such models is in the level of traceability: occurrences in one of the models can be traced to occurrences in the other.

The model overview (Figure 11.1) constitutes the starting point for producing the more detailed model of the company (Figure 11.2).

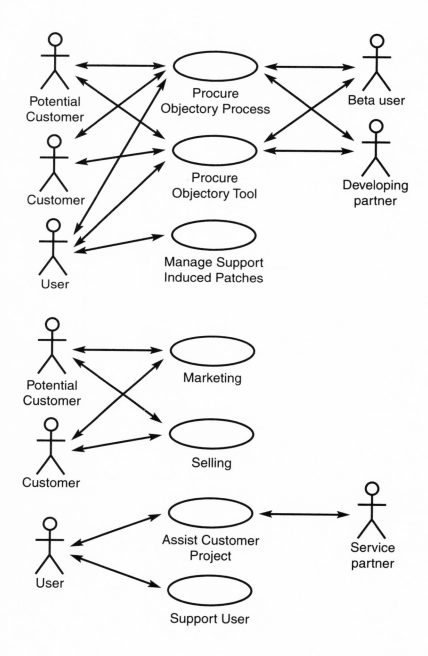

Figure 11.2 *The Objectory AB detailed use-case model.*

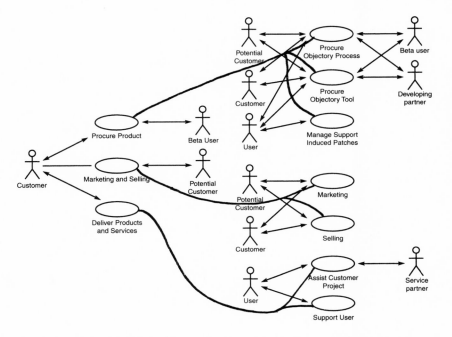

Figure 11.3 *Traceability between the overview and Objectory AB's more detailed use-case model.*

The handler category that owns the more abstract model uses it to communicate with the category (or categories) that owns the concrete model.

What do we mean when we say that the relation between the models is in the level of traceability? Figure 11.3 shows how occurrences in an abstract model can be traced to occurrences in a concrete model. The use case Procure Product in the overview can be traced to three use cases in the more detailed model: Procure Objectory Process, Procure Objectory Tool and Manage Support-Induced Patches. The actor Customer can be traced to the actors Customer and User. However, the traceability relation is not always as simple as in our example, since it is a many-to-many relation.

The technique with two use-case models at different levels of abstraction is also applicable if you want to reengineer your business one process at a time. First, you make a use-case model overview of the entire business, then prioritize the use cases in the overview and make a detailed use-case model of the highest priority use cases. Finally, you reengineer these use cases.

11.3 Business system areas

The technique for modelling processes that we presented in Chapter 5 can be used for companies that have a single business area and whose business activities are concentrated geographically at one location. For larger companies that have several business areas or are distributed at several locations, it may be necessary to scale up the technique.

11.3.1 Superordinate and subordinate use-case model

We expand our existing use-case model with two new constructs: business system area and sub-use case. We start with a schematic example. Assume that we have a use-case model for Corporation A, shown in Figure 11.4.

The company has several business areas, each of which is an independent profit centre. If these are entirely autonomous, there is no real reason to describe them in the same model; they are handled more appropriately as individual business systems. Here, we assume that these different business areas together serve a particular type of customer, and identify for each business area a business system area. We then divide the previously identified use cases into sub-use cases. Each sub-use case is

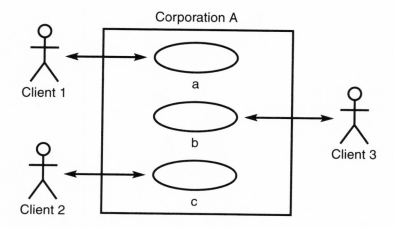

Figure 11.4 *Use-case model for Corporation A.*

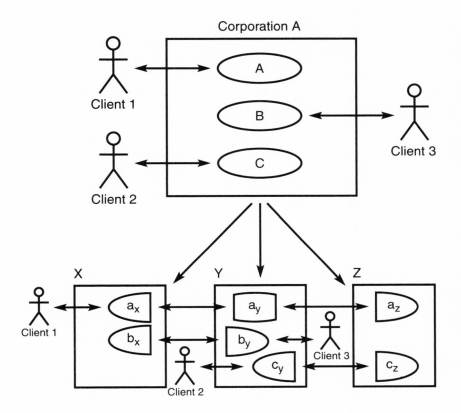

Figure 11.5 *Business system areas and sub-use cases.*

part of a superordinate use case that falls within the realm of a certain business system.

The simple use-case model in Figure 11.4 has been expanded in Figure 11.5. Corporation A has been divided into three business system areas, X, Y and Z, and the use cases a, b and c have been subdivided into a_x, a_y, a_z, b_x, b_y and c_y, c_z, where a_x is the sub-use case that originates from use case a and falls within the area X and so on. The discussion below applies even in the special case where a use case in the top model (Figure 11.4) is allocated entirely, without being subdivided, to a single business system area in the lower model (Figure 11.5).

How should we interpret this expanded model? The simple use-case model is now called the superordinate use-case model and the expanded part (the lower part in Figure 11.5) is the subordinate use-case model. The relation between the superordinate model and the subordinate model is interpreted as if they were equivalent as seen from the original actor's perspective. For example, the behaviour of Corporation A towards Client 1 is equivalent in the superordinate use-case model and the subordinate use-case model. This means that use case a on its own and the three use cases a_x, a_y and a_z put together perform an equivalent behaviour towards Client 1.

There is thus a type of equivalence relation between the superordinate use-case model and the subordinate use-case model. Each actor in the superordinate use-case model corresponds exactly to an actor in the subordinate model. Each use case in the superordinate use-case model corresponds to a set of sub-use cases in a subset of the business system areas in the subordinate use-case model. Sub-use cases are linked together via communication associations. A sub-use case does not need to be linked to every other sub-use case. Thus, in our schematic example, a_x and a_z are not associated with each other, but each sub-use case is associated with at least one other sub-use case. When we talk about sub-use cases, we mean those that originate from the same use case in the superordinate use-case model. There is a special case that should be mentioned. It is quite possible for a use case in the superordinate use-case model to correspond in its entirety to one sub-use case in the subordinate use-case model, that is, the use case is not really divided into sub-use cases. Finally, each actor that is associated with a use case in the superordinate use-case model is usually associated with only one sub-use case in the subordinate use-case model (theoretically, there is no reason why there cannot be more than one sub-use case, but it is usually impractical).

You should describe how each use case in the superordinate use-case model is composed of sub-use cases in the subordinate use-case model, so that the same behaviour is experienced by the actors in the environment. It is especially important to identify the interface between associated sub-use cases.

When you have come this far in the modelling, you can proceed with each individual business system area. Each business system area is treated as a business system and all of its sub-use cases as use cases in this system, for example as in Figure 11.6.

Business system area X is handled as an individual business system with use cases a_x and b_x. Two new actors have been added, Client a_y and Client b_y. These behave from X's perspective in a way equivalent to how use cases a_y and b_y behave. We could say that Client a_y and Client b_y simulate a_y and b_y from X's point of view.

Now, business system X is developed with the use cases a_x and b_x as a new system. We identify the objects required to realize the use cases,

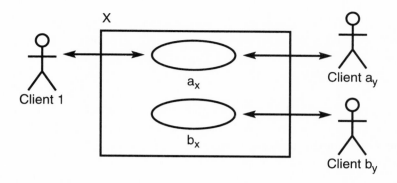

Figure 11.6 *A business system area itself becomes a business system at the next level.*

exactly as described in Chapter 5; thus, X is handled in the way described there.

In this section we have shown how to build up a use-case model recursively. The technique allows you to continue the division indefinitely. We believe, however, that even very large organizations can be described with only one division, as described here.

11.3.2 Staffing

What is the division of responsibility in this sort of organization? Principally, process owners are appointed for processes for the entire business. Thus, in our schematic example process owners are appointed for a, b and c. These process owners are responsible for ensuring that the use cases are composed of suitable sub-use cases, concentrating especially on specifying the interface between sub-use cases. Further, process owners are appointed for each of the sub-use cases. Depending on how you want the organization to appear, you can find different solutions. If the superordinate model represents a conglomerate and the business system areas represent subsidiaries with different functions, the process owners at the top level have a responsibility for the whole picture and for ensuring that the interface is suitably described. The process owners at the lower level are responsible for ensuring that the processes within the subsidiaries are carried out in an acceptable way.

It is probably unusual to appoint process leaders for the super-ordinate use cases. However, process leaders are appointed for every instance of sub-use cases. Ultimate responsibility for the businesses lies with the managers of each business area. They not only have a resource owner role, but are also responsible for ensuring that the work within their area is performed in the correct way and in line with their colleagues. The environment should be treated as actors. For your own business, you have full operational responsibility, as is usual for a chief executive officer.

11.3.3 An example

Let us explain the discussion with an example. Telecom Inc. offers customers all over the world complete networks of products within the field of telecommunications. Customers may look different; an individual customer may wish to purchase:

- a switching system for public telecommunication,

- a system for a private company,

- transmission equipment for a telecommunication network,

- a mobile telecommunication network.

There may also be an individual customer that wishes to purchase a complete network using a combination of these products.

Telecom Inc. is a large company with many thousands of employees. Three business areas may be identified:

- Public Telecommunication, which supplies products — switching systems and transmission products — for the public telecommunication network.

- Business Communication, for which the customers are private companies.

- Mobile Communication, which is the supply of mobile networks.

Each business area is an autonomous unit within Telecom Inc. It is clear that several processes cross several business areas. 'Product Development: from requirements to product' demands interaction of

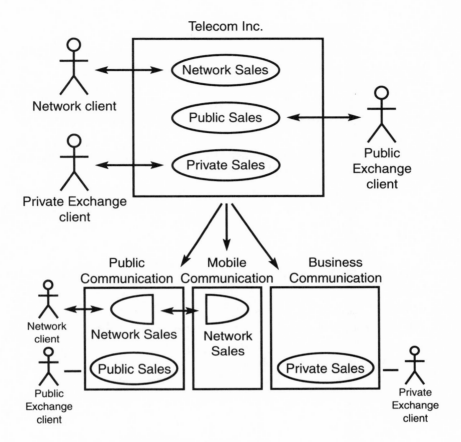

Figure 11.7 *A use-case model of Telecom Inc.*

all business areas if a complete network, perhaps including private exchanges, is to be developed. Thereafter, there are a number of other processes. Here, for simplicity, we concentrate on the sales processes. Each business area has responsibility for its own products, whether it applies to development or order handling. Parts of the business areas are responsible for the interaction between the different process parts. In the case of a customer only wishing to purchase part of a total network, for example a mobile network, this can be handled using a process that is entirely contained within Mobile Communication.

A use-case model of Telecom Inc. could appear as shown in Figure 11.7.

Telecom Inc. comprises three business area systems. In the model in Figure 11.7, we have only concerned ourselves with sales processes. We have identified three different use cases, all of type Sales: from lead to order. Network Sales deals with Public and Mobile Communication, while Public Sales and Private Sales affect only Public Communication and Private Communication, respectively. The superordinate use case Network Sales has been divided into two sub-use cases — one for each of the business area systems Public Communication and Mobile Communication. Together these two sub-use cases realize the superordinate use case. In order to differentiate between these different use cases, we call the superordinate use case 'Network Sales in Telecom Inc.' and the sub-use cases 'Network Sales in Public Communication' and 'Network Sales in Mobile Communication', respectively. Within Mobile Communication, there is probably also a use case Mobile Sales, which is not shown in Figure 11.7. Let us look more closely at Public Communication (Figure 11.8).

We move down a level and consider the business area system Public Communication as an individual system with its use cases, Network Sales and Public Sales. In the previous model, both of these were sub-use cases of the superordinate use cases, but are now use cases themselves. The next step in the modelling work should be to describe each use case. We will not do this here, but instead will reflect a little on this task. It is probable that there are many similarities between Network Sales and Public Sales. Both work with the same product. The generation of quote information is probably very similar. There are, of course, important differences; for example, Network Sales must collate documentation from Mobile Communication and take total responsibility towards the

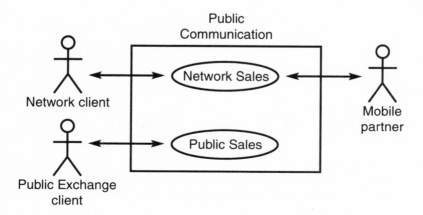

Figure 11.8 *The business area system Public Communication.*

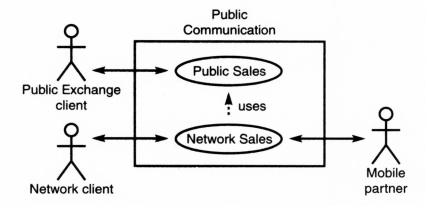

Figure 11.9 *Clarified use-case model for Public Communication.*

customer, whereas Public Sales does not need to bother with this. Therefore, we conclude that the use-case model shown in Figure 11.9 is approximately the one required for Public Communication.

An alternative would be to identify a new use case that contains the similarities between Public Sales and Network Sales, and then let both these use cases have uses associations to the new use case.

Further work in the modelling of Telecom Inc. continues from the individual business area systems. For each of them, an object model is produced, as described in Chapter 5.

To summarize, we have discussed how to model large companies by dividing them into business system areas. Use-case models become expanded. They will consist of two related parts, one comprising the whole business with its global use cases, and one that shows all business area systems and how the superordinate use cases are composed of sub-use cases in individual business area systems.

11.4 Layered business models

Another technique that can be used to comprehensively describe a business is layering. This technique allows you to master the complexity of large businesses. It is particularly powerful when used to model activities other than business processes, such as infrastructural processes. Nowadays, the layering technique is used to structure complex systems in general, systems that can be developed in software, hardware or 'humanware'.

11.4.1 What is a layered architecture?

In a layered architecture, the underlying layers relate to the implementation, that is, the different types of resources, while the upper layers relate to the business. Figure 11.10 shows a schematic example of a layered architecture. A business system may well have more layers than the ones shown in Figure 11.10, and it can also have layers in several dimensions, so that one layer can itself be layered.

- The *resource layer* contains the different concrete resources you have for realizing your organization. Here you will find human resources with different kinds of skills — education, management, experience, and so on — and different types of equipment such as information systems and machines.

- The *infrastructure layer* consists of objects generic to the type of business being modelled. Here you will find objects to support management processes, accounting processes, personnel administration, office administration, and so on.

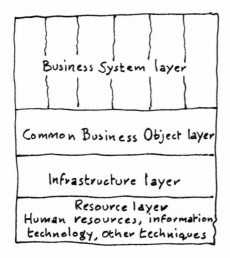

Figure 11.10 *An example of a layered business system architecture.*

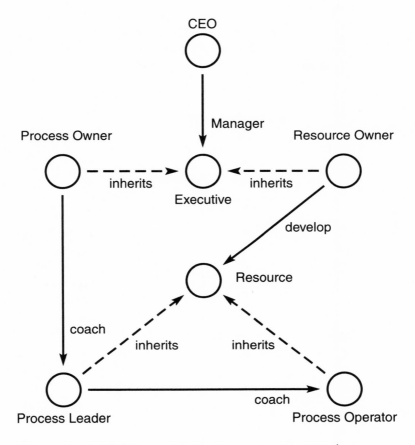

Figure 11.11 *Modelling a management process using entity objects.*

If you model this layer you will find, even in a small company, a large number of objects. Therefore, you will normally only model parts of it and only parts that are critical in some respect. The following example models some of the different types of human resources and their static relations in an organization (Figure 11.11).

Both process owners and resource owners are executives. They report to the president of the company being modelled. A resource owner develops his/her resources, which might be process leaders or process operators, and a process owner has a relation to a process leader which is different from the traditional boss–employee relationship. A process owner coaches his/her process leaders.

- The *common business object layer* contains objects generic to the type of business modelled. These objects can be used by many different businesses or business system areas within the company being modelled.

- Finally the *business system layer* consists of the objects specific to a business subsystem.

For example, in the common business object layer a bank would contain those objects – such as customer, account, loan, branch office – that are used by several banking subsystems. The different banking subsystems could, for instance, be operations concerned with customers depositing money, lending operations and operations dealing with the transfer of funds from different parts of the world. These are specific to the bank being modelled. The business processes of a bank will primarily be visible in the highest layer. It is this layer that will differentiate between different banks. The layer with the common business objects could to a large extent be common to several banks.

Another business, for example an insurance company, would be able to use the same basic object layer as the bank, but the higher layers would be quite different.

11.4.2 Developing a layered architecture

A layered architecture is normally developed during a long period of time – iteratively and incrementally. To aid understanding we present here a simplified view, a recursive approach which would, in practice, hardly work. A layered system must be modelled both top-down and bottom-up. It may actually be more correct to say that you model bottom-up first so that you know how to anchor your top-down model.

The different activities are:

- *Step 1*: start with the whole business system.

  - Make a use-case model of the whole business system. In this model the actors will be the normal actors of the business system, and the use cases will be the business processes of the company.

- Make an object model corresponding to the use-case model. If you want to have several object models of the business, proceed with the next one at this stage.

- *Step 2*: proceed recursively with the next layer.

  - Make a use-case model for the business system corresponding to the next layer and all of its subordinate layers. Actors of this use-case model are found in the object model of step 1. Note that these actors must not be confused with the actors of the information system, which we discussed in Chapter 9. The actors we are talking about here are similar to the actors that simulate the surrounding business system areas in Section 11.3.1. Here, they simulate objects in a higher layer.

  - Make an object model for this use-case model.

- *Step 3*: continue with analogous activities for every layer.

11.4.3 Relations between different layers

In systems with a layered architecture it is important to define the interfaces between the various layers. Object-oriented technology provides an elegant way of doing this. Every layer is a composite object consisting of its constituent objects alone. The interface to a layer is made up of the interfaces to its public objects. How a layer can be used by layers higher up in the structure is an important architectural decision. There are several such types of layer relations to choose from. Here, we present two:

- *The use of objects in the lower layers is encapsulated in the objects of the higher layer.* The design of the higher layers uses the public interfaces of the basic object layer as primitives; this is because the interface is encapsulated in the overlying layer's objects, and can only be seen in these objects' implementation parts. The interface should not be used in the documentation, which describes the interaction between objects in the higher layers. A larger business system consists of thousands of objects that communicate with one another in an extremely intensive way; by concealing the communication with underlying objects inside the objects in their own layer, all documentation will be simplified.

Since they are designed to be reused extensively, basic objects should be managed in a very different way compared to business objects: they should be carefully tested before being released, they should not be allowed to change until all business objects dependent on them have also been changed, and so on.

- *Objects in the lower layer need not only be encapsulated in objects of the higher layer but can be used in the design documentation of the higher layer; however, they cannot be changed by the designers of the higher layer.* The common business object layer grows and matures during the development of several different business subsystems. It should contain the objects in common for an entire business, and it should, therefore, become relatively stable after a number of releases. The layer should be managed in a different way to the business system layer, but in a similar way to the infrastructure layer. An important difference, compared to the objects in the infrastructure layer, is that it is necessary to show the objects in the common business object layer when describing the business subsystems; it is not enough to use these objects only in the implementation part of the objects in the business subsystems. When designing a business subsystem, you may show the common business objects you are using, but you are not allowed to make any changes to them whatsoever. You are only allowed to make changes to your own objects, that is, objects to realize your business subsystem. If a common business object is to be changed, all business subsystems using that object will need to be changed at the same time.

11.4.4 Relations between different subsystems

Every layer can be divided into subsystems using the technique described in Chapter 5. The subsystems in the highest layer are relatively large and independent of each other. They could also be business system areas as described in Section 11.3.

Business system areas and layering are complementary. You can apply both techniques to describe a complex organization. First, you use the business system area technique to find the different business system areas and then you develop a layered architecture as described in Section 11.4.2. The layers below the highest will be used for all of the business system areas.

11.5 Summary

We have extended our basic technique for business modelling with a number of new constructs.

- Use-case models can be developed at different levels of abstraction. A use-case model can be developed for the executives of the company such that it gives an overview of its business processes. Another more detailed model can be developed for the process managers. The two models are related through traceability relations.

- Use-case modelling has been extended with two new constructs: business system areas and sub-use cases, which allow you to model large companies with several business areas.

- A business system model can be given a layered structure to support extensively reusable objects and to manage the complexity of large companies by hiding resource allocation and infrastructure − building problems from business process modelling.

Glossary

When objects are discussed in the glossary, unless otherwise stated we mean instances of objects.

Abstract class A class with the purpose of being inherited by other classes.

Acquaintance association Defines how one object has knowledge of another object.

Actor (to a business system) An actor defines one or a set of roles that someone or something in the environment can play in relation to the business.

Actor (to an information system) An actor defines one or a set of roles that someone or something in the environment can play in relation to the information system. An example of an actor is a user of the information system.

Aggregate An identifiable set of objects which has meaning. The aggregate itself is usually modelled as one object composed of the identifiable set of objects, each of which is considered as part of the aggregate object.

Architecture (of a modelling language) The different types of architecture that our modelling language allows us to show.

Architecture (of a business) The most important static, or long-lived, structures within the business.

Association A directed binary relation between objects. An association always links together two objects (instances or classes). It is always the associating object that acts upon and knows of the associated object, never the other way around.

Attribute Represents properties you wish to attach to an object.

Benchmarking An activity that analyzes and exchanges knowledge with the best of other businesses, with the objective of validating that one's own process goals surpass those of one's competitors.

Beta test To let a product be used by a carefully selected set of customers before it is released.

BPR   Business Process Reengineering.

Business system   The modelling construct we use to symbolize a business.

Cardinality   A property of an association which indicates how many instances of the associated class each instance of the associating class may point out.

Class   Contains a definition that all objects belonging to the class can follow.

Class association   An association linking two classes.

Communication association   Defines that one object that uses the interface offered by another object.

Contract   Specifies the stimuli that can be communicated between two instances of two different classes.

Control object (in a business system)   Represents a set of tasks in a business. These tasks should be performed by one resource instance, which typically is a specialist or a routine worker, not dealing directly with the customer.

Control object (in an information system)   An object that encapsulates functionality specific to one or a few use cases.

Deliverable   An output from a process that has a value – material or immaterial – for a customer.

Dynamic association   Communication association.

Encapsulation   The only visible parts of an object are the services that are offered, not how they are performed. The information contained in an object, and how the operations are performed, are not visible from outside the object.

Entity object (in a business system)   Represents occurrences such as products, deliverables, documents, and other things that are handled in the business.

Entity object (in an information system)   An object that manages some piece of information or some resource and its access.

Extends association   Spcifies how one use case description extends another use case description. When performing a use case, it might be performed either with or without the extended description according to some condition.

Forward engineering   Describes the new business processes.

Handler   A party that has an interest of or is a resource in the system. Usually a handler needs one or more models of the system. A handler can be human, but it can also be another system. A system can be a business system or an information system. Example of a handler to a business system is a customer and to an information system a user of it.

Ideal design   To develop an ideal-object model.

Ideal object   An object in an ideal-object model.

Ideal-object model (of a business)   Contains only those objects required to perform the use cases. The ideal objects describe how the business would operate in the best possible way.

Ideal-object model (of an information system)   An object-model that is ideal in the sense that it is independent of the implementation environment.

Implementation   The realization of a model.

Implementation model (of an information system)   The code produced when implementing the system.

Information system   A software system used to support the activities in a business.

Inheritance association   A relationship between two classes, meaning that the definition of the operations and attributes of one class is also used in the inheriting class which might do additions and redefinitions.

Instance   All objects that are created to conform to the description of a particular class are said to be instances of that class. When an instance is created, the class is said to be instantiated.

Instance association   An association linking two instances.

Interaction diagram   A diagram showing how a use-case is realized by communicating objects.

Interface object (in a business system)   Interface objects represent a set of operations in the business, each of which should be performed by one and the same resource. This task involves communicating with the environment of the business.

Interface object (in an information system)   An object that encapsulates the functionality to manage some system interface.

IT   Information Technology.

Meta association   An association linking a class to an instance or vice versa.

Model (of a business)   A business model is a model of a company that shows the company's function in the world, what it does, how and when. It is designed to serve the needs of one or more types of handler and it should contain the information these handlers need – no more and no less.

Multiple Inheritance   When a class inherits properties from several other classes.

NVA   Non Value Adding activities, in this context used to label activities in a business process that do not give anything of value to a customer. The opposite of VA.

Object   An identifiable, encapsulated entity that provides one or more services that can be requested.

Object model   A model that is described using an object-oriented language.

Object orientation   Here we mean techniques that are based on the following key concepts: Object, Class, Instance and Inheritance.

OOSE   Object-Oriented Software Engineering.

Operation   One identifiable entity that denotes a service that can be requested by an object (OMG) definition.

Process leader   Has responsibilities for an instance of a process, and may in many ways be similar to a project leader.

Process operator   The individuals working to perform a process. Each individual may take part in one or several business processes.

Process owner   Has the responsibility for a process in the business. This responsibility entails defining the process, determining the interface of the process, defining goals of the process, planning the budget, appointing process leaders, allocating resources, and developing the process itself.

QA   Quality Assurance.

Real design   To develop a real-object model.

Real object   An object in a real-object model.

Real-object model (of a business)   As opposed to the ideal-object model, the restrictions on the business are taken into consideration.

Real-object model (of an information system)   In the real-object model of the information system, you take the implementation environment (implementation language, capabilities, database handlers), its problems and limitations, into consideration.

Reengineering   Reverse engineering of an existing process followed by forward engineering of the new process.

Requirements analysis   To develop a requirements model, including a use-case model, of an information system.

Requirements capturing   To gather necessary information needed to be able to build a requirements model.

Resource owner   Owns the resources in the business. This responsibility means making sure all individuals are allocated somewhere, solving resource conflicts, establishing development plans for each individual, and also to take care of recruitment.

Reverse engineering   Developing an abstract model of an existing business and its processes. This encompasses a number of activities with the objective of gaining understanding of the business, and also communicating this understanding.

Semantic gap   The difference between the model and what it represents.

Signature (of an operation)   Describes the legitimate values of request parameters and returned results of an operation.

State (of an object)   Tells you where an object is in its life cycle, and what events can make it change to a new state.

State transition diagram   A diagram showing the states and the transitions that an object may pass through during its lifetime.

Static association   Acquaintance, consistsOf or inheritance association.

System   Delimits the 'world' of which we are building models.

Testing   Verification; checking whether the system agrees with the specification.

Test case   A way to test the functionality of a system. Each possible instantiation of a use case will correspond to one test case.

Test model   A set of test cases.

Use case (in a business system)   A sequence of transactions in a system whose task is to yield a result of measurable value to an individual actor of the business system.

Use case (in an information system)   A behaviourally related sequence of transactions performed by an actor in a dialogue with the system to provide some measurable value to the actor.

Use-case model A set of use cases, actors and their relations.

Uses association A relationship defining one use case description that uses another use case description as part of its own description.

VA Value Adding activity, in this context used to label activities in a business process that, from the customer's perspective, increases the value of the final product.

Index